# Sensational
# buttercream
# decorating

# Sensational buttercream decorating

## 50 projects for luscious cakes, mini-cakes & cupcakes

### Carey Madden

*Robert*
**ROSE**

**For complete cataloguing information, see page 362.**

*Disclaimer*
The recipes in this book have been carefully tested by our kitchen and our tasters. To the best of our knowledge, they are safe and nutritious for ordinary use and users. For those people with food or other allergies, or who have special food requirements or health issues, please read the suggested contents of each recipe carefully and determine whether or not they may create a problem for you. All recipes are used at the risk of the consumer.

We cannot be responsible for any hazards, loss or damage that may occur as a result of any recipe use.

For those with special needs, allergies, requirements or health problems, in the event of any doubt, please contact your medical adviser prior to the use of any recipe.

Design and production: Daniella Zanchetta/PageWave Graphics Inc.
Editor: Sue Sumeraj
Recipe editor and tester: Jennifer MacKenzie
Proofreaders: Sheila Wawanash and Kelly Jones
Indexer: Gillian Watts
Photographer: Lou Manna
Prop stylist and photo assistant: Joan O'Brien

Cover image: Chrysanthemum cupcakes (page 164)

Lace illustration © iStockphoto.com/ajuga

Traditional Rose Tattoo template (page 351) used for the Embroidered Tattoo project (pages 184–189) with permission from The Tattoo Pin (www.tattoopin.com).

Flowered Monogram B template used for the Monogram project (pages 246–249) with permission from Mary Corbet's Needle 'n Thread (www.needlenthread.com).

The publisher gratefully acknowledges the financial support of our publishing program by the Government of Canada through the Canada Book Fund.

Published by Robert Rose Inc.
120 Eglinton Avenue East, Suite 800, Toronto, Ontario, Canada M4P 1E2
Tel: (416) 322-6552 Fax: (416) 322-6936
www.robertrose.ca

Printed and bound in China

1 2 3 4 5 6 7 8 9 PPLS 22 21 20 19 18 17 16 15 14

..........................................................

*To my mother, who supported me both emotionally and financially through my multiple college majors and career tracks. Thank you for always recognizing my creative talents, even though neither of us knew where those abilities would lead or if I would ever make a reasonable living from them.*
*I think this choice is going to stick, Mom!*

&

*To my father, who, even in an abbreviated life, taught me that the power of persistence is equal to, if not greater than, innate talent or intelligence. This book is for you, Dad.*

..........................................................

# Contents

# Introduction

Few foods are more exquisite than a magnificently decorated cake, and few cakes taste more divine than those swathed in buttercream. *Sensational Buttercream Decorating* will help you create stunning cakes you can be proud of, with expert advice on everything you need to know along the way. This comprehensive guide offers equipment information, delicious cake and icing recipes, invaluable instructions on cake decorating fundamentals and techniques, hundreds of step-by-step photographs and 50 fabulous projects to choose from. And because everyone deserves to have their cake and eat it too, regardless of dietary restrictions, there are even gluten-free and vegan options!

Making a cake from scratch is an act of love, whether it's a stolid English fruitcake, an instant cake from a box or an elaborate tiered cake. Decorations transform a cake into a blank canvas on which the decorator can express creativity and personalize a cake in honor of a loved one or a significant event. In an increasingly fast-paced society where convenience and speed reign supreme, a lovingly baked and decorated cake is a throwback to a slower time when connections and relationships were nurtured and rituals celebrated. Regardless of the results — flawless and intricate, or lopsided and well intentioned — a decorated cake's loving message remains a constant.

Although there are many mediums suitable for cake decoration, buttercream icing is indisputably the most delicious. Decorations are often considered extraneous: pretty to look at but not all that tasty. When made with buttercream, though, even the most elaborate decorations are creamy, fluffy and full of flavor. Buttercream icing is real food, invented for the sole purpose of being devoured and only later developed into a decorating medium. *Sensational Buttercream Decorating* takes buttercream in an entirely new and exciting direction, applying contemporary design and innovative techniques to a traditional decorating medium.

Buttercream's popularity can be attributed to its simple sweetness, versatility, resiliency and ease. Essentially, in its simplest form, buttercream icing is made by creaming butter and powdered sugar. This traditional American style of buttercream is fluffy and very sweet, since its structure is derived from sugar. This book uses the Swiss meringue style of buttercream. Because Swiss buttercream is satiny and smooth, and its sweetness is subtle and well balanced, it is the perfect medium for decorating cakes. In addition to sugar and butter, Swiss buttercream relies on whipped egg whites for texture and structure. Nothing compares to the flavor and satiny smooth quality of Swiss buttercream — though I think I've come close with my vegan version, developed specially for those who avoid all animal products.

If you love food as much as I do, and have a special appreciation for baked goods, buttercream decorating is the perfect channel for your creativity and self-expression. As with learning any new skill, decorating with buttercream requires time and practice. Be patient with yourself as you develop your coordination and muscle memory. Start by making some of the less complicated cakes featured in this book, then work up to the more intricate projects. When you start to feel confident about your cake decorating abilities, use the techniques you have learned here to create your own sensational designs.

Most importantly, have fun — it's only cake, after all. If your creation doesn't live up to your high expectations, there's always consolation to be found in consumption!

*Carey Madden*

# Chapter 1

# Tools and Supplies

A perfectly golden brown exterior is usually a worthy ambition when it comes to baked goods, but not when you're baking a cake meant for layering and icing. Once the finished cake is cut into slices, you do not want the cake layers to be edged in crisp brown. What looks good on a muffin or croissant looks overbaked on a cake and detracts from the overall esthetic appeal. Glass, nonstick and dark pans tend to brown items faster.

**Two in One!**

Heavy glass measuring cups with handles are particularly useful, as they can act as both bowl and liquid measuring cup — meaning fewer dishes to wash! I have glass measuring cups in 2-cup (500 mL), 4-cup (1 L), and 6-cup (1.5 L) capacities.

# Baking Supplies

Before you can decorate a cake, you need to bake one and make the icing! You'll find cake and icing recipes in Chapter 2. To get started, you really only need a few basic tools — an electric mixer, some bowls, assorted cake pans, parchment paper and a double boiler — plus an assortment of other handy supplies. You may already own many of these supplies; others are readily available at kitchen and baking supply stores or online.

## Electric Mixer

A quality stand mixer is an invaluable piece of equipment that will ensure light, airy cakes and satiny smooth icing. It is a high-powered machine that can soften difficult-to-whip cream cheese with ease and can withstand the mixing time for Swiss buttercream icing without overheating or burning out. For all these reasons, a stand mixer is the equipment of choice for the cake and icing recipes in this book. If you don't have a stand mixer, however, the recipes can be made using a good-quality, heavy-duty handheld mixer instead, though some adjustments will be required. Each of the recipes specifies what adjustments you'll need to make if using a handheld mixer instead of a stand mixer.

## Bowls

For all-around general use, my go-to bowls are a set of melamine plastic bowls in 1-quart (1 L), 2-quart (2 L), 3-quart (3 L) and 4-quart (4 L) capacities. These bowls nest, so they are easy to store, and they have contoured spouts for pouring liquids and rubber non-slip rings on the bottom for stability. Melamine doesn't react with acidic foods, ensuring that flavors stay true.

I also keep a variety of other bowls on hand for various specific uses. Tiny light metal bowls are ideal for holding small quantities of premeasured ingredients, such as spices. A bowl with high sides is a good choice when you're whisking liquid ingredients, to ensure that the liquid does not spill over the top. When you're sifting dry ingredients into a bowl, choose a bowl with a wide opening, to capture all the drifting particles.

For whipping cream or egg whites, avoid plastic bowls and opt for stainless steel, glass or ceramic. Do not use an aluminum bowl for whipping egg whites, as it could turn the whites grey. Copper bowls are ideal for whipping eggs and help you create tremendous volume and stiffness in less time.

# Cake Pans

Cake pans come in various sizes, shapes and materials, and most are capable of effectively baking a cake. Aluminum, silver-anodized, hard-anodized, silicone, nonstick and glass pans are some of the most popular options for baking cakes. Avoid steel pans, as they do not conduct heat well and can cause inconsistencies in baking. Thick-gauge aluminum pans are an excellent choice. If you choose nonstick, glass or dark-colored pans, reduce the oven temperature by 25°F (10°C), as these pans absorb more heat.

Cake pans come in depths of 2 inches (5 cm), 3 inches (7.5 cm) or 4 inches (10 cm). I prefer a 3- to 4-inch (7.5 to 10 cm) deep pan, as it allows for more options when it comes to slicing layers. You can bake a single thin layer or add more batter and bake a tall cake that can be sliced into two or three layers.

The decorating projects in this book use cakes baked in round cake pans that are 4 inches (10 cm), 6 inches (15 cm) or 8 inches (20 cm) in diameter, but feel free to adapt the decorations to suit your needs or your cake pans. It's a good idea to have two cake pans in each size so you can bake more than one layer at a time.

# Parchment Paper

Once you use parchment paper for the first time, you'll wonder how you ever managed without it. When parchment is used to line the bottom of a cake pan, there's no need to go through the process of greasing and flouring the pan; a light coat of nonstick baking spray on top of the parchment and on the sides of the pan will suffice. Parchment paper ensures clean removal of the cake from the pan, so you'll never have to worry that your perfectly baked cake will break apart as you lift it out.

# Muffin Pans and Cupcake Liners

Just about any muffin pan can be used to bake cupcakes, and expensive, professional-grade pans do little to improve results. I do recommend keeping your eye out for pans with features that make the cupcake-baking experience a little easier: handles and a nonstick surface. Handles are helpful for removing hot pans from the oven. I find that when I use muffin pans without handles, a corner of my bulky pot holder inevitably swipes a cupcake or two, marring the top surface. And if your cupcakes happen to spill over the top of the liner and onto the pan, it is much easier to remove the cupcakes if the pan is nonstick.

## Parchment Rounds

Parchment rounds are available in the most common pan sizes at baking supply stores or online (see the Source Guide, page 354). But it's easy to make your own if you don't have any on hand. Simply trace the bottom of the pan on a piece of parchment paper, then cut out the traced round, making sure to cut inside the traced line.

## Make the Most of Down Time

While you're waiting for butter, eggs and liquids to come to room temperature, use the time to cut multiple parchment rounds to line your baking pans. A reserve stock of parchment rounds will come in handy in the future.

If you don't have a
double boiler, fill a
medium saucepan
with 1 inch (2.5 cm)
of water and place
a deep, heatproof
bowl on top, making
sure the bowl does
not touch the water
(it is the steam that
will gently heat the
mixture inside
the bowl).

When it comes to lining those pans, there is a proliferation of patterned paper cupcake liners available on the market today. I have collected more than I will likely use in my lifetime — there are just so many cute stripes, flowers, polka dots, toiles and laser-cut laces. It's good fun to try to match the liner to the decoration you're planning, but keep in mind that, once the cupcakes are baked and the oil has saturated the liners, the pattern is less visible, especially if the cupcakes are chocolate or dark-colored.

# Double Boiler

A double boiler allows you to gently heat a delicate liquid without burning, scorching or curdling it. When you're making Swiss buttercream icing, the egg whites must be heated to destroy any hazardous bacteria. The goal is to heat them without cooking them, since you don't want any solid bits of egg in your icing!

# Other Handy Supplies

- **Measuring cups:** You should have two types of measuring cups on hand: a set of dry, nesting-style measuring cups, and a glass measuring cup with a handle and spout. Use the nesting-style cups to measure dry ingredients, such as sugar and flour, and moist ingredients, such as brown sugar and coconut. Use the glass measuring cup to measure liquid ingredients, such as milk and water.

- **Measuring spoons:** For quantities under $\frac{1}{4}$ cup (60 mL), use measuring spoons to get an accurate measure. Because measuring spoons are used for both dry and liquid ingredients, make sure to always measure the dry ingredients first. If you measure the wet ingredients first, the dry ingredients will stick to the spoon.

- **Sifter or fine-mesh sieve:** Sifting the dry ingredients aerates the mixture, resulting in a lighter cake with a more consistent crumb. Sifting also eliminates lumps and helps ensure that the ingredients are evenly combined. If you don't have a sifter, you can use a fine-mesh sieve: holding the sieve above a wide-mouth bowl, pour the ingredients into the sieve, tapping the rim of the sieve against your palm (much like playing a tambourine) to agitate the ingredients and force them through the mesh.

- **Wire whisk:** A whisk does for liquid ingredients what a sifter does for dry ingredients: it incorporates air, removes lumps and blends ingredients until smooth. A standard-size wire balloon whisk is appropriate for most tasks. I also have a beloved tiny whisk, just $5\frac{3}{4}$ inches (14 cm) long, that is handy for blending ingredients in small bowls and measuring cups.

- **Rubber or silicone spatula:** Use a sturdy rubber or silicone spatula to help pour the batter into the cake pan and scrape as much as possible from the bowl into the pan. Once all the batter is in the pan, use the spatula to smooth the top.

- **Nonstick baking spray:** Baking spray works with the parchment paper used to line the pan to ensure easy removal of the cake after baking. Spray both the parchment liner and the sides of the pan.

- **Toothpick, skewer or cake tester:** A toothpick is inserted into the center of a cake to test for doneness. When a cake is fully baked, the toothpick will come out clean. If it has batter clinging to it, the cake needs to continue baking. A skewer or cake tester can be used in place of the toothpick.

- **Wire cooling racks:** Placing a cake on a wire rack helps it cool quickly and evenly. First place the cake, still in the pan, on the rack for 5 to 10 minutes. This cooling period allows the cake to cool enough that it's comfortable to touch, but does not

## Ensuring Accurate Measurements

Accurate measurements are very important in baking, as even small inaccuracies can alter the texture and flavor of a baked good. Here are some tips that will help you get precise results:

- Flours tend to be light and fluffy, and how you fill the measuring cup can dramatically affect the quantity of the flour in the cup. Using a measuring cup to scoop flour directly out of the bag packs the flour in too tight. The best method is to spoon the flour into the measuring cup until it overflows the top and creates a rounded mound, then use the straight edge of a spatula or knife to scrape off the mound so that the flour is flush with the top of the measuring cup.

- Icing (confectioners') sugar is measured much like flour, but must be sifted to remove lumps before it is measured.

- Brown sugar should be packed snugly into the measuring cup. If packed correctly, the sugar will retain the shape of the cup when it is dropped into the bowl.

- When you're measuring liquid ingredients, the glass measuring cup should be sitting on a level surface, such as a countertop. Pour the ingredients into the cup and squat down so that you can ascertain at eye level whether the liquid reaches the specified mark.

- When measuring ingredients — especially liquids — into measuring spoons, do not do so in the air above a bowl full of other ingredients. Any slip or overly ambitious pour can ruin the ingredients already in the bowl.

Flip the pan upside down onto the cooling rack and lift the pan off the cake so that the cake rests upside down on the rack. You can flip the cake right side up at this point, but be careful not to break it, as it's still delicate while warm. Alternatively, you can just leave it to cool upside down. Don't worry about the grid imprint on the top of the cake; you will likely be slicing off the top to level the cake, and even if you aren't, it will be covered by icing.

**DIY Cardboard Rounds**

Don't have a cardboard round? Make your own. Use a cake pan to trace the diameter of the cake onto clean cardboard, then cut out the round with heavy-duty scissors. Wipe both sides of the round with a soapy damp cloth, rinse with a damp cloth with no soap, and let dry.

permit the butter or cooking spray to cool entirely, seize up and cement the cake to the pan. Once the cake is cool enough to touch (it should still be quite hot, but not hot enough to burn), transfer it from the pan to the rack to cool completely (see sidebar, at left). A cake should always be completely cool before it is sliced and filled.

- **Offset spatulas:** This tool gets its name because the thin, blunt blade is offset from (lower than) the handle. It is the perfect tool for transferring cakes and cake layers, and for spreading filling. Offset spatulas also have many uses when it comes to icing and decorating cakes (see page 17).

- **Long serrated knife:** Serrated knives come in multiple lengths. Choose a knife that is at least a little longer than the diameter of your cake. A serrated knife is my preferred tool for leveling the top of a cake and slicing layers, but you can also use a cake leveler (a metal tool strung with serrated wire that can be adjusted in height and fixed in place to level and slice clean and even layers).

# Decorating Supplies

When you start browsing in a baking supply store, or looking at all of the options available online, it might seem like cake decorating requires a vast array of tools and supplies. There are certainly a lot of handy specialized tools out there, but when it comes right down to it, all you really need to assemble a basic cake decorating starter kit is some cardboard rounds, a variety of spatulas, some pastry bags and couplers, a set of decorating tips and a turntable.

## Cardboard Rounds

Cardboard rounds are simple circular pieces of cardboard that are the same diameter as the cake. They are placed under the bottom layer after the cake is sliced but before it is filled and iced. They make it easier to move the cake on and off the turntable and into and out of the refrigerator, and they allow you to use glue or double-sided mounting tape to securely affix the cake to the presentation surface. Cardboard rounds are optional for 4-inch (10 cm) cakes because of their diminutive size and weight, but are imperative for larger cakes. An 8-inch (20 cm) cake with multiple layers can be quite heavy, and if you attempt to pick it up with a spatula, the cake will break from its own weight and the layers could slide.

# Spatulas

An assortment of spatulas in different shapes, sizes and materials are used in cake decorating. Each has a variety of functions, some of which overlap.

- **Offset spatulas:** A small offset spatula is used to apply buttercream icing, to smooth icing and to correct decorating mistakes. For small quantities of icing, it can also be used to mix color into icing (using the spatula method) and to fill pastry bags. A large offset spatula is used to transfer an iced cake from the turntable to the presentation surface, and to mix color into icing and fill pastry bags when a full bag of icing is required.

- **Small tapered offset spatula:** A tapered offset spatula, as you might expect, has a blade that tapers toward the rounded end. Its small tip makes it the perfect tool for reaching into small spaces and for correcting mistakes without disturbing other nearby decorations. It can also be used to fill pastry bags.

- **Straight blade spatulas:** These spatulas (also called straight edge spatulas) have a flat blade that juts straight out from the handle rather than being offset. Straight blade spatulas are used to apply and smooth buttercream icing, to break the icing seal between cake and turntable after icing a cake, and to scrape icing off a cake for the reductive decorating technique. I keep a selection of 6-inch (15 cm), 8-inch (20 cm) and 10-inch (25 cm) straight blade spatulas on hand. Shorter spatulas are easier to control when you're working with a 4-inch (10 cm) or 6-inch (15 cm) cake. A longer spatula is best when you're icing a larger cake, because it stretches across the entire top surface, allowing you to make long, clean sweeps with fewer stroke marks, for a smoother finish.

- **Rubber or silicone spatulas:** These spatulas are useful for scraping icing from a bowl or other container, mixing color into icing, stirring icing to remove air bubbles, filling pastry bags and applying icing. I keep different sizes on hand for various tasks.

## Heat Resistance Is a Plus

Although cake decorating tasks do not generally require heat-resistant spatulas, if you're purchasing new rubber or silicone spatulas anyway, you may as well opt for ones you can use for a wide variety of cooking tasks. Heat-resistant rubber or silicone spatulas tolerate high heat without melting. I'm all for experimenting with unusual ingredients while baking, but melted plastic is not one of them!

# Pastry Bags and Couplers

The pastry bag is to a cake decorator what the paintbrush is to an artist. It is your primary tool for decorating with buttercream icing, and there are several options available, so make sure to choose the bags that best suit you.

## Coated Cloth Bags

Coated cloth bags are the Cadillacs of pastry bags. They are light and flexible, and they last for years. Not all coated bags are created equal, and spending a little more upfront will save you money in the long term. You want a fabric-coated bag that is not too thick, bulky or stiff. Most importantly, you want a bag that will not allow the icing to seep through and coat the bag, and your hand, in grease. I recommend Wilton's Featherweight pastry bags or Bakery Crafts' BakeMate pastry bags.

## Disposable Bags

Disposable bags are a handy option for light decorating work because, let's face it, cleaning pastry bags is not a particularly fun task. The majority of disposable bags are plastic. They can be used as is or the end can be cut off and a tip or coupler inserted. I find that their often asymmetrical shape and plastic seam can make them stiff and slightly awkward to use. They also become slick and difficult to grip once they meet with any buttercream on the outer surface. I rarely use disposable bags for these reasons, but refraining from adding more non-biodegradable plastic to landfills is another good reason.

## Parchment Bags

A bag made from parchment paper is hand folded (see box, opposite) and holds a relatively small amount of buttercream. A parchment bag can be a handy tool when small amounts of icing are required, such as when you're placing dots in the center of flowers or writing an inscription.

Unless you're a paper engineer and a whiz with scissors, you are limited to a round hole as the tip for a parchment bag, as it is difficult to pair a coupler and decorating tip with one. The beauty of the parchment bag is that you can snip off the tip to create any size opening you wish. But cut conservatively — if the opening is bigger than you intended, there's no going back.

I tend to use a coated cloth bag even for small jobs because a parchment bag doesn't always hold its round tip. But if you choose to use a parchment bag and the tip becomes malformed or closes, you can use the tip of a toothpick to gently reshape it.

If your bag feels a little loose and is threatening to unravel, secure it with a bit of tape. *Do not* secure a parchment bag with staples. If a loose staple slips into the buttercream, it becomes a health hazard.

**Filling a Parchment Bag**

Here's a handy way to fill a parchment bag: Set a full roll of paper towels on one end. Place the parchment bag in the hole made by the cardboard core. The paper towel roll will securely suspend the pastry bag so you have two free hands to fill the bag.

**Closing a Parchment Bag**

Rotate the bag so that the seam is facing away from you. Squeeze the top of the bag together, fold the two top corners in toward the center and roll the top of the bag down, forcing the buttercream into the tip. As buttercream is depleted, continue to roll the bag down to maintain pressure, much as you would with a tube of toothpaste.

# How to Fold a Parchment Pastry Bag

With a little practice, folding a parchment bag will become second nature.

Cut a piece of parchment paper into a triangle that is 8 to 12 inches (20 to 30 cm) wide on its longest side. ■ You can do this by taking a square or rectangular piece of parchment paper and cutting it in half diagonally. ■ The angles don't need to be perfectly equal. ■

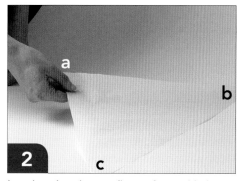

Lay the triangle on a flat surface with the right-angled point of the triangle (corner A) pointing toward your stomach. ■

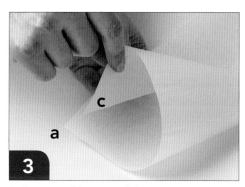

Roll corner C in toward the center so that corners A and C are approximately lined up and a pointy tip is created. ■

Pinch corners A and C between your thumb and index finger to secure them. ■ Lift the parchment slightly, maintaining the orientation. ■

Wrap corner B up and over the top of the cone and around the back so that all three corners are approximately lined up. ■

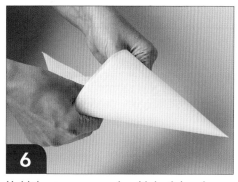

Hold the cone securely with both hands, with your thumbs inside. ■

*continued...*

# How to Fold a Parchment Pastry Bag *(continued)*

Using an up and down motion, rub the layers of the cone between your fingers until they are snug and the tip is perfectly pointy and closed. ■

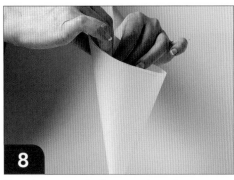

Keeping your grip firm, reorient the cone so that the tip is facing down. ■

In a single motion, fold all three corners down toward the center of the cone. ■

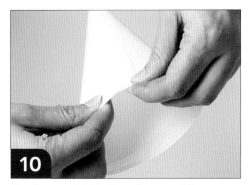

Continue to fold in the edges until the cone is secure. ■

*Note:* You can make a parchment bag almost any size, depending on what size triangle you start with. To avoid buttercream squeezing out the top of the bag, fill it no more than half full.

## Bag Size

Obviously, the bigger the bag, the more buttercream it can hold, but wielding a big bag requires the strength and coordination to match. In my professional life, I prefer a 16-inch (40 cm) bag, but I often fill it just half to three-quarters full. For home use, a 14-inch (35 cm) bag will cover most needs. A smaller 8-inch (20 cm), 10-inch (25 cm) or 12-inch (30 cm) bag is handy for inscriptions and small, detailed work, but a larger bag can always be partially filled, making it a more versatile option.

# How to Clean Cloth Pastry Bags

If coated cloth pastry bags aren't properly washed and stored, you can end up with bags slick with residual grease and smelling like limburger cheese.

1. Place a large pot of water on the stovetop and add a generous squeeze of dish soap. Bring the water to a boil.

2. Meanwhile, empty the bags of any icing.

3. Wearing rubber gloves if desired, hold the bags one at a time under the faucet and run hot water (as hot as you can stand) through them, washing out most of the visible icing.

4. Remove any tips or couplers that remain in the bags. Turn the bags inside out. Drop them into the boiling water, reduce the heat to low and simmer for 10 to 15 minutes.

5. Drain the pot and rinse the bags individually with hot water.

6. Squeeze and wring out the bags, then hang them to drip dry. Do not store the bags until they are *completely dry*, to avoid a mildew smell.

*Note:* About every third time I wash pastry bags, I use a little bleach to remove any food coloring stains. *Do not soak the bags in bleach*, as this will eat away the fabric lining of the bag. As the bags are simmering on the stovetop, drop 1 teaspoon (5 mL) bleach into the pot 2 to 3 minutes before removing it from the stove. Be careful not to breathe in the bleach-infused steam.

## Couplers

A coupler is a brilliant tool that allows you to switch between decorating tips on the same pastry bag without emptying the bag. A coupler consists of two parts — the base and the ring — and can be made of either plastic or metal. Plastic couplers are more affordable, but metal ones are exceptionally sturdy and will last forever. A metal coupler also has a nice weight, lending balance to the bag.

### How to Hold a Pastry Bag

Pastry bags are held in the palm of your dominant hand, with the twisted-off portion clasped in the squishy part between your thumb and forefinger and the excess bag draped over the back of your hand. Place the index finger of your non-dominant hand near the narrow opening of the bag and use it to steady and guide the bag.

### Cutting the Bag to Fit the Coupler

There's little more disheartening than having to discard an expensive cloth pastry bag because you've cut too big a hole in the tip and the coupler falls through. Cut conservatively, then drop the coupler in to test the opening: half or less of the coupler's threads should push through the hole. If the hole is too small, make another small cut, then test again.

# Decorating Tips

When paired with cloth or disposable pastry bags, decorating tips open up a world of cake decorating possibilities. Essentially, these tips are small cones with openings cut in various shapes, creating distinctive decorations when buttercream icing is pushed through.

Depending on the brand, tips may be made of stainless steel, nickel-plated brass or, occasionally, plastic. They come in a huge array of sizes and shapes, and are identified by a number stamped into their surface. The industry-standardized numbers make for easy identification and ordering.

Most tips can be paired with a coupler for quick and easy tip changes on the same pastry bag, though some large tips (such as the #124 and #125 rose tips) will not fit with a coupler. If you are using one of these large tips, or if you prefer not to use a coupler, any tip can simply be inserted directly into the bag instead.

Tips can be purchased individually or in a set. A set is an affordable way to start your collection with the most frequently used tips. Tip sets usually come in a plastic container, perfect for long-term storage. Consider purchasing multiples of your favorite tips to avoid washings between bag and color changes.

Tips are broken into families: round tips, star tips, petal tips and many more. All of the tips in a particular family produce a similar decoration, or a decoration used for a common purpose, with the openings varying in size and perhaps slightly in shape. The tips included in the list below are the ones used in this book; this is by no means an exhaustive list of the tips available.

## Round Tips

The smallest round tip I use is the #1, as buttercream icing tends to become unmanageable when you try to push it through smaller tips. The largest round tip I use is a #12. If I need a larger round opening, I just use a coupler with no tip attached.

- **Small round tips (#1, #2, #3, #4):** Used for inscriptions, smooth scallop borders, flower centers, dots, embedded dots, Swiss dots, grape hyacinths, dot daisies, dot borders, piped lines, swags, tassels, outlines, embroidery
- **Medium round tips (#5, #6, #8, #10, #12):** Used for inscriptions, smooth scallop borders, flower centers, dots, embedded dots, Swiss dots, sprinkled rolled dots, dot borders, piped lines

## Star Tips

Open star, deep star, fine cut, stellar — the variety of star tips is mind-boggling. Play with various tips to find your favorites, or just use what you have on hand; they all create pleasing results. The size of the decoration I want to create often dictates which star tip I use.

- **Star tips (#14, #16, #18, #32):** Used for ridged scallop borders, ridged dollop borders, rosettes, drop flowers

## Petal Tips

These are the tips that set my heart aflutter with thoughts of sumptuous buttercream flowers. Learn to manipulate these tips and you will create awe-inspiring cakes.

- **Petal tip (#61):** Used for lotus flower petals
- **U tips (#80, #81):** Used for long horizontal petals, short vertical petals, cupped flowers, lilies of the valley, sheep ears
- **Rose tips (#101, #102, #103, #104, #124, #125):** Used for ribbon borders, bows, classic flat petals, petal daisies, rosebuds, feathers, poppies

## Leaf Tips

These tips make leaves in various shapes and sizes. I find that #352 suits most of my leafy needs, but there are many more leaf tips available. When I want to make a tiny, delicate leaf, I use #352's baby sister, #349.

- **Leaf tips (#349, #352):** Used for leaves, sunflower petals

## Drop Flower Tips

I could kiss the feet of the person who invented drop flower tips. The results are so pretty, easy and elegant that no tip collection is complete without one. I primarily use tip #131.

- **Drop flower tip (#131):** Used for drop flowers, wisteria, lilacs, hyacinths

## Specialty Tips

These tips are a fun bunch, and they make tremendously inventive decorations.

- **Basket weave tip (#48):** Used for a basket weave pattern
- **Ribbon (or oval) tip (#45, #301):** Used for inscriptions, oval dots, bamboo stalks
- **Grass tip (#233):** Used for grass, bird's nest

**Finding Your Favorite Tips**

Certain tips in my collection have been weathered by time and use because, like my favorite wooly winter sweater, I go back to them time and again. I know I can depend on them to make consistent decorations. Often, the tips you begin decorating with will be the tips you wind up preferring, but if you're going to be doing a lot of cake decorating, try different brands to find the tips you like best.

## How to Clean Decorating Tips

Hot water will remove most visible buttercream icing from a tip, but although it may look clean, a stubborn film of grease may remain. Here's how to remove all traces of grease.

1. Place the tips in a pot of water and bring to a boil.

2. Give the tips a stir, then reduce the heat to low and simmer until the buttercream is released from inside the tips and floats to the surface.

3. Dump the tips into a strainer and rinse them with hot water. Rinse the pot. Return the tips to the pot, add more water and a squeeze of dish soap, and bring to a boil.

4. Rinse the tips again in the strainer.

5. Place the tips in the center of a dish towel, bring the ends of the towel together and gently massage the tips. Open the towel and separate any tips that have nested together. Let the tips air-dry on the towel overnight.

*Notes:*
Be careful not to leave tips at the bottom of your sink while they wait to be washed. Contact with a heavy saucepan or frying pan can bend and deform tips to the point where they are no longer usable.

Tips can rust, so make sure they are completely dry before storing them.

### Caring for Your Turntable

If your turntable is sticking and spins only with great effort and at a slow pace, it likely needs to be cleaned and oiled. A turntable that is well used — or one that sits unused for long periods — may need to be cleaned of an accumulation of gummy oil, dust and frosting. Cleaning the socket and the post with soap and water will not do the trick; they require a vigorous scrub with an abrasive sponge or scouring pad. After cleaning, dry the turntable thoroughly and lubricate the socket with a professional food-grade lubricant (you can use a cooking oil, but it will not be as efficient and will gum up faster). Avoid using a mechanical oil such as WD-40.

# Turntable

A good-quality turntable may be the largest investment in your collection of decorating tools, but it is well worth the cost. If your turntable does not rotate easily, evenly and smoothly, then icing a cake smoothly will be nearly impossible. A quality turntable is made of metal, is quite heavy, and is well balanced so that it does not hitch and jump when spun.

Turntables have two parts: a round table top and a base. The top surface is typically 12 inches (30 cm) in diameter. If you think you might ever ice a cake larger than that, consider purchasing a turntable with spines on the bottom of the table surface — they will help you spin the table when a cake extends beyond its edges.

# Other Handy Supplies

- **All-purpose glue or double-sided mounting tape:** When a cake board is being used as the presentation surface, all-purpose glue is used to secure the cardboard round underneath the cake to the cake board. When a plate, platter or cake stand is being used as the presentation surface, double-sided mounting tape is used to secure the cardboard round to the presentation surface.

- **Cake comb:** A cake comb is dragged across the surface of an iced cake to create a uniform pattern. There are cake combs for making simple lines, scallops, intricate ridges and fat waves. Combs can be found in cake supply stores or online, or, with a pair of scissors and heavy card stock, you can make your own, limited only by your imagination.

- **Garland maker:** This small, lightweight plastic tool transfers dotted garland outlines onto the side of a cake, using preset depth and width markers to ensure that the garlands ringing the cake are consistent in size and shape. Look for garland makers at baking supply stores, craft stores and online retailers.

- **Cookie cutters:** Cookie cutters come in many different shapes and sizes, from simple rounds and ovals to complex shapes and character outlines. In cake decorating, cookie cutters are used to imprint a design onto an iced cake, creating an outline that you can pipe over with buttercream icing. If you're just starting a cookie cutter collection, you'll get the most use out of round cookie cutters in various sizes.

- **Ruler:** The thin edge of a ruler can be used to imprint straight lines on an iced cake that you can pipe over with buttercream icing. It is also helpful when you are trying to leave an equal amount of space between decorations.

- **Toothpicks or skewers:** You can use a toothpick or skewer (either wooden or metal, as long as the point is very sharp and small) to trace around a template, creating an outline that you can pipe over with buttercream icing, or to help you plan out a freehand design before you start piping. For example, you might dot the shape of a winding vine onto the iced cake and make sure you are happy with the design and placement of it before you pipe over it with icing. Toothpicks and skewers are also very helpful when it comes to fixing cake decorating mishaps.

- **Templates:** A template is a great way to transfer a complex design onto a cake when you're not confident enough in your artistic abilities to draw the design freehand. See page 71 for instructions and tips on using templates.

## Cookie Cutter Substitutes

I have a fairly wide collection of cookie cutters, but I'm just as likely to scour the kitchen for a randomly sized object that will suit my needs perfectly. Items I commonly use to make an imprint on a cake include drinking glasses, takeout food containers and their lids, screwbands from canning jars, spice container lids and cardboard rounds.

## Free Online Templates

The internet is a fantastic resource for just about any template you can imagine. Simply type "free printable," plus the name of the shape you're looking for, plus "template" into your search engine, and you'll get back hundreds of options to choose from. For example, if you were looking for a star template, you would type in "free printable star template."

## Taste-Testing Embellishments

Some sugar pearls and dragées are incredibly, filling-cracking hard. Before chomping down on a mouthful, you might want to give one a gentle test bite. I was surprised to find that some of the larger decorations are actually gumballs!

## The Traditional Use for Rose Nails

Rose nails are traditionally used to create large buttercream flowers. The shaft is rotated between the thumb and forefinger, allowing for symmetrical placement of petals. The flower is then lifted from the nail with kitchen scissors and placed on the cake. This technique is not used in the projects in this book, but several online videos are available to show you how it's done. Experiment with the technique to create your own fabulous designs!

- **Tweezers:** When you're placing small decorations such as sugar pearls on a cake, and particularly when you're trying to place them in a particular spot on the cake (as opposed to just scattering them), tweezers make the task much easier, allowing for much greater precision in small areas than your fingers are capable of.

- **Sugar pearls and dragées:** These small round candies come in many different colors and several sizes, ranging from 3 to 10 millimeters. When they are coated in a metallic finish, they are often called "dragées." They can be used to embellish a buttercream icing design or to create a design on their own. The most common colors are readily available in baking aisles. Baking supply stores carry a wider selection, and you'll find even more options to choose from through online retailers.

- **Sprinkles:** These teeny tiny candies are available in a huge array of individual colors, color assortments and shapes. Round sprinkles are often called "nonpareils." They can be sprinkled on top of a cake or cupcake, either randomly or as part of a design, or patted around the bottom edge of a cake. They are also used to make sprinkled rolled dots.

- **Rose nail (aka flower nail):** In the projects in this book, a rose nail is used to make sprinkled rolled dots. Rose nails are usually made of stainless steel but are also available in plastic. They consist of a round, flat platform, ranging in diameter from $\frac{1}{2}$ to 3 inches (1 to 7.5 cm), attached to a thin, pointed shaft that resembles a construction nail. I find that a rose nail with a $1\frac{1}{2}$- to 2-inch (4 to 5 cm) diameter suits all my decorating needs. Rose nails are available at bakery supply stores, craft stores and online retailers. When purchasing a rose nail, make sure the shaft has threads (like a construction screw) and is not perfectly smooth — a smooth shaft is exceptionally difficult to rotate once your hands are slippery with buttercream.

- **Kitchen scissors:** These scissors should be reserved solely for use with food. In cake decorating, they are used to help transfer sprinkled rolled dots and flowers from the rose nail to the cake.

- **Other household scissors:** You'll need a separate set of scissors for cutting out your printed templates. Make sure not to use the same scissors on both paper and food.

- **Damp cloths:** Keep several damp clothes nearby when you're decorating a cake — they're very useful for wiping spatulas clean, removing icing from the tip of a toothpick or skewer when correcting mistakes, and numerous other small tasks.

- **Apron:** Buttercream has a way of getting on everything, and because the primary ingredient is butter, it takes more than a bit of dabbing to remove it from clothing. Save time, a headache and your clothing by wearing an apron while baking and decorating.

# Presentation Supplies

Before beginning the decorating process, you will need to decide on the type of presentation surface you will use. The first factor to consider is size. To protect the cake from damage during transport (even just into and out of the refrigerator), the diameter of the presentation surface should be 2 inches (5 cm) larger than the cake. For a 4-inch (10 cm) cake, you will need a 6-inch (15 cm) presentation surface, and so on. A larger presentation surface is fine, but if you use a smaller surface, there's nowhere for fingers to grasp and you're sure to stick a thumb in the cake.

You'll also want to make sure your chosen presentation surface is both attractive and practical. Below are a handful of options for presenting your cake.

## Cake Boards

The simplest way to present a cake is on a silver cake board, a cardboard round covered in silver foil. Cake boards are available in several different thicknesses, and can have smooth or scalloped edges. Cake boards that are $\frac{1}{2}$ inch (1 cm) thick offer the greatest stability and a more formal appearance. Silver cake boards can be found in most craft stores and cake decorating supply stores, and through online retailers.

## Plates or Platters

A plate or platter is a popular option for presenting a cake because the possibilities are endless. One of my favorite pastimes is frequenting antique and thrift shops — fantastic places to pick up inexpensive vintage plates with a ton of character. I often purchase plates and store them until the perfect occasion arises. I have even used plates as inspiration for a cake decoration! If I'm bringing a cake to a celebration, I'm happy to leave the plate for the host to keep, since I picked it up for a song.

An excellent alternative is to purchase a set of simple white plates in appropriate sizes. You will never be at a loss for a presentation surface, as these plates will match any cake and are perennially elegant.

It is best if the cake rests completely within the flat center of the plate, not on the angled rim or edge. You can place a cardboard round, or multiple cardboard rounds that have been glued together, in the center of the plate to raise up a cake that is wider than the flat center, but this makes it difficult to add a border, and especially a ribbon border, around the bottom edge of the cake. For the same reason, avoid plates with textured, crenulated or wavy edges, or edges with a raised pattern.

## Dressing Up Your Cardboard Rounds

Cardboard rounds can also be used to present the cake if they are dressed up with a doily. Make sure the doily is glassine or sealed in some way to prevent oil from the cake from seeping into it. Attach the doily to the cardboard round with a spiral of glue under the part of the doily where the cake will sit.

## Decorating a Cake Board with a Ribbon

If you use a thick cake board, you can dress it up by gluing a ribbon around the outside edge. Choose a ribbon that matches the cake decorations and is the same width as the board. Cut the ribbon $\frac{1}{2}$ inch (1 cm) longer than the circumference of the board. Squeeze beads of glue around the edge of the board and spread the glue with an offset spatula. Wrap the ribbon around the board, overlapping the ends and securing the top end with glue. The ribbon can be adjusted slightly while the glue is still wet.

## Attaching the Cake to the Presentation Surface

If your decorated cake has a cardboard round supporting the bottom, you can use all-purpose glue or double-sided mounting tape to affix the round to the presentation surface. The cardboard can be removed from the presentation surface and the glue washed off after the cake has been eaten. If the cake does not have a cardboard round beneath it, place a dollop of buttercream icing on the presentation surface before setting the cake down. Always be careful when moving a cake, to ensure that it does not slide around on the presentation surface. For detailed instructions on how to transfer an iced cake to its presentation surface, see page 96.

# Cake Stands

Cake stands are a particularly good option if the cake will be displayed with other desserts or as part of a buffet. The stand lends height to the cake, spotlighting it and adding interest to the entire spread.

The number and variety of stands available these days is astonishing, and the detail and craftsmanship can be stunning. Stands for both cakes and cupcakes can be purchased in craft stores or cake supply stores, but the selection will be limited and they tend to look mass-produced. For an amazing array of cake stands in any number of colors and materials, I recommend browsing around on Etsy's website (www.etsy.com). Etsy is an online artisan marketplace with innovative products, and I love the idea of supporting other artists and interacting with the actual artisans. I found my birch slab cake platter on Etsy's site, but you can also find cake stands made from materials such as reclaimed wood, whole tree trunks, sculpted metal and blown glass.

Discount retailers such as HomeGoods, Century 21, Marshalls and T.J. Maxx are another great source for cake stands, so long as you don't have a particular style in mind. I always seem to find an attractive stand or two whenever I visit one of these stores.

# Chapter 2
# Cake and Icing Recipes

# Moist Yellow Cake

**Makes
2 cake layers**

## Hints and Tips

If you don't have a stand
mixer, you can use a
heavy-duty handheld
mixer to make this cake.
Use the mixer and a
large bowl for step 3,
then use a silicone
spatula or wooden spoon
to incorporate the flour
and buttermilk mixtures
by hand in step 4.

The addition of potato
starch to the flour reduces
the overall protein
content, allowing enough
gluten for structure but
not so much that the
cake becomes tough
and chewy. The result
is a cake that is tender
and moist, with a fine,
even crumb. For more
information on potato
starch, see page 354.

If not using both cake
layers immediately,
store the extra layer as
directed on page 345.

*There is nothing better than a simple, moist, delicate and
versatile yellow cake. This one fits the bill on all points. Enjoy!*

- Preheat oven to 350°F (180°C)
- Stand mixer, fitted with paddle attachment (see hints and tips, at left)
- Two 6-inch (15 cm) or 8-inch (20 cm) round cake pans, bottoms lined with parchment paper, paper and sides of pan sprayed with nonstick spray

### For 6-inch (15 cm) cake layers

| | | |
|---|---|---|
| 1½ cups | all-purpose flour | 375 mL |
| 3 tbsp | potato starch | 45 mL |
| 1 tsp | baking powder | 5 mL |
| ¾ tsp | baking soda | 3 mL |
| ½ tsp | salt | 2 mL |
| 1 cup | buttermilk | 250 mL |
| 1½ tsp | vanilla extract | 7 mL |
| 1 cup | superfine granulated sugar (see hints and tips, at right) | 250 mL |
| ½ cup | unsalted butter, softened | 125 mL |
| 2 | large eggs | 2 |
| 1 | large egg yolk | 1 |

### For 8-inch (20 cm) cake layers

| | | |
|---|---|---|
| 2¾ cups | all-purpose flour | 675 mL |
| ⅓ cup | potato starch | 75 mL |
| 2 tsp | baking powder | 10 mL |
| 1 tsp | baking soda | 5 mL |
| 1 tsp | salt | 5 mL |
| 2 cups | buttermilk | 500 mL |
| 1 tbsp | vanilla extract | 15 mL |
| 2 cups | superfine granulated sugar (see hints and tips, at right) | 500 mL |
| 1 cup | unsalted butter, softened | 250 mL |
| 3 | large eggs | 3 |
| 2 | large egg yolks | 2 |

1. Using a fine-mesh sieve, sift together flour, potato starch, baking powder, baking soda and salt into a medium bowl.

2. In a measuring cup or small bowl, combine buttermilk and vanilla. Set aside.

3. In stand mixer bowl, cream sugar and butter on low speed until blended. Increase speed to medium and beat until light and fluffy. Reduce speed to medium-low. Beat in eggs, one at a time, beating well after each addition, then beat in yolk(s) until well blended.

4. With the mixer on low speed, alternately beat in flour mixture and buttermilk mixture, making three additions of flour and two of buttermilk, and beating just until blended. Divide batter equally between prepared cake pans, smoothing tops.

5. Bake in preheated oven for about 35 minutes for 6-inch (15 cm) cakes or 40 minutes for 8-inch (20 cm) cakes, or until a toothpick inserted in the center comes out clean.

6. Let cool in pans on wire racks for 10 minutes, then remove from pans and let cool completely on racks before slicing and filling.

---

### Variations

**For four 4-inch (10 cm) cake layers:** Prepare the batter for the 6-inch (15 cm) cake layers and divide it equally among four prepared 4-inch (10 cm) round cake pans. Bake for 25 to 30 minutes, then let cool as directed. If not using all four cake layers immediately, store the extra layers as directed on page 345.

**For 24 cupcakes:** Line 24 cups of muffin pans with paper liners. Prepare the batter for the 6-inch (15 cm) cake layers and divide it equally among prepared muffin cups. Bake in upper and lower thirds of oven for about 18 minutes, switching pans between racks halfway through, then let cool as directed.

---

## Hints and Tips

Sugar acts not only to sweeten and flavor a cake, but also to provide structure. When sugar is creamed with butter, air is incorporated, creating volume and lightness. The finer the sugar crystal, the lighter and fluffier the batter. Do not substitute icing (confectioners') sugar for superfine sugar; they are definitely not the same thing. Popular as a quick-dissolving sweetener for iced tea, superfine sugar is frequently available at grocery stores, but you can make also make it at home by pulsing regular granulated sugar in a food processor.

When separating the yolks for this cake, be sure to save the egg whites for making buttercream (see recipe, page 46). Store egg whites in an airtight container in the refrigerator for up to 3 days or in the freezer for up to 3 months. Let thaw overnight in the refrigerator before using. Be sure to label the container with the number of egg whites and the date.

# Rich Chocolate Cake

**Makes
2 cake layers**

## Hints and Tips

If you don't have a double boiler, fill a medium saucepan with 1 inch (2.5 cm) of water and place a deep, heatproof bowl on top, making sure the bowl does not touch the water (it is the steam that will gently heat the chocolate).

If you don't have a stand mixer, you can use a heavy-duty handheld mixer to make this cake. Use the mixer and a large bowl for step 4, then use a silicone spatula or wooden spoon to incorporate the flour and sour cream mixtures by hand in step 5.

*There's nothing subtle about this cake. It's moist, packed with flavor and full of chocolaty goodness, without being too dense or heavy.*

- Preheat oven to 350°F (180°C)
- Double boiler (see hints and tips, at left)
- Stand mixer, fitted with paddle attachment (see hints and tips, at left)
- Two 6-inch (15 cm) or 8-inch (20 cm) round cake pans, bottoms lined with parchment paper, paper and sides of pan sprayed with nonstick spray

### For 6-inch (15 cm) cake layers

| | | |
|---|---|---|
| 1 tsp | instant coffee granules | 5 mL |
| ⅓ cup | boiling water | 75 mL |
| 1½ oz | unsweetened chocolate, coarsely chopped | 45 g |
| 1 cup | all-purpose flour | 250 mL |
| ⅓ cup | unsweetened cocoa powder | 75 mL |
| 1 tsp | baking soda | 5 mL |
| ½ tsp | salt | 2 mL |
| ⅓ cup | sour cream | 75 mL |
| 1½ tsp | vanilla extract | 7 mL |
| ½ tsp | white vinegar | 2 mL |
| 1 cup | packed brown sugar | 250 mL |
| ¼ cup | unsalted butter, softened | 60 mL |
| 2 | large eggs | 2 |

### For 8-inch (20 cm) cake layers

| | | |
|---|---|---|
| 2 tsp | instant coffee granules | 10 mL |
| 1 cup | boiling water | 250 mL |
| 3 oz | unsweetened chocolate, coarsely chopped | 90 g |
| 2 cups | all-purpose flour | 500 mL |
| ⅔ cup | unsweetened cocoa powder | 150 mL |
| 2 tsp | baking soda | 10 mL |
| 1 tsp | salt | 5 mL |
| 1 cup | sour cream | 250 mL |
| 1 tbsp | vanilla extract | 15 mL |
| 1 tsp | white vinegar | 5 mL |
| 2 cups | packed brown sugar | 500 mL |
| ½ cup | unsalted butter, softened | 125 mL |
| 3 | large eggs | 3 |

1. In the top of the double boiler, over simmering water, whisk together coffee granules and boiling water until coffee is dissolved. Add chocolate and heat gently, whisking often, until chocolate is melted. Remove from heat and set aside to cool slightly.

2. Using a sieve, sift together flour, cocoa, baking soda and salt into a medium bowl.

3. In a measuring cup or a medium bowl, whisk together sour cream, vanilla and vinegar. Whisk in slightly cooled coffee mixture. Set aside.

4. In stand mixer bowl, cream brown sugar and butter on medium-low speed until well blended. Beat in eggs, one at a time, beating well after each addition, until well blended.

5. With the mixer on low speed, alternately beat in flour mixture and sour cream mixture, making three additions of flour and two of sour cream, and beating just until blended. Divide batter equally between prepared cake pans, smoothing tops.

6. Bake in preheated oven for about 35 minutes for 6-inch (15 cm) cakes or 40 minutes for 8-inch (20 cm) cakes, or until a toothpick inserted in the center comes out clean.

7. Let cool in pans on wire racks for 10 minutes, then remove from pans and let cool completely on racks before slicing and filling.

## Hints and Tips

You can replace the boiling water and instant coffee granules with 1 cup (250 mL) strongly brewed coffee.

If not using both cake layers immediately, store the extra layer as directed on page 345.

### Variations

**For four 4-inch (10 cm) cake layers:** Prepare the batter for the 6-inch (15 cm) cake layers and divide it equally among four prepared 4-inch (10 cm) round cake pans. Bake for about 25 minutes, then let cool as directed. If not using all four cake layers immediately, store the extra layers as directed on page 345.

**For 24 cupcakes:** Line 24 cups of muffin pans with paper liners. Prepare the batter for the 6-inch (15 cm) cake layers and divide it equally among prepared muffin cups. Bake in upper and lower thirds of oven for about 18 minutes, switching pans between racks halfway through, then let cool as directed.

# Pink Velvet Cake

## Hints and Tips

If you don't have a stand mixer, you can use a heavy-duty handheld mixer to make this cake. Use the mixer and a large bowl for step 6, then use a silicone spatula or wooden spoon to incorporate the flour and buttermilk mixtures by hand in step 7.

Freeze-dried strawberries can sometimes be found at local grocery stores or health food stores, and are available at large online retailers. You'll need just under 1 oz (30 g) for 1⅓ cups (325 mL) and just under 2 oz (60 g) for 2⅔ cups (650 mL). For more information on freeze-dried strawberries, see page 355.

If not using both cake layers immediately, store the extra layer as directed on page 345.

*This scrumptious cake delivers vibrant strawberry flavor, for a little bit of summer sweetness in every bite!*

- Preheat oven to 350°F (180°C)
- Mini chopper or food processor
- Stand mixer, fitted with paddle attachment (see hints and tips, at left)
- Two 6-inch (15 cm) or 8-inch (20 cm) round cake pans, bottoms lined with parchment paper, paper and sides of pan sprayed with nonstick spray

### For 6-inch (15 cm) cake layers

| | | |
|---|---|---|
| 10 oz | unsweetened frozen strawberries, thawed, juice reserved | 300 g |
| 1⅓ cups | freeze-dried strawberries (optional; see hints and tips, at left) | 325 mL |
| 1½ cups | all-purpose flour | 375 mL |
| 3 tbsp | potato starch | 45 mL |
| 1½ tsp | baking powder | 7 mL |
| ½ tsp | salt | 2 mL |
| ½ cup | buttermilk | 125 mL |
| 2 tbsp | freshly squeezed lemon juice | 30 mL |
| 1½ tsp | vanilla extract | 7 mL |
| 1 cup | superfine granulated sugar (see hints and tips, page 31) | 250 mL |
| ½ cup | unsalted butter, softened | 125 mL |
| 4 | large egg whites | 4 |

### For 8-inch (20 cm) cake layers

| | | |
|---|---|---|
| 1¼ lbs | unsweetened frozen strawberries, thawed, juice reserved | 625 g |
| 2⅔ cups | freeze-dried strawberries (optional; see hints and tips, at left) | 650 mL |
| 3 cups | all-purpose flour | 750 mL |
| 6 tbsp | potato starch | 90 mL |
| 2 tsp | baking powder | 10 mL |
| 1 tsp | salt | 5 mL |
| 1 cup | buttermilk | 250 mL |
| ¼ cup | freshly squeezed lemon juice | 60 mL |
| 1 tbsp | vanilla extract | 15 mL |
| 2 cups | superfine granulated sugar (see hints and tips, page 31) | 500 mL |
| 1 cup | unsalted butter, softened | 250 mL |
| 8 | large egg whites | 8 |

1. In a small saucepan for the 6-inch (15 cm) cakes or a large saucepan for the 8-inch (20 cm) cakes, bring thawed frozen strawberries and juice to a simmer over medium heat, mashing occasionally. Reduce heat and simmer, stirring often, for about 5 minutes or until soft. Strain strawberries through a sieve, using a spatula to press juices and thin pulp through into a bowl. Discard any pulp and seeds left in sieve.

2. Return strawberry juice to saucepan and bring to a boil over medium heat, stirring. Reduce heat and boil gently, stirring constantly, for about 10 minutes or until reduced to about $\frac{1}{3}$ cup (75 mL) for the 6-inch (15 cm) cakes, or for about 15 minutes or until reduced to about $\frac{2}{3}$ cup (150 mL) for the 8-inch (20 cm) cakes. Measure the exact amount in a liquid measuring cup and set aside to cool completely (reserve any extra for another use).

3. If using freeze-dried strawberries, process them in the mini chopper until fairly fine and powdery. Measure $\frac{1}{3}$ cup (75 mL) for the 6-inch (15 cm) cakes or $\frac{2}{3}$ cup (150 mL) for the 8-inch (20 cm) cakes.

4. Using a clean, dry fine-mesh sieve, sift together flour, potato starch, baking powder and salt into a medium bowl. Stir in strawberry powder (if using).

5. In a measuring cup or a small bowl, combine buttermilk, lemon juice and vanilla. Whisk in cooled strawberry purée. Set aside.

6. In stand mixer bowl, cream sugar and butter on low speed until blended. Increase speed to medium and beat until light and fluffy. Reduce speed to medium-low. Beat in egg whites, one at a time, beating well after each addition, until well blended.

7. With the mixer on low speed, alternately beat in flour mixture and buttermilk mixture, making three additions of flour and two of buttermilk, and beating just until blended. Divide batter equally between prepared cake pans, smoothing tops.

8. Bake in preheated oven for about 40 minutes for 6-inch (15 cm) cakes or 50 minutes for 8-inch (20 cm) cakes, or until a toothpick inserted in the center comes out clean.

9. Let cool in pans on wire racks for 10 minutes, then remove from pans and let cool completely on racks before slicing and filling.

## Variation

**For four 4-inch (10 cm) cake layers:** Prepare the batter for the 6-inch (15 cm) cake layers and divide it equally among four prepared 4-inch (10 cm) round cake pans. Bake for 30 to 35 minutes, then let cool as directed. If not using all four cake layers immediately, store the extra layers as directed on page 345.

**For 24 cupcakes:** Line 24 cups of muffin pans with paper liners. Prepare the batter for the 6-inch (15 cm) cake layers and divide it equally among prepared muffin cups. Bake in upper and lower thirds of oven for about 20 to 25 minutes, switching pans between racks halfway through, then let cool as directed.

# Mama Suzanne's Carrot Cake

## Hints and Tips

If you don't have a stand mixer, you can use a heavy-duty handheld mixer to make this cake. Use the mixer and a large bowl for step 2, then use a silicone spatula or wooden spoon to incorporate the flour mixture by hand in step 3.

If not using both cake layers immediately, store the extra layer as directed on page 345.

*Ever since I met my friend Ryan, I have been hearing about his mother's scrumptious carrot cake. Ryan had reason to boast: Suzanne's carrot cake is indeed outstanding, chock full of all the delicious chew and crunch one expects from a carrot cake. Soaking the cake in a sweet buttermilk glaze ensures that it's moist and flavorful. Thank you, Suzanne!*

- Preheat oven to 350°F (180°C)
- Stand mixer, fitted with paddle attachment (see hints and tips)
- Two 6-inch (15 cm) or 8-inch (20 cm) round cake pans, bottoms lined with parchment paper, paper and sides of pan sprayed with nonstick spray

### For 6-inch (15 cm) cake layers

| | | |
|---|---|---|
| 1¼ cups | all-purpose flour | 300 mL |
| 1 tsp | baking soda | 5 mL |
| 1 tsp | ground cinnamon | 5 mL |
| ¼ tsp | ground ginger | 1 mL |
| ½ tsp | salt | 2 mL |
| 1 cup | granulated sugar | 250 mL |
| 2 | large eggs | 2 |
| ⅓ cup | vegetable oil | 75 mL |
| ⅓ cup | buttermilk | 75 mL |
| 1 tsp | vanilla extract | 5 mL |
| 1 cup | grated carrots (about 2) | 250 mL |
| ⅓ cup | drained canned crushed pineapple | 75 mL |
| ½ cup | sweetened flaked coconut | 125 mL |
| ½ cup | chopped pecans or walnuts | 125 mL |
| | Buttermilk Glaze (see recipe, opposite) | |

### For 8-inch (20 cm) cake layers

| | | |
|---|---|---|
| 2¼ cups | all-purpose flour | 550 mL |
| 2 tsp | baking soda | 10 mL |
| 2 tsp | ground cinnamon | 10 mL |
| ½ tsp | ground ginger | 2 mL |
| 1 tsp | salt | 5 mL |
| 2 cups | granulated sugar | 500 mL |
| 3 | large eggs | 3 |
| ¾ cup | vegetable oil | 175 mL |
| ¾ cup | buttermilk | 175 mL |
| 2 tsp | vanilla extract | 10 mL |
| 2 cups | grated carrots (3 to 4) | 500 mL |
| 1 | can (8 oz/227 mL) crushed pineapple, drained (¾ cup/175 mL) | 1 |

| 1 cup | sweetened flaked coconut | 250 mL |
| 1 cup | chopped pecans or walnuts | 250 mL |
|  | Buttermilk Glaze (see recipe, below) |  |

1. Using a fine-mesh sieve, sift together flour, baking soda, cinnamon, ginger and salt into a medium bowl.

2. In stand mixer bowl, combine sugar, eggs, oil, buttermilk and vanilla. Beat on medium speed until smooth.

3. With the mixer on low speed, gradually add flour mixture in two additions, beating just until blended.

4. Using a spatula, fold in carrots, pineapple, coconut and nuts by hand, just until evenly distributed. Divide batter equally between prepared cake pans, smoothing tops.

5. Bake in preheated oven for about 40 minutes for 6-inch (15 cm) cakes or 45 minutes for 8-inch (20 cm) cakes, or until a toothpick inserted in the center comes out clean.

6. Immediately drizzle Buttermilk Glaze evenly over cakes, using about $\frac{1}{3}$ cup (75 mL) for each 6-inch (15 cm) layer or $\frac{3}{4}$ cup (175 mL) for each 8-inch (20 cm) layer.

7. Let cool in pans on wire racks for 15 minutes, then remove from pans and let cool completely on racks before slicing and filling.

# Buttermilk Glaze
## Makes about 1$\frac{1}{2}$ cups (375 mL)

| $\frac{3}{4}$ cup | granulated sugar | 175 mL |
| 1$\frac{1}{2}$ tsp | baking soda | 7 mL |
| $\frac{1}{2}$ cup | buttermilk | 125 mL |
| $\frac{1}{2}$ cup | unsalted butter | 125 mL |
| 1 tbsp | light (white) corn syrup | 15 mL |
| 1 tsp | vanilla extract | 5 mL |

1. In a heavy saucepan, combine sugar, baking soda, buttermilk, butter and corn syrup. Bring to a boil over medium-high heat, stirring often. Reduce heat and boil, stirring often, for 4 minutes. Remove from heat and stir in vanilla.

2. Use immediately or cover and refrigerate for up to 3 days. If refrigerated, reheat gently in a saucepan or in the microwave, stirring often, until warmed before using.

**Variations**

**For four 4-inch (10 cm) cake layers:** Prepare the batter for the 6-inch (15 cm) cake layers and divide it equally among four prepared 4-inch (10 cm) round cake pans. Bake for about 30 minutes, drizzle each layer with 2$\frac{1}{2}$ tbsp (37 mL) glaze, then let cool as directed. If not using all four cake layers immediately, store the extra layers as directed on page 345.

**For 24 small cupcakes:** Line 24 cups of muffin pans with paper liners. Prepare the batter for the 6-inch (15 cm) cake layers and divide it equally among prepared muffin cups. Bake in upper and lower thirds of oven for about 20 minutes, switching pans between racks halfway through, then let cool as directed. Omit the glaze.

# Sweet Potato Spice Cake

**Makes
2 cake layers**

## Hints and Tips

The sweet potatoes can be baked and mashed a day or two in advance. Refrigerate mashed potatoes in an airtight container for up to 2 days. Let warm to room temperature before adding to batter.

If you have a potato ricer, you can press the sweet potatoes through the ricer to mash them in step 2. Don't be tempted to use a food processor or blender, as that may create an undesirable texture for this cake.

This cake is particularly delicious with Cream Cheese Icing (page 50).

If not using both cake layers immediately, store the extra layer as directed on page 345.

*Like the sweet potatoes themselves, this confectionery creation bakes up particularly light and fluffy. The aromatic ground cinnamon, ginger, nutmeg and cloves and the chewy goodness of crystallized ginger make this a perfect cake for holiday gatherings and cold winter nights.*

- **Preheat oven to 350°F (180°C)**
- **Baking sheet, lined with foil**
- **Stand mixer, fitted with paddle attachment (see hints and tips, at left)**
- **Two 6-inch (15 cm) or 8-inch (20 cm) round cake pans, bottoms lined with parchment paper, paper and sides of pan sprayed with nonstick spray**

### For 6-inch (15 cm) cake layers

| | | |
|---|---|---|
| 1¼ lbs | sweet potatoes (about 2 medium) | 625 g |
| 1½ cups | all-purpose flour | 375 mL |
| 1¼ tsp | baking powder | 6 mL |
| ¾ tsp | ground cinnamon | 3 mL |
| ¼ tsp | baking soda | 1 mL |
| ¼ tsp | salt | 1 mL |
| ¼ tsp | ground ginger | 1 mL |
| ¼ tsp | ground nutmeg | 1 mL |
| ⅛ tsp | ground cloves | 0.5 mL |
| ¾ cup | packed brown sugar | 175 mL |
| 6 tbsp | unsalted butter, softened | 90 mL |
| 1 | large egg | 1 |
| ½ tsp | vanilla extract | 2 mL |
| 2 tbsp | minced crystallized ginger | 30 mL |

### For 8-inch (20 cm) cake layers

| | | |
|---|---|---|
| 2 lbs | sweet potatoes (3 to 4 medium) | 1 kg |
| 3 cups | all-purpose flour | 750 mL |
| 2¼ tsp | baking powder | 11 mL |
| 1½ tsp | ground cinnamon | 7 mL |
| ¾ tsp | baking soda | 3 mL |
| ¾ tsp | salt | 3 mL |

| | | |
|---|---|---|
| ½ tsp | ground ginger | 2 mL |
| ½ tsp | ground nutmeg | 2 mL |
| ¼ tsp | ground cloves | 1 mL |
| 1½ cups | packed brown sugar | 375 mL |
| ¾ cup | unsalted butter, softened | 175 mL |
| 3 | large eggs | 3 |
| 1 tsp | vanilla extract | 5 mL |
| 3 tbsp | minced crystallized ginger | 45 mL |

1. Using a fork, prick holes all over sweet potatoes. Place on prepared baking sheet and bake in preheated oven for about 1¼ hours, turning occasionally, until very soft and pliable. Remove from oven, leaving oven on, and let cool completely.

2. Peel cooled sweet potatoes and place in a large bowl. Mash with a potato masher or fork until smooth and no large lumps remain. Measure 1⅓ cups (325 mL) for the 6-inch (15 cm) cakes or 2½ cups (625 mL) for the 8-inch (20 cm) cakes (reserve any extra for another use).

3. Using a fine-mesh sieve, sift together flour, baking powder, cinnamon, baking soda, salt, ground ginger, nutmeg and cloves into a medium bowl.

4. In stand mixer bowl, cream brown sugar and butter on low speed until blended. Increase speed to medium and beat until light and fluffy. Reduce speed to medium-low. Beat in egg(s), one at a time, beating well after each addition, until well blended. Beat in vanilla.

5. With the mixer on low speed, alternately beat in flour mixture and mashed sweet potato, making three additions of flour and two of sweet potato, and beating just until blended. Using a spatula, fold in crystallized ginger by hand. Divide batter equally between prepared cake pans, smoothing tops.

6. Bake for about 35 minutes for 6-inch (15 cm) cakes or 40 minutes for 8-inch (20 cm) cakes, or until a toothpick inserted in the center comes out clean.

7. Let cool in pans on wire racks for 10 minutes, then remove from pans and let cool completely on racks before slicing and filling.

**Variation**

**For four 4-inch (10 cm) cake layers:** Prepare the batter for the 6-inch (15 cm) cake layers and divide it equally among four prepared 4-inch (10 cm) round cake pans. Bake for about 25 minutes, then let cool as directed. If not using all four cake layers immediately, store the extra layers as directed on page 345.

# Gluten-Free Chocolate Cake

**Makes
2 cake layers**

## Hints and Tips

If you don't have a double boiler, fill a medium saucepan with 1 inch (2.5 cm) of water and place a deep, heatproof bowl on top, making sure the bowl does not touch the water (it is the steam that will gently heat the chocolate).

If you don't have a stand mixer, you can use a heavy-duty handheld mixer to make this cake. Use the mixer and a large bowl for step 4, then use a silicone spatula or wooden spoon to incorporate the flour and sour cream mixtures by hand in step 5.

You can replace the boiling water and instant coffee granules with 1 cup (250 mL) strongly brewed coffee.

Check the labels for all ingredients to be sure they do not contain any gluten. It's best to check each time you buy a product, as formulas and labels can change, so something that was gluten-free the last time you bought it may, indeed, contain gluten.

*This luscious cake bakes up light and fluffy, perfect for slicing and layering.*

- Preheat oven to 350°F (180°C)
- Double boiler (see hints and tips, at left)
- Stand mixer, fitted with paddle attachment (see hints and tips)
- Two 6-inch (15 cm) or 8-inch (20 cm) round cake pans, bottoms lined with parchment paper, paper and sides of pan sprayed with nonstick spray

### For 6-inch (15 cm) cake layers

| | | |
|---|---|---|
| 1 tsp | instant coffee granules | 5 mL |
| 1/3 cup | boiling water | 75 mL |
| 1 1/2 oz | unsweetened chocolate, coarsely chopped | 45 g |
| 1 1/3 cups | Gluten-Free Flour Mix (see recipe, opposite) | 325 mL |
| 1/3 cup | unsweetened cocoa powder | 75 mL |
| 1 tsp | baking soda | 5 mL |
| 1/2 tsp | salt | 2 mL |
| 1/2 cup | sour cream | 125 mL |
| 1 1/2 tsp | vanilla extract | 7 mL |
| 1/2 tsp | white vinegar | 2 mL |
| 1 cup | packed brown sugar | 250 mL |
| 1/4 cup | unsalted butter, softened | 60 mL |
| 2 | large eggs | 2 |

### For 8-inch (20 cm) cake layers

| | | |
|---|---|---|
| 2 tsp | instant coffee granules | 10 mL |
| 1 cup | boiling water | 250 mL |
| 3 oz | unsweetened chocolate, coarsely chopped | 90 g |
| 2 2/3 cups | Gluten-Free Flour Mix (see recipe, opposite) | 650 mL |
| 2/3 cup | unsweetened cocoa powder | 150 mL |
| 2 tsp | baking soda | 10 mL |
| 1 tsp | salt | 5 mL |
| 1 cup | sour cream | 250 mL |
| 1 1/2 tsp | vanilla extract | 7 mL |
| 1 tsp | white vinegar | 5 mL |
| 2 cups | packed brown sugar | 500 mL |
| 1/2 cup | unsalted butter, softened | 125 mL |
| 3 | large eggs | 3 |

1. In the top of the double boiler, over simmering water, whisk together coffee granules and boiling water until coffee is dissolved. Add chocolate and heat gently, whisking often, until chocolate is melted. Remove from heat and set aside to cool slightly.

2. Using a sieve, sift together flour mix, cocoa, baking soda and salt into a medium bowl.

3. In a measuring cup or a medium bowl, whisk together sour cream, vanilla and vinegar. Whisk in slightly cooled coffee mixture. Set aside.

4. In stand mixer bowl, cream brown sugar and butter on medium-low speed until well blended. Beat in eggs, one at a time, beating well after each addition, until well blended.

5. With the mixer on low speed, alternately beat in flour mixture and sour cream mixture, making three additions of flour and two of sour cream, and beating just until blended. Divide batter equally between prepared cake pans, smoothing tops.

6. Bake in preheated oven for about 35 minutes for 6-inch (15 cm) cakes or 40 minutes for 8-inch (20 cm) cakes, or until a toothpick inserted in the center comes out clean.

7. Let cool in pans on wire racks for 10 minutes, then remove from pans and let cool completely on racks before slicing and filling.

# Gluten-Free Flour Mix

*After searching high and low for a gratifying gluten-free mix, I came up with this winning combination. You can double or triple this recipe to make larger cakes or just to keep on hand; just be sure to use a very large bowl so you can thoroughly whisk the ingredients.*

**Makes about 2$\frac{2}{3}$ cups (650 mL)**

| | | |
|---|---|---|
| 1 cup | certified gluten-free oat flour | 250 mL |
| 1 cup | potato starch | 250 mL |
| $\frac{1}{3}$ cup | almond meal (almond flour) | 75 mL |
| 1 tsp | xanthan gum | 5 mL |

1. In a bowl, whisk together oat flour, potato starch, almond meal and xanthan gum until well blended.

2. Use immediately or store in an airtight container in a cool dark place for up to 1 month.

## Variations

**For four 4-inch (10 cm) cake layers:** Prepare the batter for the 6-inch (15 cm) cake layers and divide it equally among four prepared 4-inch (10 cm) round cake pans. Bake for 25 to 30 minutes, then let cool as directed. If not using all four cake layers immediately, store the extra layers as directed on page 345.

**For 24 cupcakes:** Line 24 cups of muffin pans with paper liners. Prepare the batter for the 6-inch (15 cm) cakes and divide it equally among prepared muffin cups. Bake in upper and lower thirds of oven for about 20 minutes, switching pans between racks halfway through, then let cool as directed.

# Gluten-Free Blueberry Lavender Cake

**Makes
2 cake layers**

## Hints and Tips

If you don't have a stand mixer, you can use a heavy-duty handheld mixer to make this cake. Use the mixer and a large bowl for step 4, then use a silicone spatula or wooden spoon to incorporate the flour and buttermilk mixtures by hand in step 5.

Make sure to purchase high-quality food-grade lavender buds that are free from pesticides and additives. Lavender buds and lavender extract can sometimes be found at grocery stores, but you might have better luck at gourmet food stores or large online retailers.

Check the labels for all ingredients to be sure they do not contain any gluten. It's best to check each time you buy a product, as formulas and labels can change, so something that was gluten-free the last time you bought it may, indeed, contain gluten.

*Fresh blueberries balance the floral notes of the lavender, giving this cake a unique, subtle flavor.*

- **Preheat oven to 325°F (160°C)**
- **Stand mixer, fitted with paddle attachment (see hints and tips, at left)**
- **Two 6-inch (15 cm) or 8-inch (20 cm) round cake pans, bottoms lined with parchment paper, paper and sides of pan sprayed with nonstick spray**

### For 6-inch (15 cm) cake layers

| | | |
|---|---|---|
| 1¾ cups | Gluten-Free Flour Mix (see recipe, page 41) | 425 mL |
| 1½ tbsp | potato starch | 22 mL |
| 1 tsp | baking powder | 5 mL |
| ¾ tsp | baking soda | 3 mL |
| ½ tsp | salt | 2 mL |
| 1 tsp | dried lavender flowers, crushed | 5 mL |
| 1 cup | buttermilk | 250 mL |
| 1 tsp | vanilla powder (optional; see hints and tips, at right) | 5 mL |
| ½ tsp | vanilla extract | 2 mL |
| 2 | large eggs, separated, whites at room temperature | 2 |
| 1 cup | superfine granulated sugar (see hints and tips, page 31) | 250 mL |
| ½ cup | unsalted butter, softened | 125 mL |
| 1 cup | blueberries | 250 mL |

### For 8-inch (20 cm) cake layers

| | | |
|---|---|---|
| 3½ cups | Gluten-Free Flour Mix (see recipe, page 41) | 875 mL |
| 3 tbsp | potato starch | 45 mL |
| 2 tsp | baking powder | 10 mL |
| 1¼ tsp | baking soda | 6 mL |
| 1 tsp | salt | 5 mL |
| 2 tsp | dried lavender flowers, crushed | 10 mL |
| 2 cups | buttermilk | 500 mL |
| 2 tsp | vanilla powder (optional; see hints and tips, at right) | 10 mL |
| 1 tsp | vanilla extract | 5 mL |
| 4 | large eggs, separated, whites at room temperature | 4 |

| 2 cups | superfine granulated sugar (see hints and tips, page 31) | 500 mL |
| 1 cup | unsalted butter, softened | 250 mL |
| 2 cups | blueberries | 500 mL |

1. Using a sieve, sift together flour mix, potato starch, baking powder, baking soda and salt into a medium bowl. Stir in lavender.

2. In a measuring cup or small bowl, combine buttermilk, vanilla powder (if using) and vanilla extract. Set aside.

3. In a medium bowl, using a handheld electric mixer or whisk, beat egg whites until firm peaks form. Set aside.

4. In stand mixer bowl, cream sugar and butter on low speed until blended. Increase speed to medium and beat until light and fluffy. Reduce speed to medium-low and beat in egg yolks, one at a time, beating well after each addition, until well blended.

5. With the mixer on low speed, alternately beat in flour mixture and buttermilk mixture, making three additions of flour and two of buttermilk, and beating just until blended. Using a silicone spatula, fold in egg whites just until blended. Gently fold in blueberries, just until evenly distributed. Divide batter equally between prepared cake pans, smoothing tops.

6. Bake in preheated oven for about 45 minutes for 6-inch (15 cm) cakes or 55 minutes for 8-inch (20 cm) cakes, or until a toothpick inserted in the center comes out clean.

7. Let cool in pans on wire racks for 10 minutes, then remove from pans and let cool completely on racks before slicing and filling.

---

### Variations

**For four 4-inch (10 cm) cake layers:** Prepare the batter for the 6-inch (15 cm) cake layers and divide it equally among four prepared 4-inch (10 cm) round cake pans. Bake for about 35 minutes, then let cool as directed. If not using all four cake layers immediately, store the extra layers as directed on page 345.

**For 24 cupcakes:** Line 24 cups of muffin pans with paper liners. Prepare the batter for the 6-inch (15 cm) cakes and divide it equally among prepared muffin cups. Bake in upper and lower thirds of 350°F (180°C) oven for about 20 minutes, switching pans between racks halfway through, then let cool as directed.

## Hints and Tips

Vanilla powder is made from finely ground dried vanilla beans and provides an intense vanilla flavor. It is available at baking supply stores, specialty food stores and online retailers. There are two varieties of vanilla powder: one that is off-white and is a mixture of vanilla extractives and other ingredients (usually sugars and/or starches); and one that is dark brown and is just ground vanilla beans, with no additives. If you have the variety without additives, use one-quarter of the amount called for in this recipe. If you can't find vanilla powder, use triple the amount of vanilla extract called for.

If not using both cake layers immediately, store the extra layer as directed on page 345.

# Vegan Banana Cake

**Makes
2 cake layers**

## Hints and Tips

If you don't have a stand mixer, you can use a heavy-duty handheld mixer or a sturdy whisk to make this cake. Use the mixer or whisk and a large bowl for step 2, then use a silicone spatula or wooden spoon to incorporate the flour mixture by hand as directed in step 3.

Bananas with brown spots are the preferred choice for baking recipes, as they are easier to mash and are particularly sweet and flavorful. Mash bananas with a fork, a potato masher or ricer or a wooden spoon — not a blender or food processor. Tasty little lumps are to be expected in the batter.

*If you doubt that a cake without butter or eggs could possibly compare to a traditional cake, this moist banana cake will turn you into a believer. As a bonus, this is a particularly easy cake to make.*

- Preheat oven to 350°F (180°C)
- Stand mixer, fitted with paddle attachment (see hints and tips, at left)
- Two 6-inch (15 cm) or 8-inch (20 cm) round cake pans, bottoms lined with parchment paper, paper and sides of pan sprayed with nonstick spray

### For 6-inch (15 cm) cake layers

| | | |
|---|---|---|
| 1½ cups | all-purpose flour | 375 mL |
| 1 tsp | baking powder | 5 mL |
| 1 tsp | baking soda | 5 mL |
| ¼ tsp | salt | 1 mL |
| ¾ cup | superfine granulated sugar (see hints and tips, page 31) | 175 mL |
| 1½ cups | mashed ripe bananas (about 4) | 375 mL |
| ½ cup | melted coconut oil or vegan buttery spread (see hints and tips, at right) | 125 mL |
| ¼ cup | coconut milk or other unsweetened non-dairy milk (see hints and tips, at right) | 60 mL |
| 1½ tbsp | white vinegar | 22 mL |
| ½ tsp | vanilla extract | 2 mL |

### For 8-inch (20 cm) cake layers

| | | |
|---|---|---|
| 3 cups | all-purpose flour | 750 mL |
| 2 tsp | baking powder | 10 mL |
| 1 tsp | baking soda | 5 mL |
| ½ tsp | salt | 2 mL |
| 1½ cups | superfine granulated sugar (see hints and tips, page 31) | 375 mL |
| 3 cups | mashed ripe bananas (about 8) | 750 mL |
| 1 cup | melted coconut oil or vegan buttery spread (see hints and tips, at right) | 250 mL |
| ½ cup | coconut milk or other unsweetened non-dairy milk (see hints and tips, at right) | 125 mL |
| 3 tbsp | white vinegar | 45 mL |
| 1 tsp | vanilla extract | 5 mL |

1. Using a fine-mesh sieve, sift together flour, baking powder, baking soda and salt into a medium bowl. Whisk in sugar.

2. In stand mixer bowl, combine bananas, coconut oil, coconut milk, vinegar and vanilla. Beat on medium-low speed until well blended.

3. With the mixer on low speed, gradually add flour mixture in two additions, beating just until moistened. The batter will be slightly lumpy. Divide batter equally between prepared cake pans, smoothing tops.

4. Bake in preheated oven for about 35 minutes for 6-inch (15 cm) cakes or 40 minutes for 8-inch (20 cm) cakes, or until a toothpick inserted in the center comes out clean.

5. Let cool in pans on wire racks for 10 minutes, then remove from pans and let cool completely on racks before slicing and filling.

---

### Variations

**For four 4-inch (10 cm) cake layers:** Prepare the batter for the 6-inch (15 cm) cake layers and divide it equally among four prepared 4-inch (10 cm) round cake pans. Bake for 25 to 30 minutes, then let cool as directed. If not using all four cake layers immediately, store the extra layers as directed on page 345.

**For 24 small cupcakes:** Line 24 cups of muffin pans with paper liners. Prepare the batter for the 6-inch (15 cm) cakes and divide it equally among prepared muffin cups. Bake in upper and lower thirds of oven for about 18 minutes, switching pans between racks halfway through, then let cool as directed.

---

## Hints and Tips

Look for a vegan buttery spread, such as Smart Balance Original Buttery Spread or Earth Balance vegan buttery spread or sticks, in the natural foods section of major supermarkets or at health food or specialty stores. These brands have a pleasant flavor and are particularly good for baking.

Use canned unsweetened coconut milk (not coconut beverage) in this recipe. When you open the can, whisk the coconut milk well before measuring to incorporate the thick cream that floats to the top.

Coconut milk adds a subtle complexity to the flavor of this cake, but any other non-dairy milk, such as soy, rice or almond, will also work well. Just be sure to use an unsweetened variety with no other flavoring.

If not using both cake layers immediately, store the extra layer as directed on page 345.

# Swiss Meringue Buttercream Icing

**Makes about 5 cups (1.25 L)**

## Hints and Tips

If you don't have a double boiler, fill a medium saucepan with 1 inch (2.5 cm) of water and place a deep, heatproof bowl on top, making sure the bowl does not touch the water (it is the steam that will gently heat the eggs).

If you don't have a stand mixer, you can use a heavy-duty handheld mixer to make the buttercream. It will take quite a long time and can get tiring to hold the mixer, so a kitchen helper to take turns with would be very handy.

Swiss meringue buttercream icing that has not been colored is naturally off-white or ivory.

*This meringue-based icing is sweet but not too sweet and light without being insubstantial, and it pairs well with just about any cake. The neutral vanilla flavor allows you to add flavorings as desired, to match (or contrast) the flavor of your icing to the flavor of your cake. This luscious confection is not only the icing on the cake but also the artist's medium. Swiss meringue buttercream has a particular ability to stretch and bend, and a pliable firmness that allows for the creation of multidimensional decorations.*

- Double boiler (see hints and tips, at left)
- Stand mixer, fitted with whisk attachment (see hints and tips, at left)

| | | |
|---|---|---|
| 1½ cups | granulated sugar | 375 mL |
| Pinch | salt | Pinch |
| 1 cup | large egg whites (about 7) | 250 mL |
| 1½ tsp | vanilla extract | 7 mL |
| 2 cups | unsalted butter, softened (1 lb/454 g) | 500 mL |

1. In the top of the double boiler, over gently simmering water, whisk together sugar, salt and egg whites. Heat, whisking constantly, until sugar is dissolved and the mixture reaches 140°F (60°C) or is uncomfortably hot to the touch.

2. Pour egg mixture into stand mixer bowl and beat on medium speed until soft peaks form and the mixture is cooled to room temperature. Beat in vanilla.

3. Meanwhile, cut butter into small cubes, about ¼ inch (5 mm) in size.

4. Add butter cubes to the cooled egg mixture, two or three at a time, beating until all of the butter is incorporated and the icing is smooth and satiny.

5. Use immediately or cover with plastic wrap directly on the surface and store at a cool room temperature for up to 24 hours.

## Egg White Hints and Tips

- The purpose of heating egg whites is not to cook them but to pasteurize them, destroying any potentially dangerous microorganisms. This is especially important for women who are pregnant or anyone with a compromised immune system. Gently heating them in a double boiler while whisking constantly ensures that the eggs reach the appropriate temperature without turning into an omelet. If you do happen to have a few particles of cooked egg in your whites at the end of step 1, run them through a fine-mesh sieve before proceeding with step 2.

- Egg whites detest grease. Even a minute trace of grease can make a botched batch of meringue. Before beginning this recipe, use a paper towel dampened with lemon juice or vinegar to wipe down all equipment that will come in contact with the egg whites.

- To determine whether the egg whites have cooled to room temperature in step 2, hold your hand against the outside of the bowl to gauge the general temperature.

- Sometimes, after you've achieved beautiful glossy peaks, the meringue begins to separate and curdle when the butter is added. Don't panic! This common occurrence is related to the temperature of the butter. The buttercream will right itself; just keep beating!

### Variations

**Chocolate Buttercream Icing:** In the top of a double boiler (or see hints and tips, page 46), over simmering water, melt 6 oz (175 g) bittersweet chocolate, whisking often. Let cool (but not to the point of solidifying), then beat into the buttercream at the end of step 4.

**Lemon Buttercream Icing:** Beat in 1 tsp (5 mL) pure lemon extract and the grated zest of 1 lemon at the end of step 4.

**Orange Buttercream Icing:** Beat in 2 tbsp (30 mL) orange liqueur and the grated zest of 1 orange at the end of step 4.

**Coconut Buttercream Icing:** Beat in $2/3$ cup (150 mL) coconut milk and 1 tsp (5 mL) coconut extract at the end of step 4. For added texture, beat in $2/3$ cup (150 mL) flaked coconut, if desired.

**Peanut Butter Buttercream Icing:** Beat in 1 cup (250 mL) smooth peanut butter at the end of step 4. Make sure the peanut butter isn't too cold and stiff, so that it blends in easily.

## Hints and Tips

For larger cakes and projects, you can double the ingredients to make 10 cups (2.5 L) buttercream, using a stand mixer. If you need more than 10 cups (2.5 L), it is best to make separate double or single batches, rather than trying to triple the recipe (or more). If you are using a handheld mixer, it is best to make multiple single batches.

I always decorate a cake with my original recipe for Swiss meringue buttercream icing, even if I have used a flavored buttercream (or another type of icing) to ice it. Be aware that some of the additions in the variations at left, such as the coconut milk or peanut butter, may result in an icing texture that is not suitable for piping decorations, and other additions, such as orange or lemon zest, will clog the tip.

# Vegan Coconut Decorator Icing

Be sure to read the special notes about vegan icing on page 49.

**Makes about 4½ cups (1.125 L)**

## Hints and Tips

Purchase the highest-quality canned coconut milk you can find. The higher the quality, the more cream will float to the top. It's best to buy two cans and chill both in case one doesn't yield enough coconut cream.

Refrigerate the remaining coconut milk in an airtight container for up to 3 days, or freeze it for up to 6 months. Let thaw, if necessary, and whisk well before using in smoothies, curries or other recipes.

Coconut oil is somewhat solid at room temperature, so can be tricky to measure. Use a stiff plastic spatula to scrape it from the jar, then pack it into the measuring cup, removing air pockets. If you have a kitchen scale, it is easier to weigh it; you'll need 12 oz (375 g). If the coconut oil is very stiff, warm it by wrapping a warm, wet tea towel around the bowl for a few minutes before beating.

*When you need a vegan option for cake decorating, this butter-like icing made with silky coconut oil and coconut cream fits the bill. Be sure to read the special notes about vegan icing on page 49.*

- Stand mixer, fitted with paddle attachment

| | | |
|---|---|---|
| 1 | can (14 oz/398 mL) coconut milk (see hints and tips, at left) | 1 |
| 1½ cups | packed virgin coconut oil (see hints and tips, at left) | 375 mL |
| 6½ cups | confectioners' (icing) sugar, sifted | 1.625 L |
| 1 tbsp | vanilla extract | 15 mL |

1. Refrigerate the can of coconut milk for at least 8 hours or overnight. Without shaking the can, open it and spoon out the thick coconut cream that has floated to the top, avoiding the thinner milk underneath. Measure ⅔ cup (150 mL) coconut cream and set aside. Reserve the remaining coconut milk for another use.

2. In stand mixer bowl, beat coconut oil on low speed until smooth and creamy. Increase speed to medium and beat until light and fluffy.

3. With the mixer on low speed, gradually beat in about half of the sugar. Beat in ⅓ cup (75 mL) of the coconut cream until incorporated. Gradually beat in the remaining sugar until incorporated. Increase speed to medium and beat until icing is smooth and fluffy. Beat in vanilla.

4. Beat in half of the remaining coconut cream until incorporated. Beat in just enough of the remaining coconut cream, 1 tbsp (15 mL) at a time, until the icing is smooth and spreadable, yet holds its shape.

5. Use immediately or cover with plastic wrap directly on the surface and store at a cool room temperature for up to 8 hours. If icing softens too much, refrigerate briefly just to firm it enough for piping.

## Variations

**Chocolate Decorator Icing:** In the top of a double boiler (or see hints and tips, page 46), over simmering water, melt 6 oz (175 g) bittersweet chocolate, whisking often. Let cool (but not to the point of solidifying), then beat into the icing at the end of step 4. If icing becomes too stiff, beat in more coconut cream, 1 tsp (5 mL) at a time.

**Lemon Decorator Icing:** Beat in 1 tsp (5 mL) pure lemon extract and the grated zest of 1 lemon at the end of step 4.

**Orange Decorator Icing:** Beat in 2 tbsp (30 mL) orange liqueur and the grated zest of 1 orange at the end of step 4.

**Peanut Butter Decorator Icing:** Beat in 1 cup (250 mL) smooth peanut butter at the end of step 4. Make sure the peanut butter isn't too cold and stiff, so that it blends in easily.

## Hints and Tips

Be aware that some of the additions in the variations at left, such as the peanut butter, may result in an icing texture that is not suitable for piping decorations, and other additions, such as orange or lemon zest, will clog the tip.

## Important Notes About Vegan Icing

Vegan Coconut Decorator Icing (page 48) is very different from Swiss Meringue Buttercream Icing (page 46) in both flavor and texture. It has the delicious sweet intensity of a classic American buttercream, with a hint of creamy coconut. It is wonderful for icing cakes and cupcakes and piping certain decorations. Because it does not include whipped egg whites to lend lightness and structure, it is better suited for decorations that lie close to the cake surface than for those that are three-dimensional.

Because coconut oil has a lower melting point than butter, the vegan icing is more susceptible to changes in temperature. If it becomes too soft, refrigerate it until it firms up, and give it a stir before refilling the bag. If it becomes too stiff, it may just need a good stir. If it is particularly chilly, run a metal spoon under very hot water, dry it off and use it to stir the icing.

A cake that has been decorated with vegan icing should be stored in the refrigerator to ensure that the decorations remain firm and intact. Let it come to room temperature only just before serving. If you plan to travel with a cake iced and/or decorated with vegan icing, make sure it is well chilled first, then keep it as cool as possible while you're en route.

# Cream Cheese Icing

## Hints and Tips

Cream cheese icing is fantastic for filling and icing cakes, and can be used to make lovely borders, but it cannot replace buttercream as a decorating medium.

This icing can easily be doubled or tripled if you are icing a larger cake. If using a handheld mixer, it may not be powerful enough to make double or triple batches, so make multiple single batches instead.

*This fast and easy frosting whips up thick and creamy, with a sweet and lively tanginess. Cream cheese icing pairs particularly well with heavier cakes, such as Mama Suzanne's Carrot Cake (page 36) and Sweet Potato Spice Cake (page 38).*

- Stand mixer, fitted with paddle attachment, or heavy-duty handheld mixer

| | | |
|---|---|---|
| 8 oz | brick-style cream cheese, softened | 250 g |
| 1/2 cup | unsalted butter, softened | 125 mL |
| Pinch | salt | Pinch |
| 1 tsp | vanilla extract | 5 mL |
| 2 cups | confectioners' (icing) sugar, sifted | 500 mL |

1. In stand mixer bowl or a medium bowl, combine cream cheese, butter and salt. Beat on low speed until blended. Increase speed to medium and beat until well blended and fluffy. Beat in vanilla. Gradually beat in sugar, 1/2 cup (125 mL) at a time, beating until icing is smooth.

2. Use immediately or cover and refrigerate for up to 3 days. Let soften at room temperature as necessary before using.

# Vegan Cream Cheese Icing

## Hints and Tips

This icing is only suitable for filling and icing cakes, not for piping decorations.

I prefer icing cakes with frosting that is firm and offers some resistance. For a stiffer consistency, make the icing before baking the cake and let it chill while you prepare, bake and cool the cake. Or make it the night before and store it overnight in the refrigerator.

*This vegan version is as smooth and creamy as the original. The lemon juice gives it the distinctive tang of the classic version.*

- Stand mixer, fitted with paddle attachment, or heavy-duty handheld mixer

| | | |
|---|---|---|
| 1 cup | cold vegan buttery spread (see hints and tips, page 45) | 250 mL |
| 1 lb | cold non-dairy vegan cream cheese | 500 g |
| 2 tsp | freshly squeezed lemon juice | 10 mL |
| 2 tsp | vanilla extract | 10 mL |
| 3 1/2 cups | confectioners' (icing) sugar, sifted | 875 mL |

1. In stand mixer bowl or a medium bowl, beat vegan buttery spread on medium-low speed just until smooth. Add vegan cream cheese and beat just until combined. Reduce speed to low and beat in lemon juice and vanilla just until blended.

2. Gradually beat in sugar, 1/2 cup (125 mL) at a time, beating until completely blended. If the icing is overly soft from mixing, cover and refrigerate to firm up.

# Chapter 3
# Decorating Fundamentals

# Leveling and Slicing the Cake

There is something delightful about a home-baked cake, roughly iced and topped with a dome. But when you're going to be decorating a cake, you want to start with a level surface, so you'll need to lop off that domed top. If the cake is tall enough, you can slice off the entire dome. If your cake is too short to remove the entire dome, slice off only as much as you feel comfortable losing.

Once the top of the cake is level, the next step is to decide how many layers you want to cut. A classic layer cake with one layer of filling is lovely, but multiple layers are an elegant option. A multilayer cake is taller and more formal in appearance, and is stunning when sliced and plated. Multiple layers also help ensure an appropriate cake-to-filling ratio. If you're using a strong-flavored, especially sweet or sturdy filling, such as flavored buttercream, fudge or cream cheese icing, you only need two layers. More layers will help you achieve a suitable cake-to-filling flavor balance when you're using a subtly flavored or delicate filling, such as jam or curd. If you want to use a sturdier filling in a multilayer cake, just make sure the layers of filling are thinner so that the flavor of the cake isn't overwhelmed by the flavor of the filling.

I use a serrated knife to slice cakes. If you're not confident in your slicing abilities, feel free to use a cake leveler, but I encourage you to work on your knife skills. With practice, you will become proficient at slicing thin, beautiful layers. Until then, you can place toothpicks or dots of icing around the circumference of the cake as guides for where to cut your layers.

Here's the most helpful trick I have learned when it comes to slicing a cake evenly: once you have set the knife blade against the cake at the appropriate spot, lock your elbow in that position and anchor it against your side or waist. Keep that elbow anchored to your side the entire time you are slicing. The eye is unreliable for making an even slice, so use the framework of your body to create an unyielding knife-wielding infrastructure.

# Filling the Cake

Once you've sliced your layers, it's time to add filling to each layer and stack the cake. There are lots of options when it comes to fillings: jams, jellies, preserves, puddings, lemon or lime curd, pastry cream, flavored buttercream icing, fudge icing, cream cheese icing. Just make sure the flavor of your filling will complement the flavor of your cake, and you're good to go.

# How to Level a Cake and Slice Layers

Place a cooled cake layer in the center of the turntable. ■ Stand directly in front of the cake (at the South position). ■ Place the blade of a long serrated knife at the East position on the side of the cake, at whatever height is necessary to create a perfectly level top, and lock your elbow against your side. ■ Place your free hand on top of the cake at the West position. ■

Applying light pressure to the cake with your free hand, rotate the turntable slowly counterclockwise as you move the knife back and forth in a sawing motion. ■

Rotate the cake as many times as needed to slice off the uneven top. ■ Do not change the angle of the knife once you have begun slicing. ■ Remove the uneven top and save it for crumbs. ■

Return the knife to the East position on the side of the cake, halfway down the side, and lock your elbow against your side. ■ Place your free hand on top of the cake at the West position. ■ Applying light pressure to the cake with your free hand, rotate the turntable slowly counterclockwise as you move the knife back and forth in a sawing motion. ■

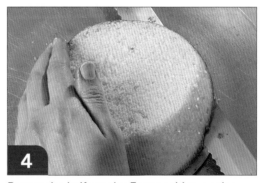

Rotate the cake as many times as needed to slice it in half. ■ Do not change the angle of the knife once you have begun slicing. ■ Using the knife to support one side of the top layer, gently lift the top layer off the bottom layer and set it aside. ■

Repeat steps 1 to 5 with another cooled cake layer, if a multilayer cake is desired. ■

*Note:* If you are left-handed, place the blade of the knife at the West position, place your free hand in the East position and spin the turntable clockwise.

**Dam Piping Options**

When creating a dam on a sliced cake layer (see step 2, page 55), you can either keep your piping hand still and rotate the turntable, or keep the turntable still and move your hand around the perimeter of the cake.

# With a Dam

Some fillings that are particularly delicate or slippery, such as jams, jellies, preserves, puddings and curds, need to be ringed with a dam of firm buttercream icing to ensure that they do not ooze out from between the layers once the cake is stacked. The dam should consist of the same icing that will be used to ice the cake. (See the information on coloring icing, pages 57–66, and on filling a pastry bag, pages 67–69.)

The goal is to create a dam large enough to securely hold the filling in place but small enough that it does not disrupt the appearance of the cake when it is sliced into individual pieces. A dam applied with a large tip or a heavy hand will squish in toward the center of the cake, practically becoming a second filling. For jams, jellies and preserves, which require only a thin schmear between each layer, I recommend using a #8 round tip for the dam. For curds and puddings, which are spread more thickly, I suggest a #10 round tip.

For cakes with multiple layers and delicate fillings, you might wish to refrigerate the filled layers individually *before* stacking them. Refrigeration will firm the filling and the dam, which will help prevent the layers from sliding and the filling from oozing out while you're stacking the layers.

To refrigerate individual layers, place a cardboard round under each layer before you add the dam and filling. As you finish filling each layer, use the cardboard round to lift it from the turntable and place it on a baking sheet, still on the cardboard round. You can place more than one layer on each baking sheet, so long as they don't overlap. When all of the layers are filled, place the baking sheets in the refrigerator until the dam is firm.

When you're ready to stack the cake, keep the cardboard round underneath the bottom layer. One at a time, carefully lift or slide each of the other layers from its cardboard round and place it on the preceding layer. Do not hold the cake layers by the edges; support the entire bottom, distributing the weight evenly over your fingers.

**Refrigeration Caution**

Do not attempt to refrigerate individual layers for cakes larger than 8 inches (20 cm), as they are prone to crack and break.

# Without a Dam

If you are using a sturdy filling, such as buttercream, fudge or cream cheese icing, a dam is not required, but do make sure the filling is whipped and smooth. Fit a pastry bag with a coupler, then fill it with the desired filling (see pages 67–69 for instructions on filling a pastry bag). Do not add a tip — the coupler is used by itself.

# How to Fill a Cake That Requires a Dam

Place a cardboard round under the first layer of the cake and place the layer in the middle of the turntable. (The round will act as added support when you move the cake.) ■

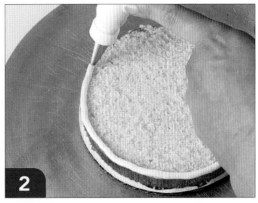

Squeezing the pastry bag with moderate pressure, create a ring of icing as close as possible to the outside edge of the cake. ■

Using a small offset spatula, scoop up some filling and plop it in the center of the cake. ■ Use the spatula to carefully spread the filling from the center of the cake out to the dam. ■

Continue spreading filling from the center out until the filling is evenly spread over the cake layer. ■

Gently place the next cake layer on top of the filling. ■

Repeat steps 2 to 6 until all the layers are filled. ■ When placing the top layer, make sure the most level and even side is facing up. ■

## How to Fill a Cake That Does Not Require a Dam

**1**

Place a cardboard round under the first layer of the cake and place the layer in the middle of the turntable. (The round will act as added support when you move the cake.) ■

**2**

Starting ¼ inch (5 mm) from the outside edge of the cake, squeeze the bag with firm pressure to make a tight spiral of filling into the center of the cake. ■ The goal is to make a ¼-inch (5 mm) thick layer of filling, so do not overlap the spirals or make a domed center. ■ The pressure of the next layer will flatten the spiral to the correct height and push it to the edge. ■

**3**

Gently place the second cake layer on top of the filling, making sure the most level and even side is facing up. ■

*Note:* If you're making a multilayer cake, make the layers of filling thinner by squeezing the bag less firmly and holding it closer to the cake surface, so the flavor of the filling doesn't obscure the flavor of the cake.

# Crumb-Coating the Cake

A crumb coating is a thin layer of icing that is spread onto the cake to lock the crumbs in place. It is an added step to the icing process, but if you've ever done battle with stubborn crumbs while icing a cake, then you know it's well worth the effort.

You may choose to place the cake in the refrigerator before applying the crumb coating, to firm up the layers or dams and reduce the risk of the layers sliding during the crumb-coating process.

## How to Crumb-Coat a Cake

1. After the cake is filled, use a small offset spatula to gently spread a thin layer of icing across the top and around the sides of the cake. It is okay for crumbs to release from the cake and mix with the icing at this point.

2. Place the cake in the refrigerator and let the crumb coating firm up before attempting to ice the cake.

*Note:* The pressure the spatula places on the cake can cause the layers to slip, so use the fingertips of your free hand to support the cake on the opposite side while crumb-coating.

# Coloring Buttercream Icing

Buttercream that has not been colored or flavored is a neutral ivory color. By adding food coloring, you can tint the icing almost any color, including fluorescents. Color mixing is part science, part art and entirely fun. With a little bit of theory, experimentation and imagination, you'll discover inexhaustible color possibilities and pairings.

## Color Theory

Let's start with the science first and get it out of the way. Color mixing has its own vocabulary, rules and formulas. Words like "rules" and "formulas" may be anathema to you, as a creative individual, but the theories involved are really very simple, and understanding them will give you the ability to mix any color imaginable and create eye-catching palettes.

Here are a few technical and descriptive words for color that will help you figure out what you need to do to mix a specific color — and leave you sounding like a color mixing pro:

- **Pigment** is the pure color substance added to a vehicle, or binder. Together, pigment and vehicle combine to make food coloring.

- **Hue** is the more technical term for the word "color." It is pure color without the addition of black or white.

**Beyond Icing**
Color theory principles apply to more than just buttercream in the realm of cake decorating. For example, if you plan to coat the edge of a cupcake with tiny sprinkles in two different colors, experiment first to make sure the colors don't combine to make an entirely different, unintended color.

- **Saturation** refers to the intensity of a color. Try not to think of saturation in terms of light or dark, but in terms of the strength or weakness of a color.

- **Value** refers to the brightness of a color — how light or dark it is, based on how near it is to white. Light blue, medium blue and dark blue are all different values of the same hue.

## Primary, Secondary and Tertiary Colors

**Primary colors** are those three magical colors that cannot be created by mixing other colors: red, blue and yellow. Primary colors can theoretically be combined to create any other color. If you could have only three colors in your toolbox, these would be the three to have.

**Secondary colors** are made when two primary colors are mixed together:

- Red + blue = purple
- Yellow + red = orange
- Blue + yellow = green

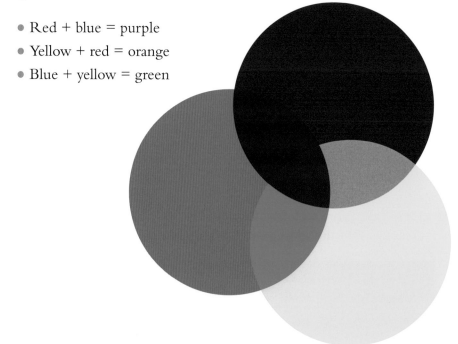

**Tertiary colors** are made when a primary and secondary color are mixed together:

- Yellow + green = yellow-green
- Green + blue = blue-green
- Blue + violet = blue-purple
- Violet + red = red-purple
- Red + orange = red-orange
- Orange + yellow = yellow-orange

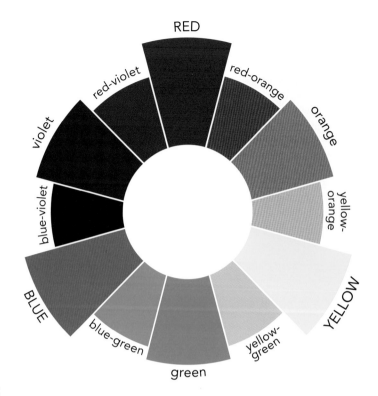

## Complementary Colors

Learning how to use complementary colors is the key to making original and difficult-to-mix colors. It is the secret to transforming saturated colors straight from the bottle into nuanced, muted shades. How do you figure out which colors are complementary? Complementary colors *always* sit directly across from one another on the color wheel.

- The complement to red is green.
- The complement to yellow is purple.
- The complement to blue is orange.

When two complements are mixed together, they neutralize one another. For example, if a pink (a derivative of red) is too bright, or is a cloying Easter pastel, add a touch of green to mute it; continue to add green, and it will turn into a muted rose color. Conversely, if you're aiming for a natural-looking green leaf, add a little pink to create a muted, complex green.

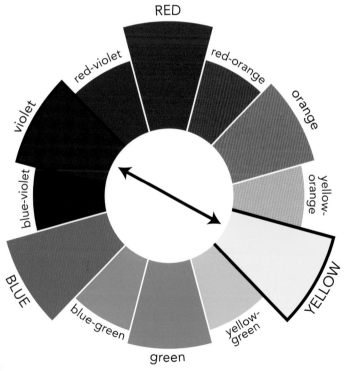

When two complementary colors are placed next to each other in decorations on a cake, they accentuate one another, and the cake will "pop" with vibrancy and interest. For example, if you want a cake that features fun, bright, bold colors, you might pair brilliant yellow sunflowers with velvety jewel-toned purple violets.

## Tinting, Toning and Shading

Learning to tint, tone and shade colors will take you one step further toward creating the color palette you envision.

- To **tint** a color means to mix a color with white to lighten it.
- To **shade** a color means to mix a color with black to darken it.
- To **tone** a color means to mix a color with a neutral or gray to neutralize it.

pure hue

tints

tones

shades

# Selecting Food Coloring

Most of the food colorings found on grocery store shelves or at cake supply stores are synthetic pigments, which are regulated by the FDA and have been deemed safe to consume. If you are concerned about eating icing colored with synthetic dyes, there is a growing selection of natural food colors available, though they tend to be more expensive, can impart a slight flavor and are more muted in color. The colors they create are very pretty, but they cannot achieve the intense, saturated color you need for an Elmo cake or a sports logo.

Food coloring is available in liquid, gel or paste form. My preference is for soft gels in squeezable plastic bottles. Adding color to buttercream with a toothpick (as is often recommended) is a tedious task unless you're making the palest of colors. Squeezable bottles allow you to do away with pesky toothpicks and color-steeped spatulas.

Color names vary among food coloring brands, but the colors listed below are staples and should be easy to find:

- Leaf green
- Pine green
- Royal blue
- Sky blue
- Egg yellow
- Lemon yellow
- Red
- Orange
- Pink
- Purple
- Black
- Brown

## No-Taste Food Coloring

Certified synthetic colors are not supposed to impart any flavor to food, but I have detected a metallic flavor in icing highly saturated with the color red. Thankfully, Wilton makes a no-taste red food coloring.

## Metallic Food Coloring, Dust and Glitter

Metallic food coloring is available but must be airbrushed onto decorations. Metallic dust and glitter disappear when added to buttercream icing.

# Blending Colors

Try to match the standard colors listed above to a cartoon character, logo or party invitation and you'll soon find yourself wanting more variety. Luckily, when you're coloring buttercream icing, it's easy to combine two or more colors, using the rules of color theory you learned above, to create pretty much any color you can imagine. Exercise restraint when blending colors, as you can always add more color, but it's impossible to take it away.

Here are the formulas for some of my favorite blended colors:

- **Beige:** A touch of brown added to the ivory icing
- **Brick:** Primarily red with a touch of green
- **Burgundy:** Primarily red with a touch of purple
- **Chartreuse:** A whole lot of lemon yellow with a touch of leaf green
- **Coral:** Pink and orange in fairly equal amounts
- **Eggplant:** A whole lot of purple with a touch of red
- **Fuchsia:** A whole lot of pink with a touch of red and purple

**When in Doubt, Add Purple**

Purple works surprisingly well to mute just about any color and make it subtler and more interesting.

- **Gold:** Egg and lemon yellow in equal amounts, with a touch of leaf green and purple
- **Indigo:** A whole lot of royal blue with a touch of purple
- **Ivory:** A touch of egg yellow added to enhance the natural ivory color of the icing
- **Lavender:** A touch of purple and a smaller touch of pink added to the ivory icing
- **Magenta:** A whole lot of pink with some purple and a touch of red
- **Navy:** Primarily royal blue with a touch of orange and black
- **Peach:** A touch of orange and a smaller touch of pink added to the ivory icing
- **Periwinkle:** A touch of royal blue, sky blue and purple added to the ivory icing
- **Rose:** Primarily pink with a touch of pine green
- **Teal:** Sky blue with some leaf green and a touch of purple
- **Terracotta:** Red and orange in equal amounts, with a touch of brown
- **Turquoise:** Primarily sky blue with a touch of leaf green

# Choosing Your Color Palette

Your color choices set a specific mood and theme for your cake. Have fun with color, search for inspiring palettes, be bold and experiment. You will soon develop favorite color combinations that express your personal artistic esthetic. Keep in mind that a palette often flounders when a multitude of random hues are selected and placed next to one another. A good way to avoid this is to limit the color palette. Here are some ways to create attractive color palettes:

- Use different shades of a single color.
- Select just two complementary colors, such as spring green and eggplant, or turquoise and terracotta.
- Limit the palette to just the primary colors: red, blue and yellow.
- Limit the palette to just the secondary colors: orange, green and purple.
- Use very pale, washed-out colors, which become almost neutral and so are easy to mix and match.
- Choose very bright, saturated colors that "pop" and vibrate with energy. The cake will be so loud and fun, no one will notice if the colors don't harmonize perfectly.

- Avoid tonal monotony and guarantee a compelling decoration by including the lightest light and the darkest dark in your palette. This doesn't necessarily mean white and black. You could use a soft butter yellow and a deep indigo blue, or a golden peach and a nearly black purple. Even a tiny amount of darkest dark — a dark brown dot in the center of a flower, for example — adds a surprising snap and vibrancy.

- Find inspiration in everyday objects. I often turn to textiles such as Indian batik fabrics, kilim rugs and hand-pressed papers.

- Let nature be your guide. Look for inspired color combinations in gardens, an autumn leaf or the nuanced shades of a single flower.

- Let the theme of the party determine your color choices, and match your cake palette to your party invitations and other decorations.

- Look for inspiration online. There are many websites devoted to color palettes. One of my favorites is Design Seeds (http://design-seeds.com). Just be careful: you may spend all your time perusing luscious color palettes instead of decorating cakes!

# Mixing Color into Buttercream

I typically use one of two methods for mixing food coloring into buttercream icing: the bowl method or the spatula method.

## The Bowl Method

The bowl method is especially useful for coloring large batches of icing, such as those that will be used to ice the cake, and when counter space is limited. I often use a plastic container instead of a bowl so that I can snap on a lid for easy cleanup and storage. If I'm coloring a very small amount of icing, I use a paper cup for easy disposal.

### How to Color Icing Using the Bowl Method

1. Squeeze small drops of food coloring into a bowl of buttercream icing.

2. Stir with a rubber spatula, ensuring that the color is evenly distributed throughout the icing.

3. Keep adding color a few drops at a time, stirring after each addition, until the desired color is achieved.

**Color Darkening**

A bowl or bag of buttercream icing that has been dyed red, blue, green or purple will darken in as little as half an hour. If the color is displeasing, simply transfer it back to the bowl (if necessary), add a bit of ivory icing and give it a good stir. In one of life's little mysteries, the color will not darken once the icing has been spread or piped onto the cake.

## The Spatula Method

The spatula method (sometimes called the slab method) refers to the technique of mixing color into buttercream icing by using an offset spatula to spread and blend the icing on a marble slab. It is a more sophisticated way to color icing that is destined for a pastry bag, and it lends itself well to creating variegated colors (see below).

This technique originated in a commercial bakery where large counters of chilled marble sat atop reach-in refrigerators. At home I use a marble cutting board, but I have also had success on Formica, granite, stainless steel and marble counters. If your counters are made of a pale stone, avoid working directly on the countertop, as the food coloring might stain the stone.

### How to Color Icing Using the Spatula Method

1. Using a rubber spatula, place a scoop of buttercream icing on the slab.

2. Squeeze small drops of food coloring onto the icing.

3. Using the flat side of an offset spatula, make generous sweeping motions to spread the icing thin. Scrape the icing back into a pile, then spread it thin again. Continue scraping the icing into a pile and spreading it thin until the color is thoroughly incorporated.

4. Keep adding color a few drops at a time, mixing in the color after each addition, until the desired color is achieved.

*Note:* Use a small offset spatula when you just need to color a small amount of icing, and a large offset spatula when you need to color enough icing to fill a pastry bag.

# Creating Variegated Colors

Mottled or streaked color adds depth and interest to your piped decorations, and can be used to simulate shadows, highlights and the patterning found in nature. Some cake decorators use a toothpick to streak a pastry bag with pure food coloring before adding the icing. I dislike this technique because it can impart deposits of liquid color onto the decoration. You will also be constrained to using the heavily saturated, harsh colors that come directly from the bottle. A better method is to mix two colors separately and place a scoop

# How to Make Variegated Icing Using the Spatula Method

1. Prepare the first color as described in the box on page 64.

2. Using the bowl method (see page 63) or a separate slab, prepare a second color that is smooth and free of air bubbles. Use a rubber or offset spatula to scoop up the second color and drop it on top of the first color.

3a. If you want the icing to feature two distinct colors, use the flat side of an offset spatula to spread the second color carefully over the entire surface of the first color.

3b. If you want to create a gradual shift in hue as you're piping, use the spatula to slightly mix the layered colors.

3c. If you want to create a ringed petal or a leaf with a stripe down the center, spread the second color in a narrow vertical line across the first color.

4. To lift the layered icing into the pastry bag, hold a large offset spatula with the thin edge touching the slab and the back raised to a 33-degree angle. Scrape the icing up with one clean single swipe and place it in the bag. The buttercream will bunch and buckle as it is lifted, but the layers of color will stay relatively undisturbed.

of each, side by side, in the pastry bag. Better still, if you are using the spatula method, you can mix the dominant color first, then layer the secondary color over it before lifting the icing into the pastry bag (see box, above). I regularly use this technique for flowers, adding a simple secondary layer of ivory icing to create the illusion of movement and highlights.

How much of each color to use is based on personal preference, with cues from nature. If I'm making a two-toned leaf with two shades of green, I use relatively equal amounts of each color. If I want to add an ivory highlight to a leaf, or a purple or red shadow, I use a larger amount of the green and just a small amount of the second color.

Your options are not limited to just two colors. You might add a schmear of both ivory and purple to a leaf to mimic nature's complex hues and the play of light. For a hydrangea flower, you might layer multiple values of the same color to mimic the various stages of maturation experienced by the blossom.

Here are some of my favorite uses for variegated buttercream icing:

- Make leaves that are darker on one side than the other, as often occurs in nature, by layering two shades of green icing.

- Mimic the varied hues of a rose leaf or an autumn leaf by adding a stripe of red over the dominant layer of green.

## The Quirks of the Medium

No matter how well-thought-out your intentions are, once buttercream icing is placed in a pastry bag, it seems to develop a mind of its own. You may get perfectly variegated leaves from the first squeeze of the bag, or you may get no variegation until you are halfway through. Just keep squeezing the icing out until you're getting the desired effect.

- Imitate eucalyptus or sage leaves by adding a silvery blue layer on top of the green layer.

- Create a luscious confectionery flower by layering pale golden peach and soft pink icing.

- Make an opulent flower with dramatic highlights by placing a thin layer of the deepest, darkest purple over scarlet red icing.

- Create a sweet, rustic flower by adding a layer of ivory over cornflower blue.

- Mimic the shifting colors of a lilac bush by layering various hues and shades of purple, from deep violet to pale lavender.

# Icing the Cake

Your cake is baked, cooled, sliced, filled and crumb-coated, and you've prepared and colored your buttercream icing — you're ready for the icing on the cake! All of the cakes in this book are iced using the Smooth Icing technique, for which you'll find complete, detailed instructions on page 82. This technique gives you a smooth, even surface that is the perfect canvas for any decorations you might have in mind.

If you are not planning on adding buttercream decorations, you can follow up the Smooth Icing technique with the Contemporary Home-Style Icing technique (page 86), the Classic Home-Style Icing technique (page 88), the Squiggle Top Icing technique (page 89), the Spiral Icing technique (page 90), the Combing technique (page 93) or the Vertical Stripes technique (page 94), to give your cake a finished look that is perfect in its simplicity.

If you are planning on adding buttercream decorations, after icing the cake it's a good idea to refrigerate it for 20 to 25 minutes, until it's well chilled, before you start decorating. (And chilling is crucial if you're using a template or the reductive decorating technique.) The icing process takes long enough that the cake is no longer chilled by the end of it, and it can be challenging to apply buttercream decorations to a warm surface. This brief chilling period will make the decorating process much easier — plus, it gives you time to prepare to decorate by filling the pastry bags with icing.

Most cakes are transferred from the turntable to their final presentation surface (see page 96) before they are placed in the refrigerator, but those that use the reductive decorating technique (see sidebar, page 69) remain on the turntable until they are fully decorated (or until the step-by-step instructions tell you to transfer the cake). In either case, make sure in advance that there is plenty of room in your refrigerator for the cake to fit — you may have to lower a shelf to accommodate it.

## How Much Icing?

Here are the icing quantities needed to ice the cakes used in the projects in this book:

- 4-inch (10 cm) cake: 3 cups (750 mL)
- 6-inch (15 cm) cake: 3½ cups (875 mL)
- 8-inch (20 cm) cake: 4 cups (1 L)

For cupcakes, here are the icing quantities you'll need:

- 24 standard-size cupcakes, iced with smooth icing: 3½ cups (875 mL)
- 24 standard-size cupcakes, iced with spiral icing: 5 cups (1.25 L)
- 24 mini cupcakes, iced with smooth icing: 1½ cups (375 mL)
- 24 mini cupcakes, iced with spiral icing: 2 cups (500 mL)

These are generous amounts, but you don't want to come up short. Any leftover icing can be used for decorating.

# Filling a Pastry Bag

The process of filling a pastry bag with buttercream icing is really a series of individual tasks: cutting off the tip of the bag, attaching the coupler and decorating tip, filling the bag with icing, then closing the bag. While all of these tasks are really very simple, I've provided some instructions, hints and tips that will make each one even easier!

## Cutting Off the Tip

If you try to insert a coupler into a brand-new pastry bag, you'll quickly realize that it doesn't fit. Pastry bag openings are made small, to accommodate all kinds of uses, and need to be enlarged to work for most decorating jobs. But some pastry bags stretch over time, so it is important not to cut off too much. Use scissors to snip about 1 inch (2.5 cm) off the tip of a new pastry bag. Although a small tip will fall through an opening this size, it will fit when combined with a coupler, and most larger tips will fit on their own without falling through. The opening is cut to the correct size when you drop the coupler base in and about half of its threads extend through the tip of the bag.

## Attaching the Coupler and Tip

Drop the base of the coupler into the pastry bag, narrow side down, aligning it so that it extends through the opening with half of the threads showing. Place a standard-size decorating tip over the part of the base that extends from the bag. Thread the coupler ring over the decorating tip and twist it onto the base, securing the tip in place. In some cases (such as filling a cake without a dam, page 56), a coupler is used alone, without a decorating tip.

## Filling the Bag

It would be so much easier to fill a pastry bag with icing if we had three arms or someone perpetually available to assist. Since the former is improbable and the latter impractical, on page 68 you'll find directions for filling a pastry bag solo, with a mere two arms.

**Icing Cupcakes**
Cupcakes are a fun, cute alternative to a layer cake, or you can making matching cupcakes to serve alongside the main event. Make sure your cupcakes are completely cool before icing them using the Smooth Cupcake Icing technique (page 85) or the Spiral Cupcake Icing technique (page 92).

**Inserting a Decorating Tip without a Coupler**
If you're using a decorating tip without a coupler, as is necessary for some large tips, simply drop it into the bag and align it so that the narrow end extends through the open tip of the bag.

## How to Fill a Pastry Bag

**If the icing is in a bowl:**

1. Use a rubber or offset spatula to collect the icing into a pile in the bottom of the bowl. Slip the spatula beneath the pile so it is prepped and ready to lift.

2. With your non-dominant hand, hold the pastry bag around the middle.

3. Fold the top of the bag down over your hand.

4. Lift the icing from the bowl and carefully drop it into the bag.

**If the icing is on a slab, cutting board or countertop:**

1. With your non-dominant hand, hold the pastry bag around the middle.

2. Fold the top of the bag down over your hand.

3. Use your free hand and an offset spatula to scoop up the icing. Lead with the thin edge of the spatula touching the slab and the back raised to a 45-degree angle. Try to scrape the buttercream up with a single large sweeping motion, then drop it into the pastry bag.

*Note:* To prevent icing from squishing out the top of the pastry bag, always leave at least 2 to 3 inches (5 to 7.5 cm) at the top unfilled.

**Diminished Icing Quality**

Buttercream icing that is left sitting in a bag for more than half an hour, or that is held in a warm hand nonstop for more than 5 or 10 minutes, will begin to diminish in quality, separating and becoming spongy and full of air bubbles. This will happen more quickly if the icing color is highly saturated. To restore the quality, squeeze the icing out into a bowl, add a dab of fresh buttercream and stir until smooth, then refill the bag.

# Closing the Bag

You may have seen pastry bags closed with a rubber band or a clip to ensure that the icing doesn't ooze out the top. This is innovative but unnecessary. To seal the bag, simply hold it with your dominant hand. With your free hand, twist the empty top portion of the bag as if you were wringing out a wet towel. Slip the twisted portion into the V between the thumb and index finger of your dominant hand.

As you decorate and the amount of icing in the bag decreases, you will begin to lose pressure inside the bag. Simply unwind the bag, slide your hand down the bag until it meets the icing, give the empty portion of the bag another twist, and you're ready to start decorating again.

# Avoiding Air Bubbles

There is little more annoying than being in the middle of piping a perfectly straight line, a stellar inscription or an impeccable rose and having the icing suddenly explode out of the bag thanks to a surprise air bubble. Air bubbles are, to a certain extent, unavoidable when decorating with buttercream, but they can be minimized. The key is to start with well-stirred icing. Air bubbles are visible in the bowl, so if you spot them, give the icing a good stir with a rubber spatula, using a back-and-forth motion, until the icing is smooth. (If you use the spatula method to mix color into the icing, that process will eliminate any air bubbles.)

Air bubbles form in pastry bags wherever there is empty space. To avoid them, squeeze a bit of icing out of the bag before beginning to decorate. Squeeze the bag whenever you fill or refill it, after setting it down and picking it back up, and whenever you change the tip.

# Decorating the Cake

When your beautifully iced cake is well chilled and your pastry bags are fitted with tips and filled with all the different icing colors you'll need, it's time for the really fun part to begin! Buttercream icing is an incredibly flexible medium that allows you to create pretty much any type of decoration you can dream up, so let your imagination lead the way, experiment with different designs, practice various techniques and, above all, enjoy the process! Remember, even if your initial decorating efforts are less than perfect, the results will still be delicious and everyone is sure to be impressed that you took the time to create a handmade cake.

The remainder of this chapter offers advice on adding embellishments such as sprinkles and sugar pearls, tracing patterns and designs onto a cake, adding inscriptions and correcting any mistakes you might make along the way. Chapter 4 provides detailed step-by-step instructions on how to make all of the basic buttercream icing decorations — including borders, dots and lines, flowers and other designs — with a photograph accompanying each step to further illustrate how to perform the technique. And in chapter 5 you'll find 50 incredible cake decorating projects to get you started. You can copy my designs exactly, or use them as a launching pad for your own ideas, color schemes and designs.

## Reductive Decorating

Reductive decorating is the process of scraping the surface of a cake after it has been decorated and chilled, to reveal a smooth, even surface with an embedded pattern. It is a little time-consuming, as it consists of multiple layers of buttercream and requires extra chilling time, but the execution is simple and the results impressive. For examples of reductive decorating, see Birch (page 140), Cheetah (page 156), Rustic Finish (page 282), Timber (page 314) and Zebra Stripes (page 338).

# Adding Embellishments

A cake doesn't need to be swathed in buttercream flowers to be considered decorated. Cake crumbs, chopped nuts, sprinkles and other tiny embellishments are an easy way to give a cake an attractive finished look in next to no time. These embellishments are traditionally sprinkled in a ring around the top of the cake, with or without a border, but they can be added around the bottom edge (see box, page 70) instead or as well. The Combed Lavender cake (page 172), for example, looks lovely with rings of dried lavender encircling the cake at both the top and the bottom. Tiny embellishments can also be pressed around

## Making Cake Crumbs

The fastest and easiest way to make crumbs is to whirl chunks of a sliced-off cake top or a whole cupcake in a food processor. If you don't own a food processor, cut the top off a cupcake and run the cupcake back and forth over a fine-mesh sieve to make crumbs.

## Toasting Chopped Nuts

Toasting nuts is not a necessary step, but it does enhance their flavor tremendously. To do so, preheat the oven to 350°F (180°C). Spread the chopped nuts out in a single layer on a rimmed baking sheet. Bake for 6 to 8 minutes or until nuts are golden and fragrant. Keep a keen eye on the nuts as they bake — they very quickly go from lightly toasted to burnt and unusable.

# How to Embellish the Bottom Edge of a Cake

Carrot cake is often ringed with chopped walnuts around the bottom edge, but this technique can be used with any iced cake and any type of tiny embellishments.

1. Pour the embellishments into a large bowl, preferably one that is shallow with a wide mouth.

2. Use a large offset spatula to lift the cake off the turntable and carefully balance the cake on the fingertips of your non-dominant hand. Slide your hand all the way under the cake and balance it over the bowl.

3. Scoop a handful of embellishments into your open hand and gently press them into the bottom edge of the cake with a lightly cupped hand.

4. Carefully rotate the cake in your hand to continue pressing embellishments into the bottom edge until it is completely ringed.

*Note:* Try to avoid sticking embellishments to the underside of the cake; these could prevent the cake from properly adhering to the presentation surface, and it might slide off when you move it.

the outer edges of cupcake icing for an elegant look, or sprinkled all over the icing for a fun look.

Decorated cakes can also be enhanced by the addition of a few well-placed larger embellishments, such as sugar pearls or dragées. I often use these round candies as the centers for my flowers, and they add vivacity and dimension as part of the pattern in the Henna Tattoo cake (page 212) and as a complement to the swags and rosettes in the Roses and Ribbons cake (page 278). The Pearls cake (page 270) is decorated entirely with sugar pearls in different sizes for an incredibly opulent look. If the embellishments you've chosen are large enough, you may be able to place them with your fingers. But for smaller sugar pearls and dragées, or when you're placing embellishments in tightly decorated areas, a pair of tweezers makes the job much easier.

# Tracing and Pattern-Making

You don't need to be a master artist to decorate cakes. But even if you have a strong artistic bent, it's a good idea to imprint a design onto the cake, then pipe the icing over it, rather than trying to pipe a design freehand. That's where cookie cutters and templates come in. Even a seemingly simple shape, such as a triangle, can be maddening if you're trying to achieve perfectly equal angles without guidelines. But if you use a triangle cookie cutter or template to create an outline of the shape beforehand, simply piping over the lines is a breeze!

## The Cookie Cutter Method

The easiest way to imprint an outline onto a cake is with a cookie cutter. These are particularly good for simple shapes such as circles, ovals, diamonds and hearts, but cookie cutters are available in an unbelievable variety of complex designs as well. To imprint the shape onto the cake, gently press the cookie cutter into the icing. Wipe the cookie cutter with a damp cloth between imprints so you don't transfer built-up icing from one imprint to another.

## The Template Method

If you don't have a cookie cutter in the shape you're looking for, you can create a template for it instead. This can be as simple as drawing the template yourself on a piece of paper, or you can look for a suitable design in a book or online, then photocopy it or print it out. You can also use a photocopier to increase or decrease the size of the image to suit your needs. Once your template meets with your approval, cut it out with a pair of household scissors.

A template is most versatile when it is made of lightweight paper, such as standard writing or copy paper. This allows it to wrap over the edge of a cake, if desired, and also makes for clean removal of the pattern from the cake.

To transfer the image to the cake, place the template in the desired location on a well-chilled cake. Smooth the template and press the edges very lightly and quickly to ensure that it adheres to the cake. Trace the image quickly with a toothpick or skewer, then peel the template off as soon as possible. If the cake warms up under the template, a layer of icing might peel away along with it. This is a particular risk if you have iced the cake with cream cheese icing, fudge icing or glaze. If any icing peels away, carefully smooth the rough area with the tip of a small offset spatula.

**Improvise!**
If you don't have a cookie cutter in the size or shape you're looking for, scan your kitchen for an improvised replacement. I often use a drinking glass or a plastic takeout container to create a circle that's just the right size. Make sure the tool you use is clean and food-safe.

**Dotting the Outline**
When tracing around a template with a toothpick or skewer (or sketching a design onto the cake freehand), you may find it easier to make a series of small dots instead of a continuous line. This will be less disruptive to the icing surface and will still give you a clear outline to pipe the icing over.

**Hands Off!**

Do not use a finger to hold down the template while you're tracing around it. The icing underneath your finger will stick to the template and peel away with it when it's removed.

**Imperfection Can Be Beautiful**

A handwritten inscription conveys a level of personal investment and sentiment that is undiminished by imperfections in the design or piping, so don't let yourself get stressed out about making your inscriptions look perfect.

If you are creating a complex design, you may find it helpful to trace the image in several stages. For example, for a car design, you might cut out the entire image of the car and trace around it. This would leave you with an accurate outline but no interior detail. The next step would be to cut the template into smaller pieces that represent distinct portions of the car — the wheels, the windows, the bumpers — and trace around those. Continue cutting ever-smaller pieces and tracing around them until you are satisfied with the level of detail you have created.

# Adding Inscriptions

An inscription is the crowning jewel on a cake. It conveys a message and records a significant moment in time. After all the work you've put into decorating the cake, it's gratifying to add a personalized inscription that matches your decorations and expresses your sentiments.

Writing with buttercream can be tricky, and creating beautiful inscriptions takes practice. Give yourself time and be patient with yourself as you develop your inscription skills.

## Tools

Writing an inscription can be as simple as filling a parchment pastry bag with buttercream, snipping off the tip and having a go at it. I prefer to use a cloth pastry bag fitted with a coupler and a round tip to ensure that the lines of icing have a consistent shape. Inscriptions can also be written using a series of connected dots or drop flowers from a star tip. For a calligraphy effect on a larger cake, you can use a #101 rose tip or a #45 ribbon tip.

Another handy tool is a letter or word press, with which you can press perfectly aligned letters and words onto the surface of the cake. You then trace the imprint of the words, producing near-perfect inscriptions. Letter and word presses come in both print and script styles, and in several sizes.

## Buttercream Quality

An important contributor to a tidy inscription is buttercream that is fresh and smooth. Icing that has been sitting in a bag for a while will begin to separate, and air bubbles will form. Air bubbles lead to foamy buttercream that breaks and pops while you're writing with it. If your icing has begun to deteriorate, squeeze the icing out into a bowl, add a dab of fresh buttercream and stir until smooth, then refill the bag.

Since the primary ingredient of buttercream is butter, it is highly susceptible to changes in temperature. If left in a warm area or held in a toasty hand, it will begin to melt and separate, leading to an oily, inconsistent inscription. Conversely, if left in a cool area, it will harden and become inflexible and prone to breakage, like a stick of butter straight from the refrigerator. Generally speaking, if you are comfortable with the temperature of a room, your buttercream will be easy to work with. If it gets so soft that it cannot be fixed by stirring in fresh buttercream, place it in the refrigerator for a few minutes to chill, then remix. If it gets too stiff for a simple fix, microwave it on Medium (50%) power in 10-second intervals until it is pliable and ready for remixing.

# Contrast

To be easy to read and really "pop," the inscription needs to be written in a color that contrasts with the color of the cake. Use a light color to write on a dark cake and a dark color to write on a light cake. The exception is when a monochromatic look is desired: an inscription that is the same color as the icing on the cake (or very similar) can look subtle and elegant.

# Speed and Pressure

Writing with buttercream is not like writing with a pen. If an inscription is written hastily, that is often reflected in its appearance. (However, as you become more familiar with the medium, you will naturally get faster at writing inscriptions.) The key is to write with consistent speed and pressure. If the speed of your hand increases without a corresponding increase in pressure, the string of buttercream will break apart; conversely, if your hand slows down but you keep the pressure the same, the string will pile up into a curly or blotchy mess.

# Stringing

Stringing is a technique that makes writing with buttercream easier and neater. To string your letters, hold the pastry bag at a 45-degree angle to the cake, with the tip lightly touching the starting point of your stroke. Squeeze the bag with moderate pressure to create an anchor of icing, then lift the tip slightly away from the surface of the cake and move your hand toward the end point of your stroke, draping a string of icing across the cake. Touch the end point with the tip of the bag and release the pressure.

**Add Pressure at the End of Each Stroke**
To make your inscription look confident and deliberate, start and end each letter or stroke with a little added pressure, creating an almost imperceptible dot or swelling of icing at the ends.

# Position and Proportion

A well-thought-out inscription is centered on the cake, with an appropriate amount of negative space around it, and is in proportion with the size of the cake: a small cake calls for small letters; a large cake should feature larger, thicker letters.

## Centering

Before beginning to write, take a moment to visualize the placement of the inscription on the cake. You want it to be centered vertically and horizontally, so that there is an equal amount of space above and below the inscription, and on either side. A helpful technique for writing a three-line inscription, such as "Happy Birthday Sally!" is to start by inscribing the middle word — in this case, "Birthday" — in the center of the cake, then write "Happy" above it and "Sally!" an equal distance below it. With practice you will learn how much space is required to write common words such as "Happy," "Congratulations," "Birthday," "Anniversary" and so on.

## Negative Space

Negative space is the empty space between the inscription and the border of the cake. A cake with negative space appears more professional and considered. A balance of used space and empty space is pleasing to the eye, and the negative space creates a quiet place for the eye to "rest." Another benefit of planning for extra space is that, if a word requires a tad more space than you expected, you don't need to scrape off the inscription and start over.

## Consistent Sizing

If the letters are all different sizes, an inscription may look like it was written by your favorite six-year-old. Consistent sizing means that all capital letters are the same height, as are all tall lowercase letters (such as "b," "h" and "t"), and that the tails of all low-hanging letters (such as "g," "p" and "y") are the same length. It may help to envision a grid of four horizontal lines on the cake: the bottom line marks the lowest point for the tails of low-hanging letters; the bottom, or belly, of each letter rests on the second line; the third line marks the top of lowercase letters such as "a," "m" and "w"; and capital letters and tall letters reach up to the top line.

**Stylizing the First Letter**

As an exception to the consistent sizing rule, you may choose to stylize the first letter of a word or phrase by making it bigger, more ornate and/or different in some other way from the rest of the letters. A stylized first letter can add character and panache to an inscription.

## Straight Lines

Unlike a ruled piece of paper, a cake has no guidelines to help you make a straight inscription. But you can create guidelines yourself using a toothpick. Lay a ruler or another straight edge across the cake, in line with where you want the bottom of your letters to fall. (To ensure that the ruler does not leave an imprint, the cake must be well chilled.) Use the toothpick to create a line of tiny unconnected dots (a solid line is often noticeable) along the straight edge. If you're using all capital letters, you can add another dotted line as the guideline for the top of your letters. For further guidance, you can even use the toothpick to sketch out the letters of the inscription.

## Vertical Orientation

Consistent vertical orientation — the direction in which your letters slant — helps to ensure a tidy, professional-looking inscription. Your letters can lean to the right, go straight up and down, or even slant to the left, but whichever style you choose, make sure to use it consistently throughout the entire inscription.

# Style

Inscriptions are all about individual personality and creativity. Letter and word presses inhibit creativity, so I recommend moving away from using them as soon as you feel comfortable with writing inscriptions freehand. For the best results when you're starting out, stick with your usual handwriting. Writing in buttercream is tricky enough without trying to develop a whole new style. When you're ready for further experimentation, these hints and tips will help you create spectacularly stylish inscriptions:

- Let the style of the cake inform the style of your writing. For an elegant anniversary cake, use a formal, curling script. For a child's birthday cake, use a round tip to write fat lowercase letters. For a masculine cake, try writing in block capitals.

- If the cake is being served at an event for which invitations were sent out, match your inscription to the font used on the invitations.

- Create long, ornate, curling tails for the letters "g," "j," "p," "q" and "y."

- Stretch all the letters horizontally, making them wider than they are tall.

**Breaking All the Rules**

Want a fun look for a children's cake or a Halloween cake? Ignore the rules about consistent sizing, alignment and orientation, and make letters that are different sizes, tilt every which way and are staggered up and down from each other.

- Stretch all the letters vertically, making them very tall and narrow.

- Add serifs — small, often perpendicular lines at the open ends of letters. For example, an A made with serifs looks like this: **A** Note the small lines at the bottom of each diagonal line. An A made without serifs looks like this: **A**

- Add fat dots in place of small serif lines. This is a style I often use for a children's cake.

- Make a particular word, such as a name or a birthday number, stand out by writing it larger and bolder than the rest of the words.

- Write an inscription in an arch instead of in a straight line. This is especially helpful when you're writing a long word or a lengthy inscription on a small cake.

- Write on an angle. A tilted inscription has a carefree feel to it.

# Making Corrections

At some point in the cake decorating process, you're bound to make a mistake or change your mind about a decoration. Luckily, most mistakes can be repaired or covered up. Repair work generally works best on a well-chilled cake.

## Smoothing Away Dotted Outlines

I always recommend using a toothpick or skewer to dot the outline of a design before piping it in icing, to minimize mistakes made when piping. But what if you make a mistake with the dotted outline itself — misspelling a word in an inscription, for example — or you realize you don't like the placement of your design and you want to move it? Is there anything you can do about all those tiny dots? Given that even a smoothly iced buttercream cake is dotted with air pockets and ridges, these small holes often just blend right in, so much of the time I don't give them a second thought. But if you can't live with them, you can fill a cup with boiling water, dip a small offset spatula into the water for a few seconds, dry the spatula, then gently slide the heated edge over the surface of the cake, melting the icing and smoothing out the embedded flaws. This works best on ivory buttercream icing and cream cheese icing. With colored buttercream, chocolate buttercream, fudge icing and glaze, the heat may cause a slight shift in color in the spots touched by the spatula.

# Removing a Decoration

When it comes to repair work, a toothpick or skewer will quickly become one of your most valued tools, as its pointy tip can go where thick, clumsy fingers cannot. If an inscription looks messy or a swag refuses to stay put, use the toothpick to pry off the errant buttercream, doing your best to disrupt the surface of the cake as little as possible. Caution is even more important with a cake that has been iced with colored or chocolate buttercream (as opposed to one iced in ivory), as any scratch or scrape will show up more clearly against the colored background. Chilling the cake increases the odds that the decoration will come off in one piece and leave less residual buttercream on the cake surface.

# Filling in Holes

If you have ever spackled a wall, you'll find this technique very similar. To fill in a hole or indentation in the cake surface, first make sure the cake is chilled. Scoop up a small amount of buttercream with the tip of a small offset spatula and spread it in and over the hole. Use the spatula to spread and scrape the icing until it is smooth and even with the surrounding area.

If you're performing this repair work on the side of the cake, hold the spatula pointed down, in line with the cake and perpendicular to the turntable. Spread and smooth the icing in a side-to-side motion; if you use an up-and-down motion, you are likely to unintentionally scrape off extra icing.

**Minimizing Dotted Outline Repairs**

When it comes to dotted outlines, your best bet for ensuring the least amount of repair work is a preventive measure: make the tiniest holes possible that you can still see to pipe over.

## Covering Up with Wisteria

Wisteria is the cake decorator's best friend, capable of covering a multitude of sins — plus it's beautiful and easy to make (see page 116 for instructions). If your cake is a little crooked, your icing is marred or you've stuck an errant thumb into the cake, wisteria will bail you out. Unlike most flowers, wisteria is just as easy to apply to the side of a cake as it is on the top, and it can cover wide swaths of area.

# Starting Over

Even for the seasoned professional, there are times when a cake just isn't worthy of a public viewing. Sometimes you decorate an entire cake, or a large portion of it, before you realize that your brilliant concept isn't translating well to reality. Don't despair. Yes, you'll need to start over, but not completely from scratch: the cake itself can be salvaged. You'll just need to take it back down to its crumb coating so that it can be re-iced.

Bring the cake to room temperature and, using a small offset spatula, remove the decoration and the layers of icing. If the icing happens to be one color or can be easily separated, set it aside for later use. If the cake has multiple layers or a delicate and slippery filling, such as jam or curd, exercise caution to ensure that the layers do not slide. Place the cake in the refrigerator until it is well chilled, then re-ice it and try, try again.

# Chapter 4
# Step-by-Step Decorating Techniques

# Decorating Terminology

Within the techniques in this chapter and the projects (pages 122–341), you will find many references to angles, clocks, compass directions, tip positions, pressure and speed. What do all these terms mean? Here are the details you need to know.

## Bag Angle

Bag angle refers to the slant of the pastry bag in relation to the surface of the cake. The angle of the bag has an impact on how the buttercream icing flows through the tip, curves and bends. Most of the techniques call for a 90-degree angle (perpendicular to the cake) or a 45-degree angle (halfway between parallel and perpendicular). When icing a cake, angles are also used to describe the slant of the spatula in relation to the surface of the cake.

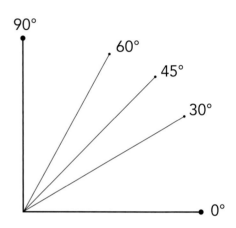

## Bag Direction

Think of the top of the cake as the face of a clock and the pastry bag as the hour hand. When the bag is held "in the 6 o'clock direction," the tip of the bag faces the center of the cake and the base of the bag points to 6 o'clock. Bag angle and bag direction work together, so a bag might be held at a 45-degree angle in the 3 o'clock direction, for example. When icing a cake, angles are also used to describe the alignment of the spatula in relation to the cake.

*Note:* The step-by-step instructions have been written for a right-handed person. If you are left-handed, look for an accompanying tip that tells you how to adjust the bag direction.

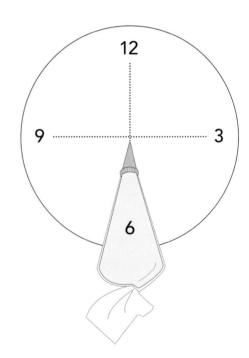

# Starting Position

Starting position refers to the point on the cake where the tip of the pastry bag should be placed to start the decoration. I use the face of a compass to refer to the starting position and to distinguish it from the bag direction. When you have a cake in front of you, North is the farthest edge, directly across from you. The bag might be held at a 45-degree angle in the 3 o'clock direction at the Northwest position, for example.

*Note:* The step-by-step instructions have been written for a right-handed person. If you are left-handed, look for an accompanying tip that tells you how to adjust the starting position.

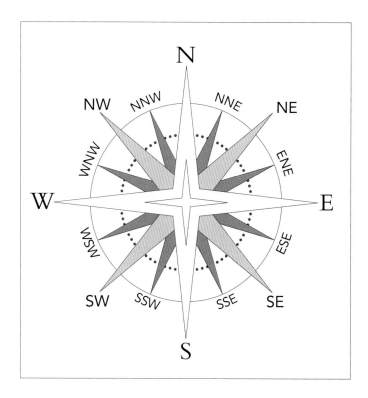

# Tip Position

Tip position tells you how to hold the tip in relation to the cake surface — usually either hovering just above the surface or lightly touching the surface. For tips with an asymmetrical opening, such as a rose tip, tip position will also tell you how to orient the opening.

# Pressure and Speed

Pressure refers to how hard you squeeze the bag. The pressure applied determines how fast the icing is released, which affects the uniformity and consistency of the decoration. Whether you are instructed to apply gentle, moderate or firm pressure, do your best to keep the pressure consistent throughout the entire motion.

The speed with which you move your hand to complete the motion should match the pressure you're applying to the bag: with gentle pressure, you move slowly; with moderate pressure, you move at a moderate pace; and with firm pressure, you move quickly. Matching pressure and speed results in a smooth, consistent stream of buttercream. With practice, this balance of pressure and speed will become intuitive.

# Smooth Icing

## What You Need

- Chilled cake, filled, crumb-coated and placed on a cardboard round
- Buttercream icing, at room temperature (see page 66 for quantities)
- Turntable
- Rubber spatula
- 8-inch (20 cm) straight blade spatula
- Damp cloth

## Hints and Tips

If you are left-handed, align the spatula in the 7 o'clock direction in step 5 and spin the turntable clockwise in step 7. Use the Southeast (SE) position in steps 8 to 10, and use the South-Southeast (SSE) position in steps 11 to 16. In steps 9 and 12, spin the turntable counterclockwise.

Any time icing accumulates on the spatula, scrape the icing into the bowl, then clean the spatula with a damp cloth.

A smoothly iced cake is the launching point for so many beautifully decorated cakes. It takes a bit of practice to master the technique, but the imperfections and handcrafted quality that make buttercream so charming allow for plenty of ridges and rough patches.

Place the cake in the center of the turntable. ■

Stir the icing with the rubber spatula until it is smooth and free of air bubbles. ■

Using the rubber spatula, pick up a large scoop of icing and plop it on top of the cake. ■

Using the straight blade spatula, spread the icing from the middle to the outside edges of the cake until it is fairly evenly distributed across the top. ■

To further smooth the top of the cake, align the spatula in the 5 o'clock direction. ■

Place the tip of the spatula at the center of the cake, with the back edge resting perfectly horizontally on the surface of the cake and the front edge at a 45-degree angle to the cake. ■

**7**

Using your free hand, spin the turntable counterclockwise while applying gentle pressure to the cake surface with the spatula. ■ Continue until the top of the cake is smooth and level. ■

**8**

Scoop up a good-sized dollop of icing with the tip of the spatula and spread it onto the side of the cake at the Southwest (SW) position. ■

**9**

Spin the turntable slightly clockwise and spread another dollop of icing at the new Southwest position. ■

**10**

Continue spinning the turntable and spreading icing at the Southwest position until the sides of the cake are covered in a rough coat of icing. ■

**11**

To smooth the sides of the cake, hold the spatula vertically at the South-Southwest (SSW) position, with the tip touching the turntable, the back edge touching the surface of the cake and the front edge at a 30-degree angle to the cake. ■

**12**

Using your free hand, spin the turntable clockwise while applying gentle pressure with the spatula. ■ Continue until the sides are smooth and vertical, and the icing creates a lip slightly higher than the top surface of the cake. ■

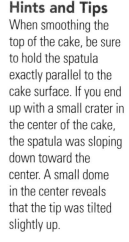

When smoothing the top of the cake, be sure to hold the spatula exactly parallel to the cake surface. If you end up with a small crater in the center of the cake, the spatula was sloping down toward the center. A small dome in the center reveals that the tip was tilted slightly up.

An iced cake should have about $1/4$ inch (5 mm) of icing on both the top and the sides, giving it a consistent and even appearance when the cake is sliced and balancing the flavors of the cake, filling and frosting.

If you remove too much icing while smoothing it, just add more and start over again.

If, at any time during the process, the cake reaches room temperature or becomes unstable, refrigerate it until chilled before continuing.

## Hints and Tips

Want to practice your icing skills without actually baking and filling a cake? Use a cake dummy. These "fake cakes" can be found in cake supply stores or online, or you can simply use a Styrofoam round. Because cake dummies have little weight, they tend to hop and slide around the turntable while you're working, so use a glue stick to put a good dab of glue on both the turntable and the bottom of the round before beginning, to create a fairly strong but temporary seal. Cake dummies are reusable. After finishing a practice session, scrape the dummy clean and wash it with warm water and dish soap. Let dry completely before reusing.

**13** To remove the lip of icing, place the back edge of the spatula horizontally at the South-Southwest position on top of the cake, with the front edge at a 30-degree angle toward the center of the cake. ■

**14** Swipe the spatula toward the center of the cake, smoothing down the lip. ■

**15** Spin the turntable slightly and make another swipe from the edge of the cake to the center. ■ Continue until the entire lip has been removed. ■

**16** To further smooth the top, hold the spatula as in step 13 and make long swipes across the top of the cake, cleaning and drying the spatula and spinning the turntable slightly between each swipe. ■ Continue until the top is very smooth. ■

# Smooth Cupcake Icing

This is the icing technique to use when the top of each cupcake will be decorated with a flower or any sizable embellishment.

## What You Need

- 24 cupcakes, cooled
- Buttercream icing, at room temperature (see page 66 for quantities)
- Pastry bag fitted only with a coupler and filled with icing
- Turntable
- Small offset spatula
- Damp cloth

## Hints and Tips

If desired, sprinkle the iced cupcakes with cake crumbs, nuts or sprinkles.

For fun, colorful cupcakes, ice the cupcakes in one color and gently roll the rounded edge in a mound of coordinating sprinkles.

Place a cupcake in the middle of the turntable. ■

Make a ring of icing on the top of the cupcake, just inside the outer edge. ■

When you reach your starting point, spiral in to the center of the cupcake, without increasing the height of the icing. ■

Using the spatula, smooth the icing, keeping the nicely rounded outer edge intact. ■

# Contemporary Home-Style Icing

## What You Need

- Chilled cake, iced using the Smooth Icing technique (page 82)
- Turntable
- 8-inch (20 cm) straight blade spatula

## Hints and Tips

If you are left-handed, place the spatula at the Northeast (NE) position in step 2 and roll it from left to right in steps 3 to 6. In step 7, gently dig the tip of the spatula into the icing at the Northeast position and, in steps 8 to 10, roll it from left to right.

If desired, sprinkle the finished cake with cake crumbs, nuts or sprinkles.

This soft, undulating pattern lends itself well to icings with more give, such as cream cheese and fudge. There's a flick of the wrist and some personal panache to the technique, and I've never seen two people create identical cakes using it. Give it a whirl to reveal your own personal style.

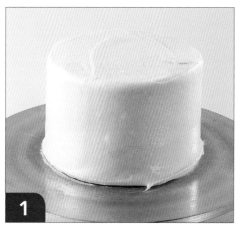

1 Make sure the iced cake is in the center of the turntable. ■

2 Reach across the cake and place the spatula at the Northwest (NW) position on the side of the cake, with the tip pointing down and touching the turntable. ■

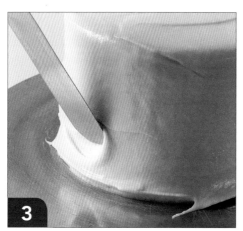

3 Gently roll the tip of the spatula in a small motion from right to left at the bottom of the cake while pulling slightly up, creating a swooping indent in the icing. ■

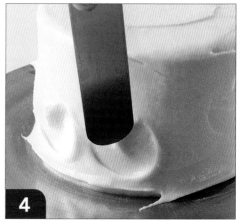

4 Spin the turntable slightly and make a second swoop directly beside the first one. ■

**5**

Continue spinning the turntable and making swoops until you have a ring of swoops around the bottom of the cake. ■

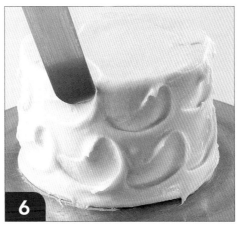

**6**

Make a second ring of swoops above the bottom ring. ■

## Hints and Tips

The swoops can be subtle, barely breaking the surface of the icing, or they can be deep and dramatic. Deep swoops make the cake appear fluffy and pillowy — the trick is to make them without digging all the way down to the surface of the cake.

If you don't plan on adding an inscription to the cake, you can continue to make concentric rings of swoops on the top of the cake, to fill the center.

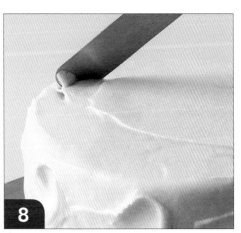

**7**

Reach across the cake and gently dig the tip of the spatula into the icing at the Northwest (NW) position on top of the cake, near the edge. ■

**8**

Gently roll the tip of the spatula in a small motion from right to left. ■

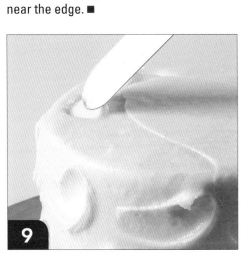

**9**

Spin the turntable slightly and make a second swoop directly beside the first one. ■

**10**

Continue spinning the turntable and making swoops until you have a ring of swoops around the top of the cake. ■

# Classic Home-Style Icing

## What You Need

- Chilled cake, iced using the Smooth Icing technique (page 82)
- Turntable
- Soup spoon
- Damp cloth

### Variation

If you plan on inscribing the cake, leave the top smooth or texturize just the top edge, leaving a smooth surface in the center.

### Hints and Tips

If you are left-handed, place the spoon at the Southwest (SW) position in step 1.

If desired, sprinkle the finished cake with cake crumbs, nuts or sprinkles.

There really is no right or wrong way to ice a cake using this technique. Have fun, knowing that imperfection is the objective.

Purposely imperfect and casual, this icing makes a cake look like it was just whipped up in grandma's kitchen.

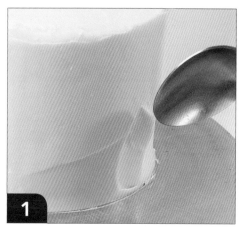

**1** With the iced cake in the center of the turntable, place the back of the spoon at the Southeast (SE) position on the side of the cake, and press gently to create an indentation. ■

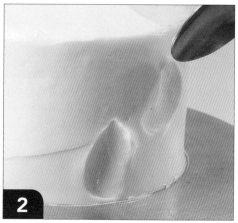

**2** Spin the turntable and make another indentation on the side of the cake, at a different height than the first one. ■ Wipe the back of the spoon with the damp cloth. ■

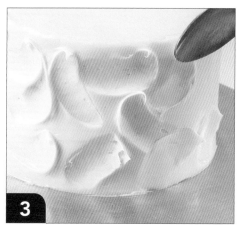

**3** Continue making indentations in a random pattern around the sides of the cake, wiping the back of the spoon as needed. ■

**4** Make a series of random indentations on the top of the cake, wiping the back of the spoon as needed. ■

# Squiggle Top Icing

It doesn't get much easier than this. The squiggle top is a go-to technique for adding vitality to a plain cake. Leave the sides of the cake plain or embellish with crumbs, nuts or sprinkles.

## What You Need

- Chilled cake, iced using the Smooth Icing technique (page 82)
- Turntable
- 8-inch (20 cm) straight blade spatula

### Hints and Tips

If you are left-handed, place the spatula at the East (E) position in step 2.

The motion made and the pattern created are similar to the effects of quickly coloring in a circle with a large felt-tip pen.

**1** Make sure the iced cake is in the center of the turntable. ■

**2** Reach across the cake and place the tip of the spatula at the West (W) position on top of the cake, at the very edge, holding the spatula at a 45-degree angle to the top of the cake. ■

**3** Applying gentle pressure, move the spatula in a sweeping back-and-forth motion across the cake, from the North edge to the South. ■

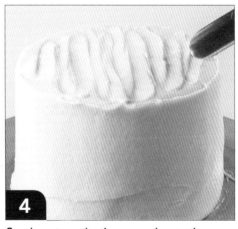

**4** Continue to make the sweeping motion while slowly moving the spatula all the way across the cake, from West to East. ■

# Spiral Icing

## What You Need

- Chilled cake, iced using the Smooth Icing technique (page 82)
- Turntable
- 8-inch (20 cm) straight blade spatula

### Variations

Draw a spiral only up the sides of the cake and leave the top smooth.

Draw a spiral only on the top of the cake and cover the sides with crumbs.

### Hints and Tips

If you are left-handed, place the spatula at the East (E) position for steps 2 to 6, and the Northeast (NE) position for steps 7 to 10. In all cases, spin the turntable counterclockwise instead of clockwise.

It's easy to transform a simple smooth cake into something quirky and fun. Spiral icing is well liked for its versatility — it can be playful when scattered with multicolored confetti or masculine with strong lines when garnished with a small pile of crumbs placed in the center.

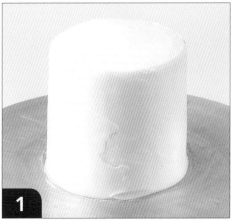

Make sure the iced cake is in the center of the turntable. ■

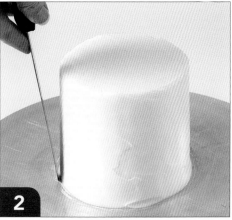

Reach across the cake and place the spatula at the West (W) position on the side of the cake, with the tip pointing down and touching the turntable and the blade angled slightly away from the cake. ■

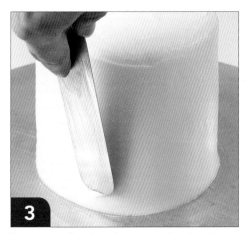

Using your free hand, start to slowly spin the turntable clockwise while applying gentle pressure to the cake surface with the tip of the spatula. ■

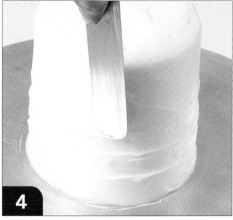

With consistent gentle pressure and slow speed, draw the tip of the spatula up the side of the cake while continuing to slowly spin the turntable. ■

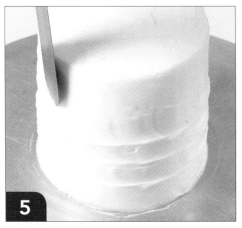

**5**

Make sure your spatula hand remains at the West position while the turntable spins. ■

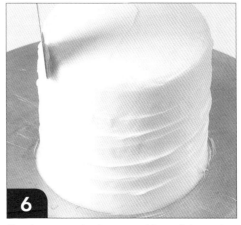

**6**

Continue to spin the turntable and draw the spatula up the side of the cake until you have reached the top edge of the cake. ■

**Hints and Tips**

This finish looks particularly lovely when you use cream cheese icing.

If desired, sprinkle the finished cake with cake crumbs, nuts or sprinkles.

**7**

Reach across the cake and place the tip of the spatula at the Northwest (NW) position on top of the cake, near the edge. ■

**8**

Start to slowly spin the turntable clockwise while applying gentle pressure to the cake surface with the tip of the spatula. ■

**9**

With consistent gentle pressure and slow speed, draw the tip of the spatula toward the center of the cake while continuing to slowly spin the turntable. ■

**10**

Make sure your spatula hand remains at the Northwest position all the way to the center of the cake. ■

# Spiral Cupcake Icing

## What You Need

- 24 cupcakes, cooled
- Buttercream icing, at room temperature (see page 66 for quantities)
- Pastry bag fitted only with a coupler and filled with icing

## Hints and Tips

If desired, sprinkle the iced cupcakes with cake crumbs, nuts or sprinkles.

Be kind to your back: ice cupcakes on a turntable to raise them higher. For speed and efficiency, you can place a half-dozen cupcakes in a ring around the surface of the turntable.

Make sure the icing does not reach beyond the edge of the cupcake or it will be marred when the cupcakes are placed next to one another on a plate or are transported.

Here's an easy and whimsical technique for icing cupcakes. Cupcakes iced with a smooth spiral are perfect left unadorned, sprinkled or decorated with small embellishments.

1 Make a ring of icing on the top of the cupcake, just inside the outer edge. ■

2 When you reach your starting point, draw your hand up as you begin a second ring of icing inside the first. ■

3 Increase the height of the icing as you spiral toward the center of the cupcake. ■

4 At the center, draw your hand up as you release pressure, to make a tapered tip. ■

# Combing

To make a combed cake, a toothed instrument is dragged across the cake, leaving behind an impression that adds texture and pattern to a cake's iced surface.

## What You Need

- Chilled cake, iced using the Smooth Icing technique (page 82)
- Turntable
- Cake comb
- Damp cloth

### Hints and Tips

If you are left-handed, rest the comb at the South-Southwest (SSW) position in step 1, and spin the turntable counterclockwise in step 2. Make your motions in steps 3 and 4 from right to left.

Once, the only cake comb available was a basic one that made simple lines. Now there are combs that make scallops, intricate ridges and fat waves. Combs can be found in cake supply stores or online, or, with a pair of scissors and heavy card stock, you can make your own, limited only by your imagination.

Any time icing accumulates on the comb, scrape the icing into the bowl and wipe the comb with a damp cloth.

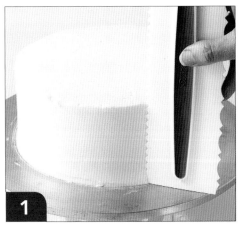

**1** With the iced cake in the center of the turntable, rest the bottom of the comb lightly on the turntable at the South-Southeast (SSE) position on the side of the cake, with the teeth just touching the cake. ■ Tilt the comb so that it is at a 45-degree angle to the cake. ■

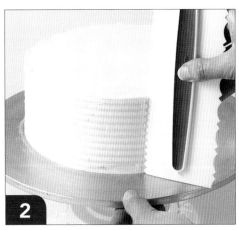

**2** Using your free hand, spin the turntable clockwise at an even speed while applying gentle pressure with the comb and keeping your comb hand still. ■ Continue until the turntable has completed a full rotation. ■

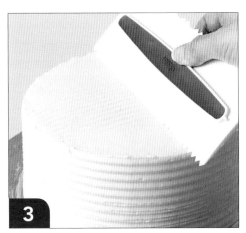

**3** Level the top of the cake by making small dragging motions with the comb from the left edge toward the center. ■ Spin the turntable halfway and repeat the small dragging motions until the toothed lines join at the center. ■

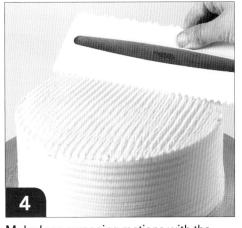

**4** Make long sweeping motions with the comb from the left edge of the cake to the right edge until the whole top is combed. ■ Make sure all the lines are heading in the same direction, perfectly parallel; overlapping is fine. ■

# Making Vertical Stripes

## What You Need

- Chilled cake, iced using the Smooth Icing technique (page 82)
- Turntable
- 8-inch (20 cm) straight blade spatula
- Damp cloth

## Hints and Tips

If you are left-handed, use the South-Southeast (SSE) position in steps 7 to 10.

Thin stripes or thick stripes? It's up to you. The more contact the spatula has with the surface of the cake as you swipe upward, the thicker the stripe will be.

Maintain a light touch when making the stripes. Heavy pressure will scrape away too much icing, revealing the cake beneath.

A cake with vertical stripes on the sides is clean and contemporary. This was one of my favorite finishes when I first started decorating cakes, because the technique is relatively simple and helps right a cake whose sides might not be perfectly vertical.

**1** With the iced cake in the center of the turntable, hold the spatula at the South (S) position on the side of the cake, with a thin edge resting on the turntable. ■

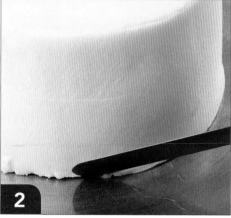

**2** Pull the top of the spatula away from the cake so that it is at a 30-degree angle to the cake. ■

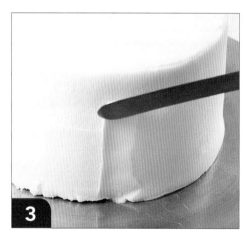

**3** With gentle and even pressure, make a rapid swipe up the side of the cake in one smooth motion. ■

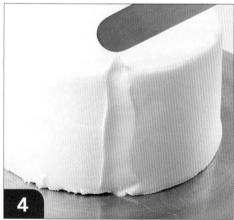

**4** Without slowing or stopping, continue the swipe past the top edge, pushing the icing up to make a ragged lip on the top of the cake. ■

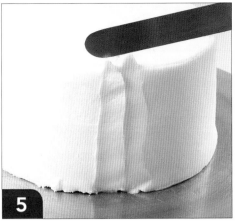

**5** Spin the turntable slightly and make a second swipe directly beside the first one. (It is okay if the stripes overlap a bit.) ■

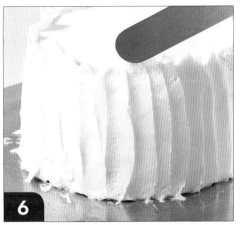

**6** Continue spinning the turntable and making swipes until you have created stripes all the way around the cake. ■

## Hints and Tips

Any time icing accumulates on the spatula, scrape the icing into the bowl, then clean the spatula with a damp cloth.

Adorn the top of the cake with Spiral Icing (page 90) or Squiggle Top Icing (page 89), or add a circle of dollops (page 100). Sprinkles, nuts or crumbs can be used alone or in addition to any of these finishes. Or you can simply leave the cake perfectly smooth and simple.

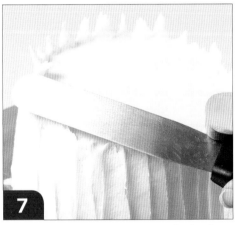

**7** To remove the lip of icing, place the back edge of the spatula horizontally at the South-Southwest (SSW) position on top of the cake, with the front edge at a 30-degree angle toward the center of the cake. ■

**8** Swipe the spatula toward the center of the cake, smoothing down the lip. ■

**9** Spin the turntable slightly and make another swipe from the edge of the cake to the center. ■ Continue until the entire lip has been removed. ■

**10** To further smooth the top, hold the spatula as in step 7 and make long swipes across the top of the cake, cleaning and drying the spatula and spinning the turntable slightly between each swipe. ■ Continue until the top is very smooth. ■

# Transferring an Iced Cake

## What You Need

- Iced cake, on the turntable
- Cake board
- Regular all-purpose school glue
- 8-inch (20 cm) straight blade spatula
- Large offset spatula

## Hints and Tips

If you are left-handed, rest the straight blade spatula on the left side of the turntable in step 2, and spin the turntable clockwise in step 5. In step 6, slide the offset spatula under the cake at the Southwest (SW) position.

Don't forget to place a cardboard round under the cake before icing it, or you will end up with a glue-glazed cake on the bottom!

If you have forgotten to place a cardboard round under the cake before icing, you can use a small dollop of icing instead of glue. This only works well if you are decorating and serving the cake in the same location. If you have to travel, take caution: that dollop of icing could heat up and become a slippery oil slick!

When a cake is iced, a seal forms between cake and turntable. Breaking this seal gives you a smooth, straight edge on the bottom of the cake and prevents excess buttercream from soiling the presentation surface. These steps show you how to transfer an iced cake to a cake board. If you are instead using a plate, platter or cake stand as your final presentation surface, place a couple of small pieces of double-sided mounting tape where the cake will sit instead of using glue.

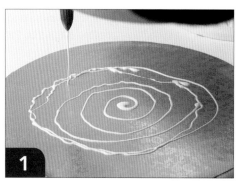

Squeeze a generous spiral of glue on the cake board, making sure it does not reach past where the cake will sit. ■ Place the cake board next to the turntable. ■

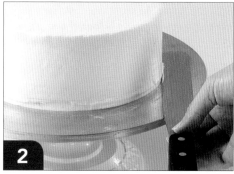

Rest the straight blade spatula flat on the right side of the turntable, with a long edge just to the side of the cake. ■

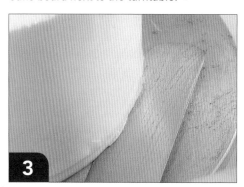

Slide the very edge of the spatula, only about ⅛ to ¼ inch (3 to 5 mm), under the cake. ■

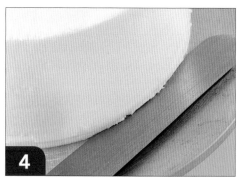

Angle the edge of the spatula that is not under the cake up ever so slightly. ■

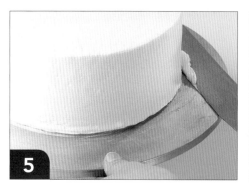

Holding the spatula in place, use your free hand to spin the turntable counterclockwise through one full rotation. ■ Remove the spatula. ■

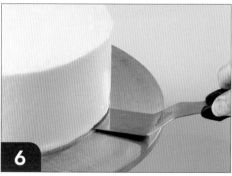

Carefully slide the offset spatula almost all the way under the cake at the Southeast (SE) position. ■

7

Begin to slowly lift the cake from the turntable. ■

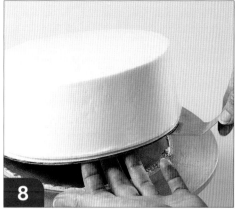

8

When it feels like the weight of the cake is equally distributed across the offset spatula, slip the fingers of your free hand under the cake to assist in the transfer. ■

## Hints and Tips

If you place a cake in a pile of glue after having forgotten to use a cardboard round, don't toss the cake out! Using a small offset spatula, scrape off as much glue as possible, then gently wipe the bottom of the cake with a damp cloth. Although I don't recommend ingesting glue, regular all-purpose school glue is nontoxic and, well... kids have been eating it for decades.

If you realize the cake is not centered after placing it on the cake board, place the tip of a small offset spatula against the barely visible edge of the cardboard round and give it a gentle push until the cake is centered. Make sure to do this quickly, before the glue has a chance to dry.

9

Carefully lift the cake off the turntable. ■

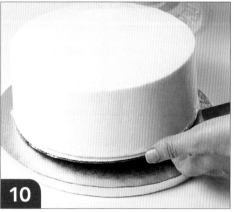

10

With the spatula and your fingers still under the cake, set the far edge of the cake gently on the cake board. ■ Eye the cake to make sure it is fairly well centered on the board. ■

11

Lower the near edge of the cake onto the cake board while slowly sliding the spatula out from under the cake. (Do not pull it out all the way.) ■ When the near edge of the cake is about 1 inch (2.5 cm) above the board, pull your fingers out from under the cake. ■

12

Use the spatula to gently lower the cake the remaining distance. ■ Gently slide the spatula out from underneath the cake. ■

# Ribbon Border

## What You Need

- Iced and chilled cake, on its final presentation surface, placed in the center of a turntable
- Pastry bag fitted with a #104 rose tip and filled with icing

## Hints and Tips

If you are left-handed, your starting position is South-Southwest (SSW). Spin the turntable counterclockwise in step 3.

A ribbon border can be made with any rose tip. For a teeny border, use #101, #102 or #103. For a wide ribbon, use #124, #125, #126 or #127.

Match the speed of the turntable to the pressure with which you squeeze the bag. Too fast, and the ribbon will tear; too slow, and the ribbon will begin to ripple. If your speed is inconsistent, there will be jogs in the ribbon.

Add a row of dots at the top of the ribbon, the bottom of the ribbon or both, mimicking the look of a picot-edge satin ribbon.

The ribbon border is a little tricky, but once mastered it has a huge payoff in expediency and appearance. This is the perfect border for a minimally decorated cake with clean, strong lines or a cake waiting to be adorned with fresh flowers. Dress up the ribbon with Swiss dots, pair it with buttercream flowers or add a bow for the sweetest little girl's cake. This technique is always done on the cake's final presentation surface.

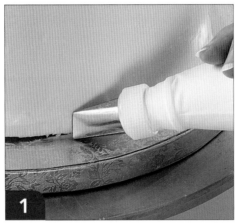

1. Holding the pastry bag horizontally, with the fat end of the tip down, set the tip firmly on the presentation surface at the South-Southeast (SSE) position on the cake, with the entire opening of the tip in contact with the cake. ■

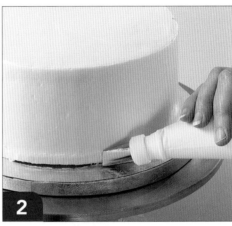

2. Tilt the bag so that it is at a 30-degree angle to the side of the cake. ■

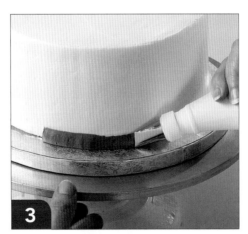

3. Holding the pastry bag steady and keeping the bottom of the tip rooted to the presentation surface, squeeze the pastry bag with firm pressure while spinning the turntable clockwise. ■

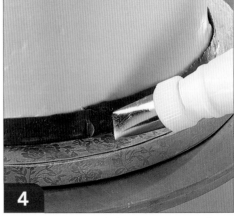

4. When you are nearly back to your starting point, reduce the pressure and slow the spinning. ■ At the starting point, pull the tip slightly away from the cake so that the ends of the ribbon overlap. ■

# Smooth Scallop Border

The elegance and versatility of the smooth scallop make it my go-to border for most cakes.

**1** Hold the pastry bag at a 45-degree angle to the top of the cake, in the 3 o'clock or 9 o'clock direction (depending on which way you want your scallops to face), and place the tip at the South (S) position so that it is lightly touching the surface. ■

**2** Squeeze the bag with moderate pressure, lifting it very slightly so that the icing fans out and begins to make a rounded dollop. ■

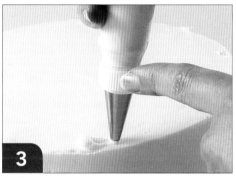

**3** Reduce the pressure and drag the tip lightly through the dollop, shifting the angle of the bag to 90 degrees to create a pretty little indent. ■ Release the pressure completely and bring the scallop to a thin point. ■

**4** Spin the turntable slightly and make another scallop directly beside the first one. ■

**5** Continue spinning and making scallops until you have a ring of scallops around the top of the cake. ■

**Variation**

***Ridged Scallop Border:*** Swap out the #8 tip for a #16 or #32 star tip. ■

## What You Need

- Iced cake, placed in the center of a turntable
- Pastry bag fitted with a #8 round tip and filled with icing

## Hints and Tips

To make a scallop border around the bottom of the cake, hold the pastry bag horizontally and at a 45-degree angle to the side of the cake. You may find it easier to work at the Southeast (SE) or Southwest (SW) position, rather than right in front of you.

Much of the versatility of a scallop border comes from the tip you choose. For a fun cake, try a fat round tip, such as a #10 or #12. For an elegant cake, try a #5 or #6 round tip.

Keep proportion in mind when choosing your tip. A #12 tip on a 4-inch (10 cm) cake will look enormous and clownish, but the same tip on a 16-inch (40 cm) cake will look just right.

## What You Need

- Iced cake, placed in the center of a turntable
- Pastry bag fitted with a #32 star tip and filled with icing

## Hints and Tips

If you are left-handed, your starting position is East (E).

Before you start making your border, you may want to mark the intended positions of the dollops with a toothpick, so that you can make sure they are evenly spaced around the cake.

---

## Variation

*Smooth Dollop:* Instead of following steps 3 and 4, make a large rosette shape (see page 120) using a #6, #8 or #10 round tip, leaving an open space in the center. Fit a pastry bag with a small round tip and fill in the center with the same filling used inside the cake, as a sneak preview. Space out the dollops as desired in a loose ring around the cake.

# Ridged Dollop Border

A cake with a combed or decorative surface may call for a finishing touch that is less elaborate than a full border. A ridged dollop border may be just the ticket.

**1** Hold the pastry bag at a 45-degree angle to the top of the cake, in the 5 o'clock direction, and place the tip at the West (W) position, hovering just above the surface. ■

**2** Squeeze the bag with moderate pressure until the icing begins to balloon out. ■

**3** Move your hand in a very slight circular motion toward the center of the cake, continuing to squeeze the bag, until you have made a small semicircle. ■

**4** Reduce the pressure and move the bag directly toward the center of the cake, shifting the angle of the bag to 90 degrees to create a nice indent and a tapered tail. ■

**5** Spin the turntable and make another dollop the desired distance away from the first one. ■

**6** Continue spinning and making dollops until you have a loose ring of dollops around the top of the cake. ■

# Mounds

Mounds are useful when you want to add volume and height to a cake or cupcake for a flower decoration. They are not decorations on their own, but rather the *base* for raised decorations to come.

## Used to Make

- Chrysanthemum (page 164)
- Hydrangea (page 226)
- Sheep (page 286)
- Sunflower (page 304)

## What You Need

- Iced cake, placed in the center of a turntable
- Pastry bag fitted with a coupler and filled with icing
- Small offset spatula (optional)

### Variation

For a smaller mound, fit the pastry bag with a #8 round tip.

**1** Hold the pastry bag at a 90-degree angle to the cake, with the tip hovering just above the surface, at the position on the cake where you want the outer edge of your mound to lie. ■

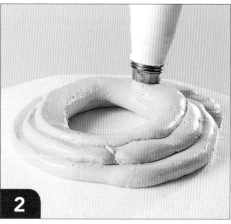

**2** Squeezing the bag with firm pressure, move your hand in a tight spiral motion toward the center of the cake, adding height to the icing as you go. ■

**3** Continue squeezing and spiraling until you have made a mound of icing in the desired size and height. ■

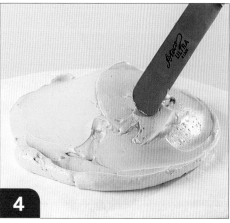

**4** If the mound is irregular in shape, use the offset spatula to even and smooth it out. ■

## What You Need

- Iced cake, placed in the center of a turntable
- Pastry bag fitted with a round tip (any size) and filled with icing

## Hints and Tips

To avoid dots that resemble a Hershey's Kiss, make sure to stop squeezing and release all pressure before removing the tip.

# Dots

Dots are the building blocks to many decorating techniques. In fact, even if all you ever learn is how to make a dot, you will know how to decorate a cake with buttercream. Making a dot is pretty intuitive, but this technique will help you perfect it.

**1** Hold the pastry bag at a 90-degree angle to the cake, with the tip hovering just above the surface. ■

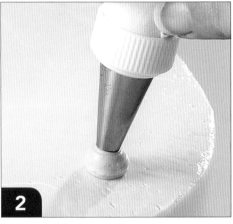

**2** Squeezing the bag with moderate pressure, move the tip slightly away from the cake until the icing begins to balloon out. ■

**3** Continue to squeeze until the nose of the tip is embedded slightly within the dot. ■

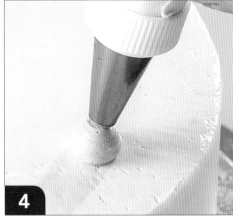

**4** Release the pressure completely and move the tip to the top of the dot. ■

**5**

Remove the tip by pulling it away to the side, to avoid a pointed top. ■

**Variation**

**Coupler Dot:** Do not attach a tip to the coupler. ■ Because coupler dots are large, if you are placing them on the side of a cake, you may choose to make them flat rather than spherical. ■ To do so, keep the coupler hovering just above the surface rather than pulling it away. ■

## Hints and Tips

If you try to make a larger dot than your chosen tip is capable of, the dot may break apart and lose its spherical shape. Either squeeze out less icing and make a smaller dot or change to a larger tip.

Embedded dots are perfect for making small eyes on a character or the spots on the back of a ladybug.

**Variation**

**Embedded Dot:** Begin with the tip inserted into the surface of the icing before beginning to squeeze, then proceed as with a standard dot. ■ The resulting dot should be even with or raised just slightly above the surface of the surrounding icing. ■

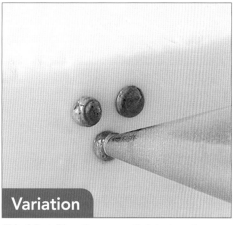

**Variation**

**Triad Dot:** Pipe three small dots together in a triangle. ■ Together, these three dots will act as a single dot in an expanded pattern. ■

# Swiss Dots

## What You Need

- Iced cake, placed in the center of a turntable
- Pastry bag fitted with a #2 or #3 round tip and filled with icing

## Hints and Tips

Swiss dots made with a #2 or #3 tip always appear elegant. For a fun look, try a larger round tip, such as a #6 or #8.

The Swiss dot pattern can be elongated to form a rectangle instead of a square.

Replace the single dots in a Swiss dot pattern with triad dots (variation, page 103) for an especially sweet look.

The simplified Swiss dot pattern is useful for small areas, such as a thin ribbon border.

The doubled Swiss dot pattern is handy for especially tall or very simple cakes. But exercise caution: too many dots can make a cake look spotted and diseased.

Swiss dots are simply a regular pattern of dots. The distance between the dots depends on the size of the surface. A small, squat cake should have more closely grouped dots than a large multilayer cake.

**1** Following the instructions on page 102, make two small dots an equal distance apart at the same height on the side of the cake. ■

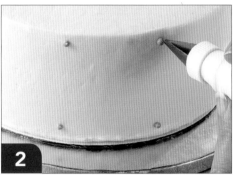

**2** Make a third dot an equal distance above the first dot, then a fourth dot an equal distance above the second dot. ■ You should now have a square of dots. ■

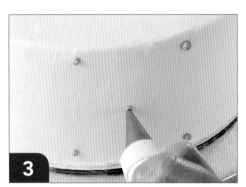

**3** Make a dot directly in the center of the square to complete the Swiss dot pattern. ■

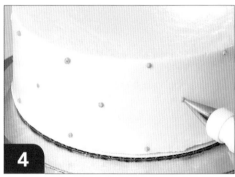

**4** To decorate a cake with Swiss dots, repeat the pattern all the way around the cake. ■

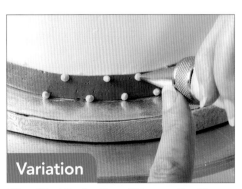

**Variation**

***Simplified Swiss Dots:*** Skip step 2, still placing the dot in step 3 where it would lie if the step 2 dots existed. ■

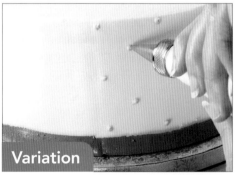

**Variation**

***Doubled Swiss Dots:*** Repeat steps 2 and 3 above the first pattern, so you have three vertical dots, two dots in the middle, then another three vertical dots. ■

# Sprinkled Rolled Dots

**Used to Make**
- Daisy centers (page 180)
- Ladybugs (page 234)

A rolled and sprinkled dot is a playful and surprising embellishment. Imagine a dot rolled in deep black nonpareils as the center of a crimson poppy or an elegant white anemone. I also like to roll pastel dots in shimmering sugar crystals to create the jewels of a crown.

## What You Need

- Iced cake, placed in the center of a turntable
- Sprinkles
- Pastry bag fitted with a #10 round tip and filled with icing
- Rose nail
- Kitchen scissors

## Hints and Tips

Placing a rolled dot on the side of a cake is a little more challenging than placing one on top. Make sure the dot is not overly large, so it doesn't tumble down from the strain of its own weight. A dot made with a #12 tip is probably okay, but a coupler dot is too large. Use your finger to aid the delivery from scissor tip to side of cake. Tap the dot gently once it is affixed, to flatten it slightly and ensure that it doesn't fall. Expect to lose a couple of dots to gravity in the process.

If the dot clings to the scissors, give it a gentle nudge and reshape it with your finger as necessary.

**1** Fill the lid of the sprinkles jar or a bowl with a generous pile of sprinkles. ■

**2** Holding the pastry bag at a 90-degree angle to the rose nail, with the tip hovering just above the surface, squeeze a large dot onto the rose nail. ■

**3** Carefully flip the rose nail upside down and gently roll the dot in sprinkles, coating thoroughly. ■

**4** If your dot becomes misshapen as you roll it, use your finger to gently tap it back into shape. ■

**5** Open the scissors and slowly close them around the base of the dot, just enough to gently lift it off of the rose nail. ■ The dot should be resting on the tip of the partially closed scissors. ■

**6** Place the tip of the scissors at the desired location on the cake. ■ Hold the scissors at a 45-degree angle to the cake and close them so that the dot slides off and into place. ■

## What You Need

- Iced cake, placed in the center of a turntable
- Pastry bag fitted with a #3 round tip and filled with icing
- Toothpick or skewer (optional)

## Hints and Tips

Buttercream can become a bit squirrelly when you use small round tips, such as a #1 or smaller. Generally speaking, the larger the tip, the easier it will be to control.

Making lines on the side of a cake is more challenging. With practice, you will discover that, for right-handed people, a line coming up from the bottom of the cake is easier if it arches to the right, and a line coming down from the top is easier if it arches to the left. Lefties will find it easier to arch their lines in the opposite directions.

# Lines

Making a line with buttercream on a cake is nothing like making a line with a pen on a piece of paper. Whereas drawing on a cake is rather tricky and can result in wobbly, uneven lines, the stringing technique described below creates smooth, gorgeous lines.

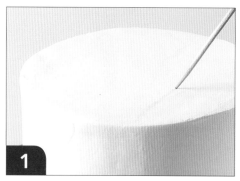

**1** If desired, use the toothpick or skewer to mark the starting and end points of your line. ■

**2** Holding the pastry bag at a 45-degree angle to the cake, with the tip lightly touching the starting point, squeeze the bag with moderate pressure to build an anchor of icing. ■

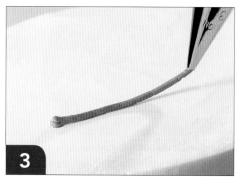

**3** Lift the tip slightly and move your hand in a straight line toward the end point, draping a string of icing across the cake. ■

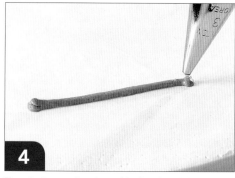

**4** Touch the end point with the tip of the bag and release the pressure. ■

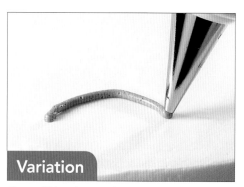

**Variation**

*Curved Line:* In step 3, move your hand in a downward or upward arch. ■

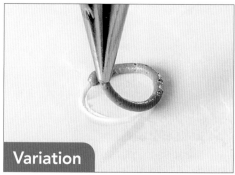

**Variation**

*Circle:* Stamp a faint circle on the surface with a round cookie cutter and trace the circle with a string of icing. ■

# Swags

Swags are a mainstay of traditional buttercream decoration. Tiered cakes decorated in the classic buttercream tradition swell with multiple crenulated swags, borders, dots and scrolls. But for me, nothing beats the airy grace of a simple string swag.

## Used to Make

- Bow and Swag (page 144)
- Chandelier (page 152)
- Roses and Ribbons (page 278)

## What You Need

- Iced cake, placed in the center of a turntable
- Pastry bag fitted with a #2 or #3 round tip and filled with icing
- Round or oval cookie cutter

## Hints and Tips

If you don't have a cookie cutter in the right size, you can substitute any round object.

The smaller and shallower the arc, the easier it will be to string a swag.

Remember, you are not drawing but stringing the icing across the cake, spanning two contact points and using the pull of gravity to form a perfect arch. A swag may make contact with the cake only at the starting and end points, dangling freely through the arch.

To decorate a cake with swags, mark off swags all the way around the cake as in step 1, then repeat steps 2 to 4 for each swag.

**1** Gently press the bottom part of the cookie cutter into the cake to make a faint impression of a swag on the side of the cake, near the top. ■

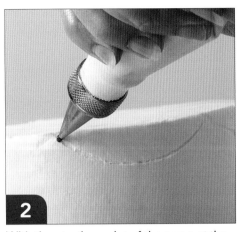

**2** With the starting point of the swag at the South (S) position, hold the pastry bag at a 45-degree angle to the cake, with the tip lightly touching the starting point. ■ Squeeze the bag with moderate pressure to build an anchor of icing. ■

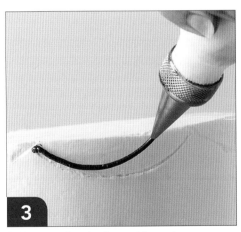

**3** Still squeezing the bag with moderate pressure, pull the tip away from the cake and move your hand in a downward and slightly outward arch toward the end point, allowing the string of icing to dangle and start to form the arch. ■

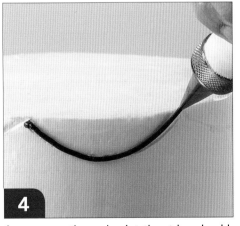

**4** As you near the end point, the string should hover directly over the imprint you made. ■ Touch the end point with the tip of the bag and give the bag an extra little squeeze to anchor the swag. ■

### Used to Make

- Golden Tassels (page 208)

## What You Need

- Iced cake, placed in the center of a turntable
- Pastry bag fitted with a #3 round tip and filled with icing
- #2 round tip

## Hints and Tips

Use quick, confident movements to make the fringe strands. Remember that you are stringing the icing, not drawing with it.

The fringe of a tassel can come straight out and down from the top knot, but I like to add a little movement by making it swoop out near the top and narrow at the bottom like an upside-down flame. Another way to add movement is to vary the lengths of the strands slightly and flip a few strands up at the ends, with a minute flick of the wrist.

Larger tassels can be made with larger round tips.

# Tassels

Buttercream makes creating fine strands easy, and a tassel composed of multiple fine strands is the ideal expression of this ability.

**1** Following the instructions on page 102, make a small dot at the South (S) position on the side of the cake, near the top. ■ This will be the top knot of the tassel. ■ Switch the tip on the pastry bag to the #2 tip. ■

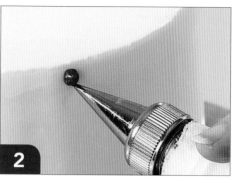

**2** Hold the bag at a 60-degree angle to the surface, with the tip lightly touching the surface of the cake just below the top knot. ■

**3** Squeezing the bag with firm pressure, pull the tip slightly away from the cake and move your hand down and to the right to create the right-hand outer strand of the fringe. ■ Release pressure when the strand is the desired length. ■

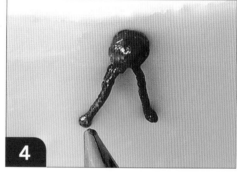

**4** Repeat steps 2 and 3, but this time move your hand down and to the left to create the left-hand outer strand of the fringe. ■ Release pressure when the strand is the desired length. ■

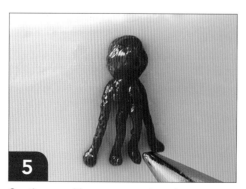

**5** Continue making as many strands as desired to fill in the fringe. ■

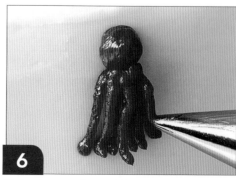

**6** Make three to four additional strands on top of the fringe to create depth and dimension. ■

# Embroidery

The embroidery technique is an elegant way to fill a design with color, and is reminiscent of ornate needlework. This is a great technique for a sports team logo (think of the logo on a baseball cap) or a monogram for a wedding or anniversary cake.

## Used to Make

- Embroidered Tattoo (page 184)
- Monogram (page 246)
- Winter Birds (page 332)

## What You Need

- Iced cake, placed in the center of a turntable
- Pastry bag fitted with a #3 round tip and filled with icing
- Template
- Toothpick or skewer
- #2 round tip

## Hints and Tips

Avoid "embroidering" over your outline. To successfully mimic needlework, the outline needs to remain visible.

Feel free to stop at any time to give your hand a rest, but avoid changing directions mid-shape. This is, however, unavoidable with certain shapes, such as the letter "H."

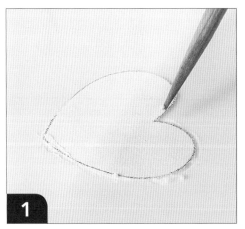

**1** Place the template in the desired location on the cake and trace around it with the toothpick or skewer. ∎

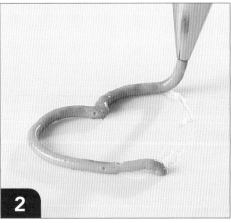

**2** Squeezing the pastry bag with gentle pressure, use the stringing technique described on page 106 to gradually outline your shape. ∎ Switch the tip on the pastry bag to the #2 tip. ∎

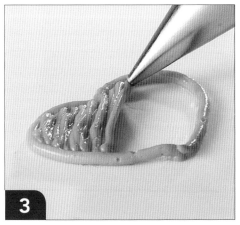

**3** Starting at one end of the shape, squeeze the bag with moderate pressure while moving your hand back and forth in an even and rhythmic motion within the outline. ∎ Add a slight arc to the movement, like a shallow, stretched-out rainbow, to accentuate the embroidered appearance. ∎

**4** Release the pressure when you have reached the end of the shape or the end of a section of the shape. ∎ Continue until the entire shape is filled in. ∎

## Variation

*Cross-Stitch:* Find a simple vintage cross-stitch pattern to copy, and use pastry bags fitted with #1 round tips to pipe the X's, following the design and colors in the pattern.

## What You Need

• Iced cake, transferred to the presentation surface

• Pastry bag fitted with a #104 rose tip and filled with icing

## Hints and Tips

When I first learned how to make bows, I put them on *everything*. These days, I reserve them for christening and baptismal cakes, simple anniversary cakes and cakes with an especially sweet flower arrangement.

# Bows

Though ubiquitous in the cake decorating medium of fondant, bows are a surprising element when made with buttercream. Bows can be made on the top of a cake or on the side. These instructions are for a bow on the side of the cake. Once you master this, a bow on the top will be, forgive the pun, a piece of cake.

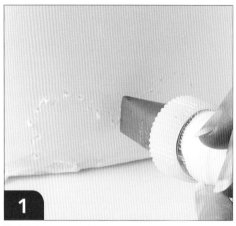

**1** Hold the pastry bag at a 90-degree angle to the side of the cake, with the fat end of the tip pointing down and the tip just touching the surface where the center of your bow will be. ■

**2** Squeezing the bag with firm pressure, move your hand up and to the right to create the top arch of the right loop. ■

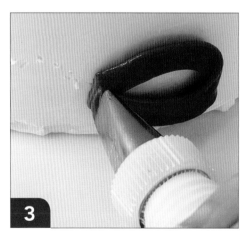

**3** Swoop down and back to the center to finish the right loop. ■

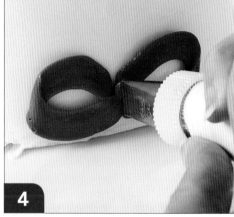

**4** Move your hand up and to the left to create the top arch of the left loop. ■ Swoop down and back to the center to finish the left loop. ■

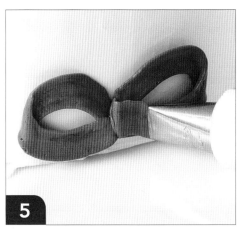

**5**

With the tip still in the center of the bow, squeeze the bag with firm pressure, moving the tip slightly to the right, then down to the presentation surface. ■

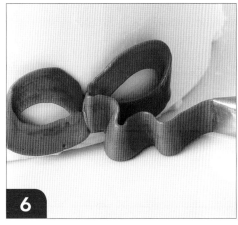

**6**

Gradually move the tip away from the cake and to the right, while making a squiggly back-and-forth motion to mimic the curled tail of a ribbon. ■

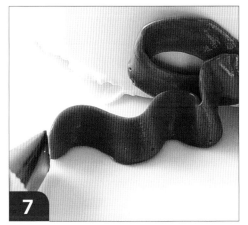

**7**

Repeat steps 5 and 6 on the left side to create the left ribbon tail. ■

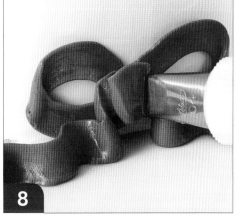
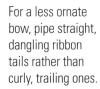

**8**

For the knot in the middle of the bow, squeeze the bag with moderate pressure to make a small horizontal line with a slight arch. ■

## Hints and Tips

I often place bows over a ribbon border. If you choose this option, use the same bag and tip for both ribbon and bow.

You can also use a round tip to make a simple bow. The technique is the same for steps 1 to 7. Make a fat dot in the center of the bow to represent the knot.

### Variation

For a less ornate bow, pipe straight, dangling ribbon tails rather than curly, trailing ones.

## What You Need

- Iced cake, placed in the center of a turntable
- Pastry bag fitted with a #352 leaf tip and filled with icing

## Hints and Tips

If you are left-handed, hold the pastry bag in the 9 o'clock direction, and move your hand toward the West (W) position in step 2.

This technique works best with a quick, confident motion of the hand. If you try to make a leaf slowly and deliberately, you'll end up with one that is thick and ripply or with a torn-off tip.

Leaves can be various lengths. Much of the time I make short, fat leaves, but if I'm going for something more tropical, I thin and elongate the leaves.

# Leaves

When making a buttercream flower, there are few occasions when the process doesn't start with a bed of leaves or end with an accent of leaves. Leaves are often the structural base of a flower, but they also anchor the flower in space, much as a shadow does for an object in a painting.

**1** Hold the pastry bag at a 45-degree angle to the top of the cake, in the 3 o'clock direction, with the tip hovering just above the starting point of your leaf. ∎

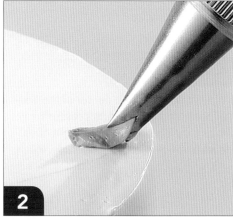

**2** Squeezing the bag with firm pressure, move your hand in a straight line toward the East (E) position on the cake. ∎

**3** When nearing the end of the leaf, shift the angle of the bag to 90 degrees and lift the tip slightly away from the surface to create a sharp, clean point. ∎

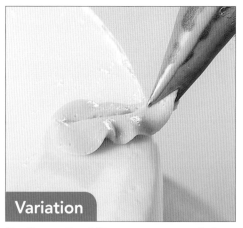

**Variation**

*Sunflower Petal:* The exact same technique is used to make a sunflower petal. ∎ Just use a sunny yellow color for the icing. ∎

# Long Horizontal Petals

## Used to Make
- Chrysanthemum (page 164)
- Gerbera Daisy (page 204)
- Lotus Flower (page 242)

Mastering the long horizontal petal is the key to making some of the most spectacular and impressive buttercream flowers.

## What You Need
- Iced cake, placed in the center of a turntable
- Pastry bag fitted with a #80 U tip and filled with icing

## Hints and Tips
If you are left-handed, hold the pastry bag in the 9 o'clock direction, and move your hand toward the West (W) position in step 3.

**1** Hold the pastry bag at a 45-degree angle to the top of the cake, in the 3 o'clock direction, with the tip hovering just above the starting point of your petal. ■

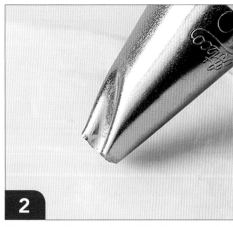

**2** Make sure the opening of the tip is oriented so that the U is right side up, like a lucky horseshoe. ■

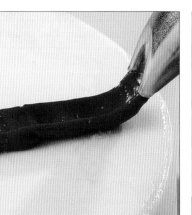

**3** Squeezing the bag with firm pressure, move your hand in a straight line toward the East (E) position on the cake, creating a petal about 1 inch (2.5 cm) long. ■

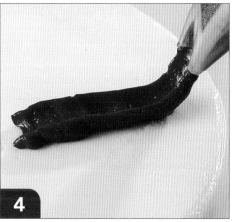

**4** When nearing the end of the petal, lift the tip slightly away from the surface to create a slightly upturned edge. ■ Release the pressure before moving the tip away from the finished petal. ■

## What You Need

- Iced cake, placed in the center of a turntable
- Pastry bag fitted with a #80 U tip and filled with icing

## Hints and Tips

When making these petals on the top of the cake, it is easiest to make them at the East (E) position if you are right-handed; if you are left-handed, it is easiest to make them at the West (W) position. Spin the turntable until the spot where you want to make the petal is oriented at the most comfortable position for your hand.

When making these petals on the side of the cake, it is easiest to make them at the South-Southeast (SSE) position if you are right-handed; if you are left-handed, it is easiest to make them at the South-Southwest (SSW) position.

# Short Vertical Petals

Cupped flowers and lilies of the valley are made exclusively of short vertical petals, but these petals also contribute detail to larger flowers, such as gerbera daisies, adding to their realism.

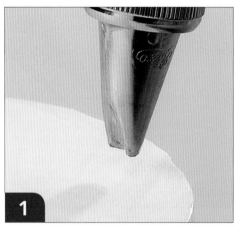

**1**

Hold the pastry bag at a 90-degree angle to the cake, with the tip hovering just above the surface where your petal will be. ■ Make sure the opening of the tip is oriented in the direction you want your petal to face. ■

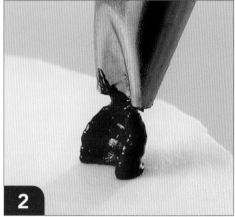

**2**

Squeezing the bag with firm pressure, move the tip away from the surface of the cake in a quick, confident motion, creating a petal about ¼ inch (5 mm) long. ■ Release the pressure before moving the tip away from the finished petal. ■

# Classic Flat Petals

The rose tip isn't just for roses: it creates a classic flat petal that can be used for any number of flowers, such as violets, pansies, geraniums, impatiens, apple and cherry blossoms, forget-me-nots and hibiscus.

## Used to Make

- Rosebuds (page 121)
- Hydrangea (page 226)
- Pansy (page 262)
- Violets (page 328)

## What You Need

- Iced cake, placed in the center of a turntable
- Pastry bag fitted with a rose tip and filled with icing

## Hints and Tips

If you are left-handed, hold the pastry bag in the 7 o'clock direction, and spin the table clockwise in step 3.

Depending on the size of flower desired, these petals can be made with a #101, #102, #103 or #104 rose tip. Each will give the flower a slightly different character. Use a #124, #125, #126 or #127 rose tip to make a large hibiscus flower.

The movement of your hand, the tip and the turntable should be very small and controlled for this technique.

1 Hold the pastry bag at a 45-degree angle to the top of the cake, in the 5 o'clock direction, with the fat end of the tip facing you and lightly touching the surface and the thin end hovering just above the surface. ■

2 Squeeze the bag with firm pressure to build an anchor of icing. ■

3 Move the tip slightly up and away from you while slowly and slightly spinning the turntable counterclockwise with your free hand. ■

4 Continue spinning the table as you return the tip to its starting point. ■ Release the pressure before moving the tip away from the finished petal. ■

**Used to Make**

- English Garden
  (page 190)
- Fairy Ring
  (page 194)

## What You Need

- Iced cake, placed in the center of a turntable
- Pastry bag fitted with a #131 drop flower tip and filled with icing

## Hints and Tips

You can also start with the tip touching the surface or a good distance from the surface. There's no one right way to make a drop flower. Experiment and have fun!

There are many drop flower tips available. My favorite is the #131, but you may find a different tip to your liking.

# Drop Flowers

There is no flower easier to make than the drop flower, and when multiple drop flowers are clustered together, there is hardly a design more beautiful.

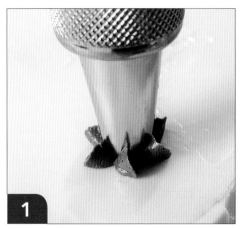

**1** Holding the pastry bag at a 90-degree angle to the cake, with the tip hovering just above the surface, squeeze the pastry bag with moderate pressure, allowing the icing to balloon out. ■

**2** Gently tap the surface of the cake with the tip and release the pressure. (The tap gives the flower a nice clean center.) ■

**Variation**

*Wisteria or Lilac:* Create a cluster of drop flowers in the shape of a bunch of grapes. ■ Layer and overlap the flowers for added dimension. ■ This technique is particularly sumptuous when draped over the side of a cake. ■

**Variation**

*Hyacinth:* Use the stringing technique described on page 106 to create a vine that starts at the bottom of the cake and reaches halfway up the side. ■ Add a tapered cylinder of drop flowers, starting at the top of the vine and moving toward the top of the cake. ■ Layer and overlap the flowers for added dimension. ■

# Dot Daisies

This sweet multipurpose flower is simply an arrangement of dots.

**1**

Following the instructions on page 102, pipe 5 or 6 dots in a tight ring. ■

**Variation**

Fill in the center of your daisy with a dot in a different icing color. ■

## Used to Make

- Calico (page 148)
- English Garden (page 190)
- Fairy Ring (page 194)
- Honey Bees (page 218)
- Vintage China (page 322)

## What You Need

- Iced cake, placed in the center of a turntable
- Pastry bag fitted with a #4 round tip and filled with icing

## Hints and Tips

Change the size of your drop daisies by changing the size of the tip.

# Petal Daisies

## Used to Make

- Daisies
  (page 180)
- English Garden
  (page 190)
- Fairy Ring
  (page 194)
- Vintage China
  (page 322)

## What You Need

- Iced cake, placed in the center of a turntable
- Pastry bag fitted with a #6 round tip and filled with icing
- Pastry bag fitted with a #124 rose tip (without a coupler) and filled with icing in a different color

## Variation

You can also use these petals on their own, as I have done in Art Deco (page 124) and Feathers (page 200).

## Hints and Tips

To help with evenly spacing the petals, start by making two petals directly across from one another. Fill in each empty half with the remaining petals.

The technique to make petal daisies on the side of the cake is the same, but in step 5, you'll have to move your hand around the center of the flower to make the petals, rather than spinning the turntable.

This technique is only slightly more challenging than the Dot Daisy (page 117). The tip used to make the petals creates an elongated shape that is more traditionally associated with a daisy.

**1** Hold the pastry bag with the round tip at a 90-degree angle to the top of the cake, hovering just above the spot where the center of your flower will be. ■

**2** Following the instructions on page 102, make a dot. ■

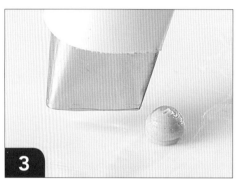

**3** Switching to the pastry bag with the rose tip, hold the bag so that opening is perfectly parallel with the surface of the cake, hovering just above the surface, with the thin end of the tip near the center of the flower. ■

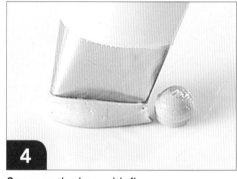

**4** Squeeze the bag with firm pressure, allowing the icing to balloon out. ■ Release the pressure before moving the tip away from the finished petal. ■

**5** Spin the turntable slightly and place a second petal next to the first. ■

**6** Continue making petals until they form a ring around the center of the flower. ■

# Cupped Flowers

## Used to Make

- Calico (page 148)
- Cherry Blossoms (page 160)
- English Garden (page 190)

On a mission to create a small, easy flower that was more delicate than the rosette and more elegant than the drop daisy, I came up with the cupped flower, inspired by the stylized rose of the Scottish art nouveau architect and artist Charles Rennie Mackintosh. The cupped flower can stand in for a traditional rose or even a cherry blossom, as in the project on page 160.

## What You Need

- Iced cake, placed in the center of a turntable
- Pastry bag fitted with a #80 U tip and filled with icing

## Variations

If there is space remaining in the center of your flower after you've made a second ring, you can create a third ring, even if it's only two or three overlapping petals.

Instead of working from the outside in, try starting the flower with a small, overlapping three-petal center and working out. The result will be slightly different — you might just like it!

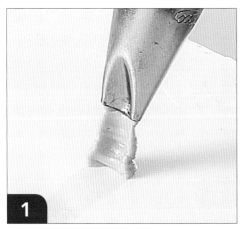

**1** Following the instructions on page 114, make a short vertical petal. ■

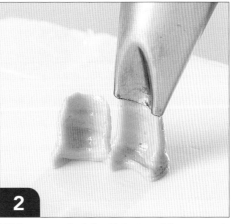

**2** With one end of the U tip touching an end of the first petal, but not overlapping it, make a second petal. ■

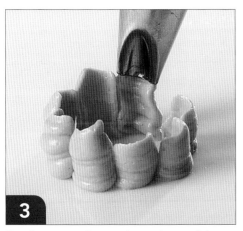

**3** Continue to make petals, end to end, in a circular shape, until you have a ring of small U shapes. ■

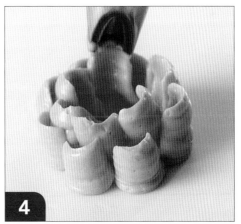

**4** Make a second ring of petals inside the first. ■ The petals may overlap a bit as your work area gets smaller. ■

## What You Need

- Iced cake, placed in the center of a turntable
- Pastry bag fitted with a #18 open star tip and filled with icing

## Hints and Tips

A rosette can be made with almost any open star tip. Play with different tips to create distinctive looks.

# Rosettes

The number of projects in this book that make use of the rosette is an indication of how easy, useful and pretty these stylized flowers are. Interestingly, a large rosette is made slightly differently than a small one, ending with the tail on the outer edge rather than in the center (see variation, below).

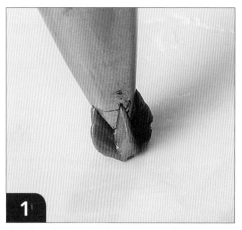

**1** Holding the pastry bag at a 90-degree angle to the cake, with the tip hovering just above the surface, squeeze the bag with moderate pressure until the icing begins to balloon out. ■

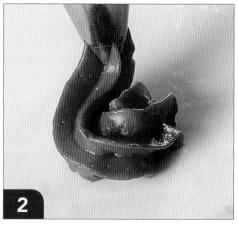

**2** Move your hand in a tight circular motion while continuing to squeeze the bag. ■

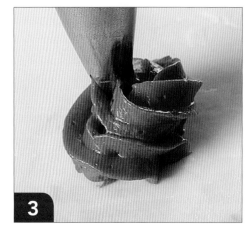

**3** As you approach the end of one complete circle, reduce the pressure and lift the tip slightly so that the icing overlaps and the narrowed tail of the flower spirals into the center. ■

**Variation**

**_Large Rosette:_** Use a #32 open star tip. ■ In step 2, move your hand in a loose circular motion. ■ As you approach the end of one complete circle, lift the tip slightly and overlap the icing on the outer edge, reducing the pressure so that the icing ends in a narrow tail on the outer edge. ■

# Rosebuds

These delicate blossoms may be tiny, but they have an oversized sweetness factor.

## Used to Make

- Fairy Ring (page 194)

## What You Need

- Iced cake, placed in the center of a turntable
- Pastry bag fitted with a #104 rose tip and filled with icing

## Variation

To make a more detailed and realistic rosebud, use green icing in a pastry bag fitted with a #2 round tip to make two calyx petals running halfway up either side of the rosebud and one up the middle. Add a green dot to the base of the bud and a trailing stem.

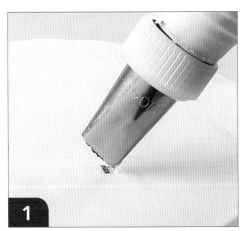

**1** Hold the pastry bag at a 45-degree angle to the top of the cake, in the 5 o'clock direction, with the fat end of the tip facing you and lightly touching the surface and the thin end hovering just above the surface. ■

**2** Squeezing the bag with moderate pressure, move the tip very slightly away from you, to the right and back to the starting point, creating a flat, upside-down triangle shape. ■

**3** Move the tip so it is butted up against bottom of the first petal, on the right side. ■

**4** Moving your hand in a very tight clockwise circle, make a second petal overlapping and slightly below the first. ■

# Chapter 5
# 50 Fabulous Projects

All of the layer cake projects in this section start with a cake that has been baked, cooled, sliced, filled and crumb-coated. For all projects, any flavor of cake, filling and icing can be used. You'll find cake recipes on pages 30–45 and icing recipes on pages 46–50. The techniques for slicing layers, filling a cake and crumb-coating a cake are covered on pages 52–56. Before you get started, you'll also want to review the information on coloring buttercream icing (pages 57–66) and on filling a pastry bag (pages 67–69).

Note that all cakes, except for Birch (page 140), Cheetah (page 156), Rustic Finish (page 282), Timber (page 314) and Zebra Stripes (page 338), should be placed on their final presentation surface, such as a cake board, serving plate, platter or cake stand, *before* they are placed on the turntable for decorating. (For clarity in the photographs, however, the cakes are shown on the turntable.)

# Art Deco

*Art deco is an influential visual arts style characterized by rich colors and bold, repetitive geometric shapes. This cake takes inspiration from the elliptical panels of the spire that tops the Chrysler Building and the cool green marble lobbies of glamorous New York City apartment buildings from the art deco era.*
**Makes one 6-inch (15 cm) layer cake.**

## Getting Started

**Ice and chill the cake:** Use medium green icing and the Smooth Icing technique to ice the cake. Transfer the cake to the presentation surface and refrigerate until well chilled.

**Fill the pastry bags:** Transfer the remaining medium green icing to a pastry bag fitted with the #6 tip, the black icing to a bag with the #104 tip, the gold icing to a bag with the #103 tip, and half the dark green icing to a bag with a #3 tip. Fit a pastry bag without a coupler with the #124 tip and fill with the remaining dark green icing.

## What You Need

- 6-inch (15 cm) layer cake, sliced, filled and crumb-coated
- 3½ cups (875 mL) medium green icing
- ¾ cup (175 mL) black icing
- ¾ cup (175 mL) gold icing
- 1½ cups (375 mL) dark green icing
- Turntable
- Presentation surface
- 5 pastry bags
- 4 couplers
- #6 round tip
- #104 rose tip
- #103 rose tip
- 3 #3 round tips
- #124 rose tip
- #301 ribbon tip
- Rainbow template (page 350)
- Toothpick or skewer

## Techniques Used

- Smooth Icing (page 82)
- Transferring an Iced Cake (page 96)
- Ribbon Border (page 98)
- Tracing and Pattern-Making (page 71)
- Lines (page 106)
- Petal Daisy petals (page 118)
- Smooth Scallop Border (page 99)

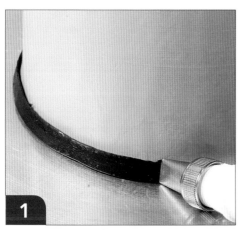

Place the chilled cake in the center of the turntable. ■ Using black icing, pipe a ribbon border around the bottom of the cake. ■

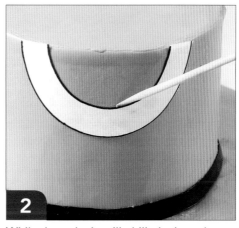

While the cake is still chilled, place the rainbow template upside down on the side of the cake, with the straight edges of the template aligned with the top edge of the cake. ■ Using the toothpick, trace the outline of the rainbow. ■

This design works best on a cake that is 4 inches (10 cm) high.

You may find that there's a little extra room between the first rainbow you trace and the last one, but don't worry: there's so much patterning in this design, a little extra space will go unnoticed. In any case, no one can view the entire circumference of a cake at once!

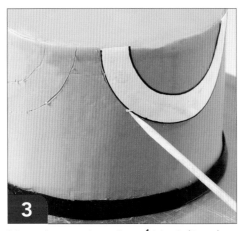

**3**

Move the template about ½ inch (1 cm) to one side of the first outline and trace another rainbow. ■ Continue tracing rainbows all the way around the top edge of the cake, spacing them about ½ inch (1 cm) apart. ■

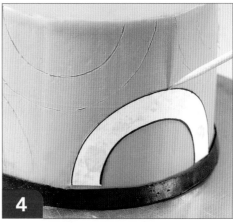

**4**

Flip the template right side up and use the toothpick to trace rainbows around the bottom edge of the cake, above the ribbon, staggering them so that the center point of each bottom rainbow lines up with the space between two top rainbows. ■

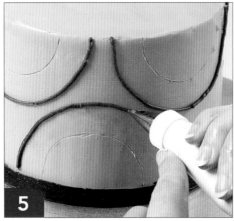

**5**

Using dark green icing from the bag with the #3 tip, outline the outer arc of all the rainbows. ■

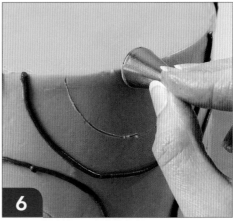

**6**

Using the back of a standard-size tip, make an imprint of a small semicircle in the center of each rainbow, top and bottom. ■

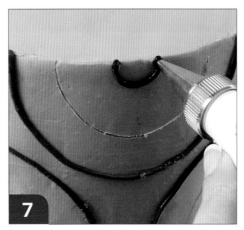

**7**

Switch the tip on the black icing to a #3 tip and outline all of the small semicircles. ■

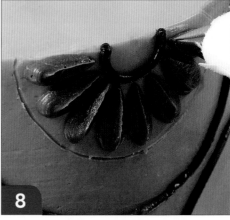

**8**

Using dark green icing from the bag with the #124 tip, make a semicircle of daisy petals fanning out from each of the small semicircles, top and bottom. ■

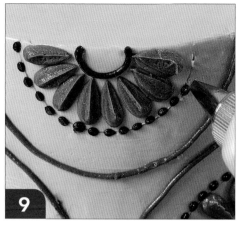

**9**

Switch the tip on the black icing to the #301 tip and pipe evenly spaced dots in a semicircle around each petal fan, following the outlined inner arc of the rainbow. ■

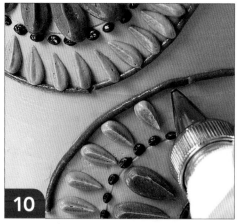

**10**

Using gold icing, make a semicircle of daisy petals fanning out from each of the dotted black semicircles. ■

## Hints and Tips

If you don't have a #301 ribbon tip to make the dotted semicircles in steps 9 and 12, you can use a #3 round tip instead, making round dots instead of ovals.

If space allows, you can pipe full circles instead of semicircles in step 11.

In step 13, the lines of dots may merge from two into one in the narrowest spaces between two rainbows.

**11**

Switch the tip on the gold icing to a #3 tip and pipe a tiny semicircle in the center of each small black semicircle at the top and bottom of the cake. ■

**12**

Using black icing, pipe evenly spaced dots in a semicircle around the outer arc of each rainbow. ■

**13**

Using medium green icing, pipe a smooth scallop border around the top of the cake. ■

**129**

# Bamboo

*The Bamboo cake is so simple, but its highly stylized decoration makes a big impact. Try making it in a brilliant red color with black bamboo stalks for a Chinese New Year cake.* **Makes one 4-inch (10 cm) layer cake.**

## Getting Started

**Ice and chill the cake:** Use green icing and the Smooth Icing technique to ice the cake. Transfer the cake to the presentation surface and refrigerate until well chilled.

**Fill the pastry bags:** Transfer the remaining green icing to a pastry bag fitted with the #103 tip, and the ivory icing to a bag with the #301 tip.

## What You Need

- 4-inch (10 cm) layer cake, sliced, filled and crumb-coated
- 3½ cups (875 mL) medium green icing
- ½ cup (125 mL) ivory icing
- Turntable
- Presentation surface
- 2 pastry bags
- 2 couplers
- #103 rose tip
- #301 ribbon tip

## Techniques Used

- Smooth Icing (page 82)
- Transferring an Iced Cake (page 96)
- Ribbon Border (page 98)

## Hints and Tips

For this project, use three 4-inch (10 cm) baked cake layers, each sliced in half then filled and stacked.

Swiss meringue buttercream icing that has not been colored is a neutral ivory color.

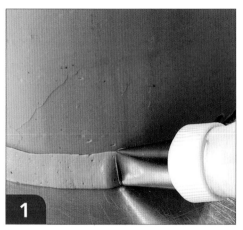

Place the chilled cake in the center of the turntable. ■ Using green icing, pipe a ribbon border around the bottom of the cake. ■

Hold the bag of ivory icing at a 90-degree angle to the side of the cake, with the tip just touching the top edge and the opening of the tip aligned horizontally. ■

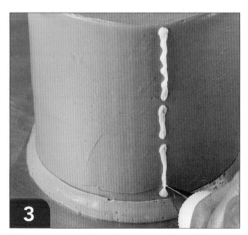

Pipe a line straight down the side of the cake in three segments of random lengths. ■ Add a little extra pressure at the top and bottom of each segment to resemble the nodes (growth rings) of the bamboo stalk. ■

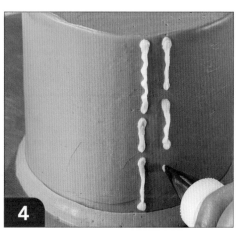

Spin the turntable slightly and make another bamboo stalk about 1 inch (2.5 cm) away from the first, varying the lengths of the segments and the widths of the stalks (see hints and tips, page 132). ■

The wonderful thing about a stylized decoration like a bamboo stalk is that it's a representation, not a reproduction. This allows for creative license and a high tolerance for imperfection. Lines no longer have to be entirely straight or leaves completely pointy to convey the object or capture the mood.

Vary the widths of the stalks by squeezing the pastry bag with more or less pressure.

You can also vary the number of segments in each stalk, making some two segments, some three and some four.

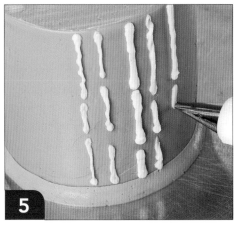

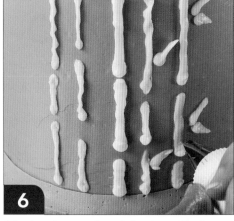

Repeat step 4 until you have a total of five stalks. ■

Aligning the opening of the tip vertically, pipe angled leaves alongside each bamboo stalk. ■ Make single leaves, or clusters of two or three with each leaf at a different angle to the stalk. ■ Place the leaves randomly, and make as many or as few as you like, but keep in mind that the overall effect should be sparse-looking. ■

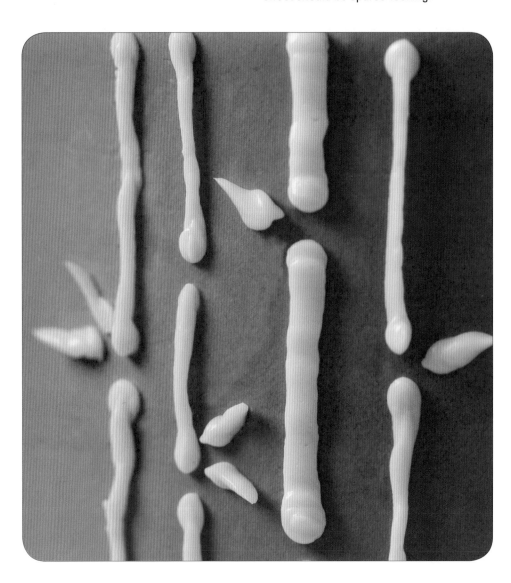

# Basket Weave

*The basket weave, a traditional buttercream technique, looks amazingly realistic and complicated, but is in fact an optical illusion of surprising ease. I updated the look with the artful placement of some cheerful red burlap flowers.* **Makes one 8-inch (20 cm) layer cake.**

## Getting Started

**Ice and chill the cake:** Use medium brown icing and the Smooth Icing technique to ice the cake. Transfer the cake to the presentation surface and refrigerate until well chilled.

**Fill the pastry bags:** Transfer the remaining medium brown icing to a pastry bag fitted with a #6 tip, and the light brown icing to a bag with the #48 tip.

## What You Need

- 8-inch (20 cm) layer cake, sliced, filled and crumb-coated
- 5 cups (1.25 L) medium brown icing
- 2 cups (500 mL) light brown icing
- Turntable
- Presentation surface
- 2 pastry bags
- 2 couplers
- 2 #6 round tips
- #48 basket weave tip
- Metal ruler

## Techniques Used

- Smooth Icing (page 82)
- Transferring an Iced Cake (page 96)
- Lines (page 106)
- Smooth Scallop Border (page 99)

**1** Place the chilled cake in the center of the turntable. ■ Holding the ruler vertically and perpendicular to the side of the cake, gently press the edge of the ruler into the icing to make an imprint of a straight line. ■

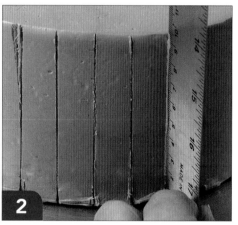

**2** Move the ruler about ½ inch (1 cm) to one side of the first line and mark another line. ■ Continue marking vertical lines all the way around the cake in ½-inch (1 cm) increments. ■

**3** Using medium brown icing, pipe over the ruler imprints, making vertical lines around the side of the cake. ■

**4** Hold the bag of light brown icing perpendicular to the cake, with the opening of the tip aligned vertically. ■ Nestle the tip against one of the vertical lines, at the top edge of the cake. ■

## Hints and Tips

Another way to mark off the vertical stripes is to use a toothpick to make small notches at the top of the cake. Gravity will help you create straight, even lines down to the bottom.

Making a vertical line on a cake is not quite like drawing a line, nor are you defying gravity by stringing the entire line of icing. It is, rather, a combination of the two: incrementally dangling a small portion of the line and overlaying it on the surface.

## Hints and Tips

When making the bands of icing, move your hand at a moderate pace to match the pressure you're applying to the pastry bag.

Work as quickly as you can while piping the icing bands, as icing that is held in a warm hand nonstop for more than 5 or 10 minutes will begin to diminish in quality, separating and becoming spongy and full of air bubbles. If that happens, squeeze the icing out into a bowl, add a dab of fresh icing and stir until smooth, then refill the bag.

**5**

Squeezing the bag with moderate pressure, move the tip toward the next vertical line, lifting the tip slightly away from the cake as it moves over and past the line. ■ Release the pressure when the tip meets the edge of the line that follows. ■

**6**

Leaving a blank space exactly the same width as the basket weave tip, make another band of icing below the first one. ■

**7**

Continue adding bands with equal spaces between them down the side of the cake. ■

**8**

For the second set of bands, begin with the tip nestled up against the center line of the first set of bands, in the space between the top two bands. ■

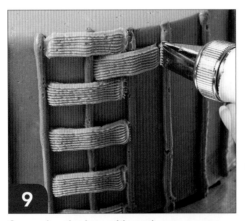

**9**

Squeezing the bag with moderate pressure, move the tip toward the next vertical line, lifting the tip slightly away from the cake as it moves over and past the line. ■ Release the pressure when the tip meets the edge of the line that follows. ■

**10**

Continue adding bands with equal spaces between them down the side of the cake to the bottom edge. ■

Continue making columns of alternating bands all the way around the cake until all the spaces are filled and the sides of the cake are covered in a basket weave of icing. ■

Switch the tip on the light brown icing to a #6 tip and pipe a smooth scallop border around the bottom of the cake. ■

## Variations

Use light brown icing to ice the cake and pipe the bands, and medium brown icing to pipe the vertical lines and the scallop border. Or, each time you make this cake, change up which browns you use where.

The basket weave also looks lovely in ivory, adorned with pastel flowers or fresh fruit.

# Birch

The beauty and perfection of nature informs the decoration of this cake. I was inspired to create it when, while flipping through a magazine, I came across a slab of birch being used as a serving plate. The birch was rustic, yet the contrast of the curling ivory bark with its black striations made it surprisingly abstract and striking. **Makes one 6-inch (15 cm) layer cake.**

## Getting Started

**Ice and chill the cake:** Roughly ice the top and sides of the cake with a thin layer of ivory icing. (This layer will eventually be entirely covered.) Cover the remaining icing and set aside. Leave the cake on the turntable and refrigerate until well chilled.

**Fill the pastry bags:** Transfer each of the light brown, medium brown and dark brown icings to a pastry bag fitted with a #8 tip. Transfer the black icing to a bag fitted with the #3 tip.

1. Starting in the center of the chilled cake, begin to make concentric rings on the top of the cake, alternating randomly between the three bags of brown icing. ■

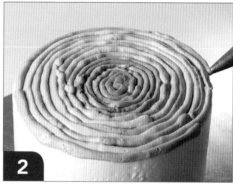

2. Continue until the top of the cake is entirely covered with brown rings. ■ Fill any gaps with icing. ■

3. Use the small offset spatula to smooth the edges of the cake, ensuring that no brown icing hangs over the sides. ■ Place the cake, still on the turntable, in the refrigerator until well chilled. ■

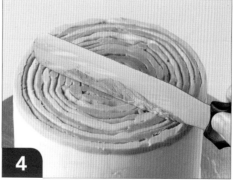

4. Using the edge of the straight blade spatula, begin to scrape the top layer of icing off the top of the cake, either by holding the spatula steady while spinning the turntable or by scraping the spatula back and forth with the turntable still. ■

## What You Need

- 6-inch (15 cm) layer cake, sliced, filled and crumb-coated
- 3 cups (750 mL) ivory icing
- 1¾ cups (425 mL) light brown icing
- 1¾ cups (425 mL) medium brown icing
- 1¾ cups (425 mL) dark brown icing
- 1¾ cups (425 mL) black icing
- Turntable
- 4 pastry bags
- 4 couplers
- 3 #8 round tips
- #3 round tip
- Small offset spatula
- Small straight blade spatula
- Damp cloth
- Paring knife

## Techniques Used

- Lines (page 106)

## Hints and Tips

Before icing the cake, make space in the refrigerator for the turntable with the cake on top. This cake is not transferred to the presentation surface until you are done decorating it.

Swiss meringue buttercream icing that has not been colored is a neutral ivory color.

## Hints and Tips

Because of the pressure exerted on the cake during the scraping process, it is important that the seal created between the cake and the turntable during the icing process not be broken, so do not remove the cake from the turntable at any time while decorating it.

Give yourself a good deal of time to create this cake. The decoration itself doesn't take too long, but the cake needs to chill for 20 to 25 minutes three different times.

If you don't have three #8 round tips, simply switch one tip between the three bags of brown icing. There's no need to clean the tip as you switch it.

This cake is gorgeous for an outdoor event. Add fresh flowers or fruit as additional decoration.

### Variation

Instead of using three shades of brown for the tree rings, just alternate between two.

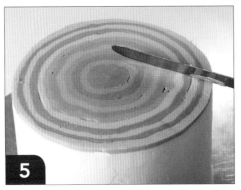

**5** Whenever a significant amount of icing accumulates on the spatula, scrape it clean and wipe it with a damp cloth. ■ Continue scraping off icing until the rings are smooth, flat and even. ■

**6** Using the straight blade spatula, add a layer of ivory icing to the sides of the cake, spreading the icing up past the top edge of the cake to create a short, jagged ledge of icing around the top. ■ Place the cake, still on the turntable, in the refrigerator until well chilled. ■

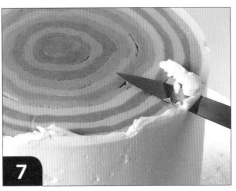

**7** Holding the paring knife parallel to the top of the cake, trim off the jagged ledge. ■ You can do this in two stages, if desired, first cutting off the big peaks of icing (or the top half of the ledge) and then cutting off the remainder of the ledge. ■ Clean the knife frequently with a damp cloth. ■

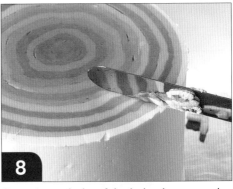

**8** Once the majority of the ledge is removed, clean and even the edge by running the edge of the straight blade spatula over it while spinning the turntable. ■

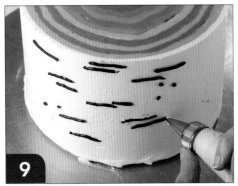

**9** Using black icing, pipe short horizontal lines and dots around the sides of the cake, placing them randomly. ■ Be conservative; you can always add more later. ■

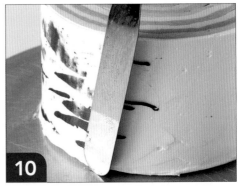

**10** Holding the edge of the straight blade spatula at an angle to the side of the cake, gently scrape the icing, spreading the black lines (some may scrape off). ■ Clean the spatula frequently. ■ Continue adding lines, spreading and scraping until the sides of the cake resemble birch bark. ■

# Bow and Swag

This cake takes the classic buttercream swag and pares it down to its simplest, most elegant form. The delicate swags, tiny bows and dots are simple enough to be clean and unfussy, but interesting enough that no further decoration is required. **Makes one 8-inch (20 cm) layer cake.**

## Getting Started

**Ice and chill the cake:** Use medium green icing and the Smooth Icing technique to ice the cake. Transfer the cake to the presentation surface and refrigerate until well chilled.

**Fill the pastry bags:** Transfer half the ivory icing to a pastry bag fitted with the #2 tip. Fit a bag without a coupler with the #125 tip and fill with the remaining ivory icing.

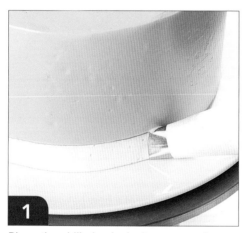

Place the chilled cake in the center of the turntable. ■ Using ivory icing from the bag with the #125 tip, pipe a ribbon border around the bottom of the cake. ■

Gently press the cookie cutter into the side of the cake to mark off 1½-inch (4 cm) wide and 1-inch (2.5 cm) deep swag imprints side by side around the top edge of the cake. ■

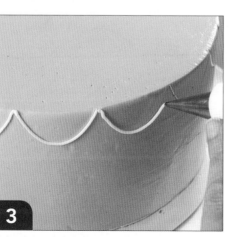

Using ivory icing from the bag with the #2 tip, pipe over the swag imprints. ■

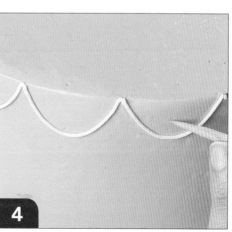

Using the toothpick, mark a point halfway between the top of the cake and the lowest part of each swag. ■

## What You Need

- 8-inch (20 cm) layer cake, sliced, filled and crumb-coated
- 4 cups (1 L) medium green icing
- 1 cup (250 L) ivory icing
- Turntable
- Presentation surface
- 2 pastry bags
- 1 coupler
- #2 round tip
- #125 rose tip
- 1½-inch (4 cm) round or oval cookie cutter
- Toothpick or skewer

## Techniques Used

- Smooth Icing (page 82)
- Transferring an Iced Cake (page 96)
- Ribbon Border (page 98)
- Swags (page 107)
- Bows (page 110)
- Dots (page 102)

## Hints and Tips

Swiss meringue buttercream icing that has not been colored is a neutral ivory color.

## Hints and Tips

If you don't have a 1½-inch (4 cm) round or oval cookie cutter, you can use a toothpick to mark off the swags in steps 2 and 6. Mark around the top edge of the cake at 1½-inch (4 cm) intervals, then mark the lowest point of each swag, 1 inch (2.5 cm) below the top edge. Use these points as guidelines for your piped swags. Similarly, in step 6, use the toothpick to mark the deepest part of each swag around the top of the cake.

This cake is particularly sweet for a baby shower, baptism or christening. You can swap out the brilliant green for a more traditional color.

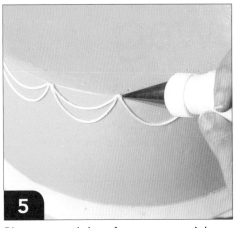

**5** Pipe a second ring of swags around the cake, the depth of the toothpick marks, with the ends joined to those of the deeper swags. ∎

**6** Gently press the cookie cutter into the top of the cake to mark off a ring of swags that are the same depth as those made in step 5. ∎

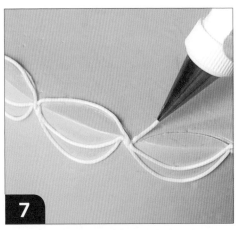

**7** Still using the bag with the #2 tip, pipe over the swag imprints on the top of the cake. ∎

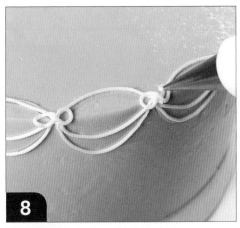

**8** Pipe the two loops of a bow between each set of swags. (No need to add the dangling ribbon ends of the bows; the idea is that the bow and swags are one continuous ribbon.) ∎

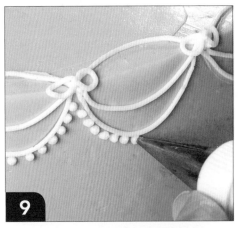

**9** Pipe small dots, very close together, around the outer edge of each of the deepest swags on the side of the cake. ∎

**10** Pipe small dots, very close together, around the top and bottom edges of the ribbon border. ∎

# Calico

This cake captures the sweetness and modesty of classic calico fabric. The soft colors make it a lovely centerpiece for a garden party or English tea. **Makes one 6-inch (15 cm) layer cake.**

## Getting Started

**Ice and chill the cake:** Use pale peach icing and the Smooth Icing technique to ice the cake. Transfer the cake to the presentation surface and refrigerate until well chilled.

**Fill the pastry bags:** Transfer the remaining pale peach icing to a pastry bag fitted with the #6 tip, the brown icing to a bag with the #2 tip, the pink icing to a bag with the #80 tip, the blue icing to a bag with the #3 tip, the dark peach icing to a bag with the #14 tip, and the dark and light green icings to bags with #352 tips.

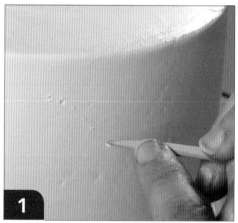

1. Place the chilled cake in the center of the turntable. ■ Use the toothpick to dot small arcs on the side of the cake, alternating between placing them near the top and near the bottom to create two rings of staggered arcs around the cake (see hints and tips, page 150). ■

2. Using brown icing, pipe over all the arcs. ■

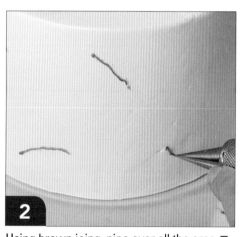

3. Using pink icing, pipe a cupped flower near the middle of each arc. ■

4. Using blue icing, pipe one or two drop daisies on each arc, placing them randomly. ■

## What You Need

- 6-inch (15 cm) layer cake, sliced, filled and crumb-coated
- 4 cups (1 L) pale peach icing
- ¾ cup (175 mL) light brown icing
- ¾ cup (175 mL) warm dark pink icing streaked with ivory
- ¾ cup (175 mL) light blue icing
- ¾ cup (175 mL) dark peach icing
- ¾ cup (175 mL) dark green icing
- ¾ cup (175 mL) light green icing
- Turntable
- Presentation surface
- 7 pastry bags
- 7 couplers
- #6 round tip
- #2 round tip
- #80 U tip
- #3 round tip
- #14 open star tip
- 2 #352 leaf tips
- Toothpick or skewer
- Tweezers
- White sugar pearls

## Techniques Used

- Smooth Icing (page 82)
- Transferring an Iced Cake (page 96)
- Cupped Flowers (page 119)
- Dot Daisies (page 117)
- Rosettes (page 120)
- Leaves (page 112)
- Smooth Scallop Border (page 99)

## Hints and Tips

For information on making variegated icing colors, see page 64.

When making the arcs in step 1, make some that curve up and some down, and some that curve right and some left.

The sugar pearls added in step 8 represent small blossoms.

### Variation

Feel free to choose different flowers to adorn the branches. Tiny wisteria tendrils (variation, page 116) or rosebuds (page 121) would also look very sweet.

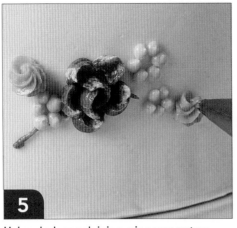

Using dark peach icing, pipe one or two small rosettes on each arc, placing them randomly. ■

Using dark green icing, pipe one or two leaves on each stem, placing them randomly. ■

Using light green icing, pipe one or two leaves on each stem, placing them randomly. ■

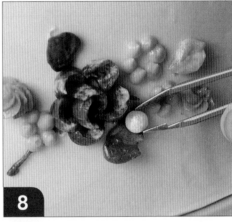

Use the tweezers to place three or four sugar pearls around each stem, placing them randomly. ■

Using pale peach icing, pipe a smooth scallop border around the bottom of the cake. ■

Pipe a smooth scallop border around the top of the cake. ■

# Chandelier

The chandelier is a popular contemporary motif, seen on everything from throw pillows to hand towels and wall stencils. Lucky for us, for a chandelier-themed cake we mostly just need to pipe lines and dots. **Makes one 6-inch (15 cm) layer cake.**

## Getting Started

**Ice and chill the cake:** Use peach icing and the Smooth Icing technique to ice the cake. Transfer the cake to the presentation surface and refrigerate until well chilled.

**Fill the pastry bags:** Transfer the remaining peach icing to a pastry bag fitted with the #6 tip, and the black icing to a bag with the #3 tip.

## What You Need

- 6-inch (15 cm) layer cake, sliced, filled and crumb-coated
- 4 cups (1 L) pale peach icing
- 1½ cups (375 mL) black icing
- Turntable
- Presentation surface
- 2 pastry bags
- 2 couplers
- #6 round tip
- #3 round tip
- #1 round tip
- Scalloped circle template (page 350)
- Toothpick or skewer
- 1½-inch (4 cm) round or oval cookie cutter

## Techniques Used

- Smooth Icing (page 82)
- Transferring an Iced Cake (page 96)
- Swags (page 107)
- Dots (page 102)
- Smooth Scallop Border (page 99)

**1** Place the chilled cake in the center of the turntable. ■ Place the scalloped circle template on the top of the cake and trace around it with the toothpick. ■

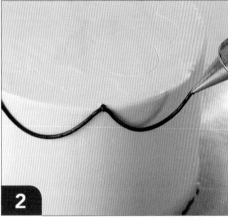

**2** Gently press the cookie cutter into the side of the cake to mark off 1½-inch (4 cm) wide and 1-inch (2.5 cm) deep swag imprints side by side around the top edge of the cake. ■ Using black icing, pipe over the swag imprints. ■

**3** Starting in the center of a swag, use the toothpick to dot the outline of a swag that is the same depth as the piped swags and that extends to the center of the next piped swag. ■ Continue to dot swag outlines all the way around the cake. ■

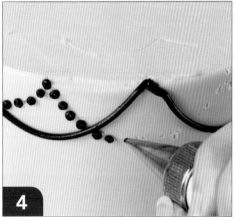

**4** Using black icing, pipe dotted lines over the second ring of swags. ■

**153**

## Hints and Tips

If you don't have a 1½-inch (4 cm) round or oval cookie cutter, you can use a toothpick to mark off the swags in step 2. Mark around the top edge of the cake at 1½-inch (4 cm) intervals, then mark the lowest point of each swag, 1 inch (2.5 cm) below the top edge. Use these points as guidelines for your piped swags.

To increase the size of the dots as you work down the swags in step 8, squeeze the pastry bag with increasing pressure.

## Variations

This cake, which is graphic and contemporary when decorated in pale peach and black, transforms into simple elegance when decorated in the palest of pastels or in shades of ivory and beige.

Add a fat dot on top of the cake at the top of each of the solid swags that ring the sides of the cake.

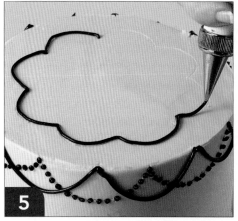

5. Pipe over the outline of the scalloped circle on top of the cake. ■

6. Pipe three dots above the point of each scallop. ■

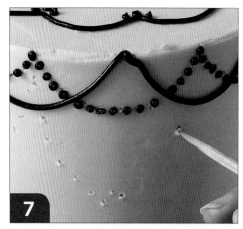

7. Use the toothpick to dot the outline of longer swags that hang directly beneath the dotted swags but are more triangular, as if a crystal were hanging from the bottom of each swag. ■

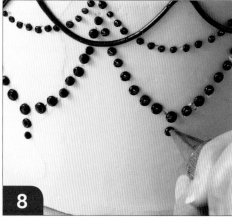

8. Using black icing, pipe dotted lines over the third ring of swags, increasing the size of the dots as they move toward the bottom of the swag (see hints and tips, at left). ■ Add two dots of decreasing size in a line below the lowest dot on each of the long swags. ■

9. Switch the tip on the black icing to the #1 tip and pipe two small dotted arcs below the point of each scallop on the top of the cake. ■

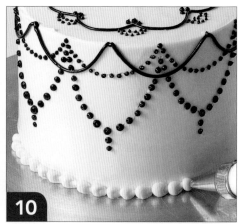

10. Using peach icing, pipe a smooth scallop border around the bottom of the cake. ■

# Cheetah

*The wonderful thing about the cheetah is that each spot is unique and amorphous in shape, so there's no wrong way to make one!*
Makes one 6-inch (15 cm) layer cake.

## Getting Started

**Ice and chill the cake:** Roughly ice the top and sides of the cake with a thin layer of brown icing. (This layer will eventually be entirely covered.) Leave the cake on the turntable and refrigerate until well chilled.

**Fill the pastry bags:** Transfer the remaining brown icing and the gold icing to pastry bags fitted with #6 tips, and the black icing to a bag with the #8 tip.

## What You Need

- 6-inch (15 cm) layer cake, sliced, filled and crumb-coated
- 6 cups (1.5 L) light brown icing (see hints and tips, page 158)
- 2 cups (500 mL) gold icing
- 2 cups (500 mL) black icing
- Turntable
- 4 pastry bags
- 3 couplers
- 2 #6 round tips
- #8 round tip
- #125 rose tip
- Straight blade spatula
- Damp cloth
- Presentation surface

## Techniques Used

- Smooth Icing (page 82)
- Transferring an Iced Cake (page 96)
- Ribbon Border (page 98)

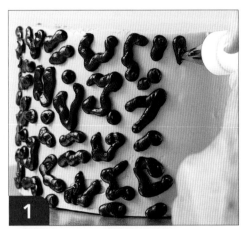

Place the cake in the center of the turntable. ■ Using black icing, pipe fat, distorted U shapes and dots of random size, shape and direction around the sides of the cake. ■

Cover the top of the cake with random U shapes and dots. ■

Using gold icing, fill in the centers of the U shapes, squeezing with firm pressure and using just one stroke for each center. ■ The centers should be fat and roughly the same height as the black icing. ■

Using brown icing, fill in all the empty spaces on the cake, squeezing with firm pressure to ensure that the height of the brown icing is similar to that of the gold and black icing. ■ Place the cake, still on the turntable, in the refrigerator until well chilled. ■

## Hints and Tips

Before icing the cake, make space in the refrigerator for the turntable with the cake on top. This cake is not transferred to the presentation surface until you are almost done decorating it.

Give yourself plenty of time to create this cake, as it needs to chill twice, for 20 to 25 minutes each time.

**157**

## Hints and Tips

The reductive scraping technique used in this project seems to bring out the undertones in icing colors. Even though this project starts out with light brown icing, it ends up looking yellow after the chilling and scraping process.

In step 4, it's okay if the brown icing pushes up against or slightly overlaps the gold icing. Just make sure there are no gaps remaining.

Because of the pressure exerted on the cake during the scraping process, it is important that the seal created between the cake and the turntable during the icing process not be broken, so do not remove the cake from the turntable before step 8.

Work quickly in steps 5 to 7, so that the cake remains chilled during the entire process, and don't be shy about applying significant pressure.

### Variation

Try this cake in shades of pink or blue for an entirely different look.

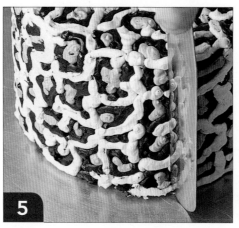

**5** Holding the edge of the straight blade spatula at an angle to the side of the cake and spinning the turntable, scrape the top layer of icing off the side of the cake. ■

**6** Using the edge of the straight blade spatula, begin to scrape the top layer of icing off the top of the cake, either by holding the spatula steady while spinning the turntable or by scraping the spatula back and forth with the turntable still. ■

**7** Whenever a significant amount of icing accumulates on the spatula, scrape it clean and wipe it with a damp cloth. ■ Continue scraping off icing until the cheetah pattern on both the top and the sides of the cake is smooth, flat and even. ■

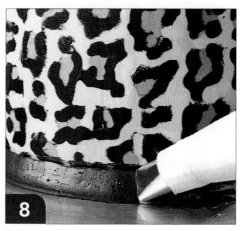

**8** Transfer the cake to the presentation surface. ■ Switch the tip on the black icing to the #125 tip and pipe a ribbon border around the bottom of the cake. ■

# Cherry Blossoms

*The cherry blossom is so esteemed in Japan that the short blooming season is tracked nightly on the national news. Creating branches heavy with buttercream flowers allows us to celebrate the cherry blossom much more often than just those few fleeting weeks each spring.* **Makes one 6-inch (15 cm) layer cake.**

## Getting Started

**Ice and chill the cake:** Use ivory icing and the Smooth Icing technique to ice the cake. Transfer the cake to the presentation surface and refrigerate until well chilled.

**Fill the pastry bags:** Transfer the light pink, medium pink and dark pink icings to pastry bags fitted with #81 tips, and the brown icing to a bag with the #3 tip.

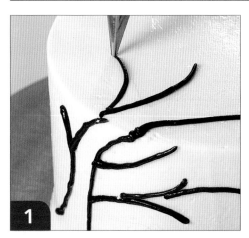

Place the chilled cake in the center of the turntable. ■ Use the toothpick to dot the outline of the branches up the side of the cake and over the top. ■ Using brown icing, pipe over the outlined branches. ■

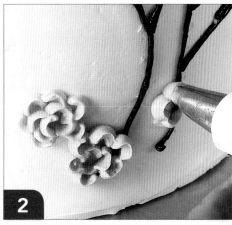

Using light pink icing, pipe cupped flowers over and around the branches, scattering them primarily at the base of the branches on the side of the cake, but with some spilling onto the top. ■

Using medium pink icing, pipe cupped flowers primarily in the center of the branches, on both the side and top of the cake. ■

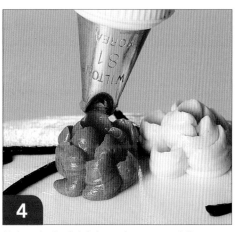

Using dark pink icing, pipe cupped flowers primarily on or near the tips of branches. ■

## What You Need

- 6-inch (15 cm) layer cake, sliced, filled and crumb-coated
- 3½ cups (875 mL) ivory icing
- 1¼ cups (300 mL) light pink icing
- 1¼ cups (300 mL) medium pink icing
- 1¼ cups (300 mL) dark pink icing
- 1¼ cups (300 mL) brown icing
- Turntable
- Presentation surface
- 4 pastry bags
- 4 couplers
- 3 #81 U tips
- #3 round tip
- #102 rose tip
- #101 rose tip
- #6 round tip
- Toothpick or skewer
- Tweezers
- Yellow sugar pearls

## Techniques Used

- Smooth Icing (page 82)
- Transferring an Iced Cake (page 96)
- Lines (page 106)
- Cupped Flowers (page 119)
- Petal Daisy petals (page 118)
- Smooth Scallop Border (page 99)

## Hints and Tips

Swiss meringue buttercream icing that has not been colored is a neutral ivory color.

## Hints and Tips

If you don't have three #81 U tips, simply switch one tip between the three bags of pink icing. There's no need to clean the tip as you switch it.

If you are right-handed, it will be easier to make branches that climb the right side of the cake and lean to the right. If you are left-handed, it will be easier to make branches that climb the left side and lean to the left.

The size of each flower's center will dictate how many pearls you add to it in step 7. Small centers might afford room for just a single pearl, but you may be able to fit several in larger centers.

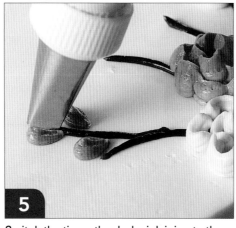

**5** Switch the tip on the dark pink icing to the #102 tip and pipe two or three daisy petals, fat end pointing out, near the tips of several branches to represent buds. ∎

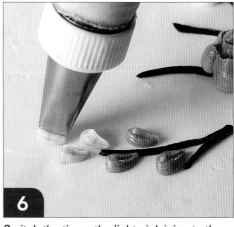

**6** Switch the tip on the light pink icing to the #101 tip and pipe two or three smaller buds on other branches or in addition to the larger buds. ∎

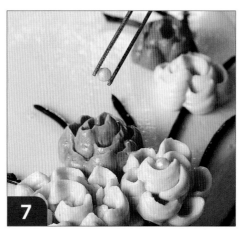

**7** Use the tweezers to place sugar pearls in the center of each cupped flower (see hints and tips, at left). ∎

**8** Switch the tip on the light pink icing to the #6 tip and pipe a smooth scalloped border around the bottom of the cake. ∎

# Chrysanthemum

*The chrysanthemum is one of the most requested flowers at the bakery. Its volume and height make it the ideal stand-alone focal point for cupcakes or a small cake.* **Makes 24 cupcakes.**

## Getting Started

**Ice the cupcakes:** Use the icing of your choice and the Smooth Cupcake Icing technique to ice the cupcakes.

**Fill the pastry bags:** Transfer the dark and light green icings to pastry bags fitted with #352 tips, the ivory icing to a bag with the #10 tip, the dark purple icing to a bag with the #80 tip, and the light purple icing to a bag fitted only with a coupler.

**1** Place a cupcake in the center of the turntable. ■ Using dark green icing, pipe a ring of evenly spaced leaves around the top of the cupcake, leaving enough space between the dark green leaves to place light green leaves. ■

**2** Using light green icing, pipe leaves in the spaces between the dark green leaves, completing the ring of leaves. ■

**3** Using ivory icing, create a tapering mound in the center of the cupcake, leaving space between the base of the mound and the inside of the ring of leaves. ■

**4** Using dark purple icing, make a long horizontal petal that starts at the base of the mound and overlaps the leaves without covering them completely. ■

## What You Need

- 24 cupcakes, cooled
- 4 cups (1 L) icing of choice
- ¾ cup (175 mL) dark green icing
- ¾ cup (175 mL) light green icing
- 1½ cups (375 mL) ivory icing
- 1 cup (250 mL) dark purple icing
- 1 cup (250 mL) light purple icing
- Turntable
- 5 pastry bags
- 5 couplers
- 2 #352 leaf tips
- #10 round tip
- #80 U tip
- Tweezers
- Yellow sugar pearls

## Techniques Used

- Smooth Cupcake Icing (page 85)
- Leaves (page 112)
- Mounds (page 101)
- Long Horizontal Petals (page 113)

## Hints and Tips

When making a ring of leaves or petals, always rotate the turntable and keep your hand in the same position for each successive leaf or petal. This will ensure a nice round flower.

If you plan to travel with your cupcakes, make sure the leaves do not reach past the edge of the cupcake or they could get damaged during transport.

## Hints and Tips

If you are right-handed, it is easiest to make the leaves and petals with your piping hand in the East (E) position on the cupcake. If you are left-handed, it is easiest to work with your piping hand in the West (W) position.

Using the same tip for different shades of the same color ensures a gradual shift in hue. When you switch a decorating tip from one pastry bag to another, squeeze the new bag over an empty bowl to release any air bubbles before continuing to decorate.

## Variations

Chrysanthemums are also stunning in classic autumn shades of burnt orange, red or yellow, or a clean and graceful ivory.

If you're short on time, these chrysanthemums look terrific in a single solid color too. You can also cut down on time and effort by making all the leaves the same color.

Don't have sugar pearls? Omit them or replace them with any type of sprinkle that coordinates with the flower. Sprinkles in a primary color would look fun on red or yellow chrysanthemums.

**5** Make a ring of these petals around the cupcake. ■ The petals should butt up against each other at the base, but angle away from each other as they move out. ■

**6** Increase the angle of the pastry bag and pipe a second ring of petals above the first, angled up rather than lying flat, and staggered so that each petal in the second ring lies between two petals in the first ring. ■

**7** Transfer the #80 tip to the bag of light purple icing. ■ Continue to make rings of petals, increasing the angle of the bag with each ring until it is nearly vertical for the final ring. ■ Leave the very center of the flower open. ■

**8** Use tweezers to drop sugar pearls into the center of the flower until they begin to cascade over the top. ■

**166**

# Climbing Roses

*Climbing roses are the acrobats of the rose world, transforming trellises, arbors and gazebos into dazzling focal points. Here, a simple stylized version transforms a cake.* **Makes one 6-inch (15 cm) layer cake.**

## Getting Started

**Ice and chill the cake:** Use light brown icing and the Smooth Icing technique to ice the cake. Transfer the cake to the presentation surface and refrigerate until well chilled.

**Fill the pastry bags:** Transfer the remaining light brown icing to a pastry bag fitted with the #6 tip, the dark brown icing to a bag with the #3 tip, the very dark pink icing to a bag with the #18 tip, the dark pink icing to a bag with the #16 tip, the medium pink icing to a bag with the #14 tip, and the variegated green icing to a bag with the #352 tip.

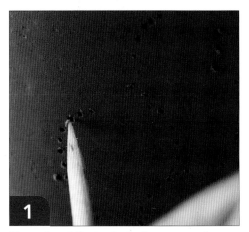

Place the chilled cake in the center of the turntable. ■ Use the toothpick to dot vines consisting of elongated C shapes up the side of the cake, alternating between backwards and forward C's (see hints and tips, page 170). ■

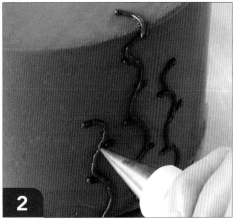

Using very dark pink icing, pipe one or two rosettes near the bottom of each vine. ■

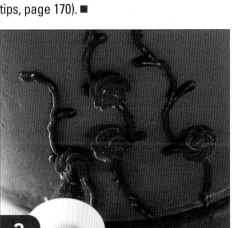

Using dark brown icing, pipe over the outlined vines, giving the bag an extra little squeeze at the end to anchor the vine to the side of the cake before removing your hand. ■

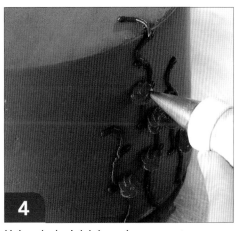

Using dark pink icing, pipe one or two rosettes around the middle of each vine. ■

## What You Need

- 6-inch (15 cm) layer cake, sliced, filled and crumb-coated
- 4 cups (1 L) light brown or chocolate icing
- 1 cup (250 mL) dark brown icing
- 1 cup (250 mL) very dark pink icing
- 1 cup (250 mL) dark pink icing
- 1 cup (250 mL) medium pink icing
- 1 cup (250 mL) medium green icing streaked with pink
- Turntable
- Presentation surface
- 6 pastry bags
- 6 couplers
- #6 round tip
- #3 round tip
- #18 open star tip
- #16 open star tip
- #14 open star tip
- #352 leaf tip
- Toothpick or skewer

## Techniques Used

- Smooth Icing (page 82)
- Transferring an Iced Cake (page 96)
- Lines (page 106)
- Rosettes (page 120)
- Leaves (page 112)
- Smooth Scallop Border (page 99)

## Hints and Tips

For information on making variegated icing colors, see page 64.

**169**

## Hints and Tips

You can make one, two or three sections of climbing roses on the cake, and as few or as many vines in each section as you like. Take a moment before starting step 1 to map out where on the cake your vines will appear, and make sure you are satisfied with the design before starting to pipe the vines. Make some short vines and some long vines, with at least one climbing all the way up the side and wrapping over the top of the cake.

For the most natural look, make your three shades of pink very similar, so that the shift from darker to lighter rosettes is subtle.

If you don't have all three open star tips, use just one and alter the size of the rosette by applying more or less pressure to the bag.

### Variations

This design also looks beautiful on top of ivory icing.

To make matching cupcakes, use the Spiral Cupcake Icing technique (page 92) to ice them, then decorate them with rosettes and leaves, omitting the vines.

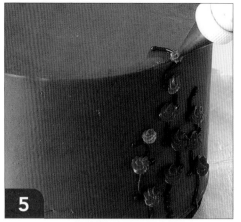

**5** Using medium pink icing, pipe one or two rosettes near the top of each vine. ■

**6** Using green icing, add a scattering of leaves to the vines, clustered in groups of two or three and pointing in different directions. ■

**7** Add a cluster of leaves at the top of the longest vine, on top of the cake. ■

**8** Using light brown icing, pipe a smooth scallop border around the bottom of the cake. ■

# Combed Lavender

*Combing is a wonderful way to quickly transform a smoothly iced cake into something unique. The only extra embellishment needed is a sprinkling of lavender.* **Makes one 6-inch (15 cm) layer cake.**

## Getting Started

**Ice and chill the cake:** Use ivory icing and the Smooth Icing technique to ice the cake. Leave the cake on the turntable and refrigerate until well chilled.

Prepare the lavender by pouring a generous amount onto a large plate or a shallow bowl with a wide mouth. ■

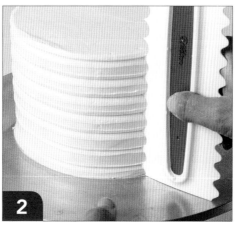

Using the cake comb, comb the sides of the cake until the pattern covers the sides evenly. ■

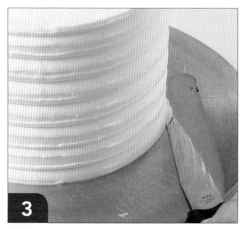

Slide a long edge of the straight blade spatula underneath the cake, angle the spatula up slightly and spin the turntable to break the icing seal between the cake and the turntable. ■

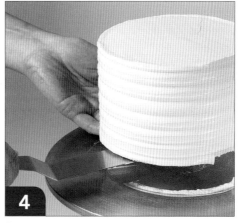

Carefully slide the offset spatula almost all the way under the cake, lift the cake off the turntable and carefully balance the cake on the fingertips of your non-dominant hand. ■

## What You Need

- 6-inch (15 cm) layer cake, sliced, filled and crumb-coated
- 4 cups (1 L) ivory icing
- Turntable
- Food-grade dried lavender
- Cake comb
- Straight blade spatula
- Large offset spatula
- Presentation surface

## Techniques Used

- Smooth Icing (page 82)
- Combing (page 93)
- Adding Embellishments (page 69)

## Hints and Tips

Swiss meringue buttercream icing that has not been colored is a neutral ivory color.

Food-grade lavender is cultivated without pesticides. If you are unable to find it at a local kitchen supply store or gourmet grocery store, you can order it online (see the Source Guide, page 354).

## Hints and Tips

Try to avoid getting any lavender on the underside of the cake, as this could prevent it from properly adhering to the presentation surface.

See Transferring an Iced Cake (page 96) for more information on the best way to lift, hold and transfer an iced cake.

## Variation

In place of the lavender, decorate the cake with rose petals, candy, nuts or sprinkles.

**5** Slide your hand all the way under the cake and balance it over the bowl of lavender. ■

**6** Scoop up a handful of lavender and gently press it into the bottom edge of the cake with a lightly cupped hand. ■

**7** Carefully rotate the cake in your hand and continue to press the lavender into the bottom edge until the cake is entirely ringed with lavender. ■

**8** Using the offset spatula for assistance, place the cake on the presentation surface. ■ Sprinkle a dusting of lavender in a ring around the top of the cake. ■

# Confetti

*Decorating this fun and quirky cake is as simple as piping dots. Because the dots are random in size and placement, there's no wrong way to pipe them, making this an ideal cake for beginners.* Makes one 8-inch (20 cm) layer cake.

## Getting Started

**Ice and chill the cake:** Use pale yellow icing and the Smooth Icing technique to ice the cake. Transfer the cake to the presentation surface and refrigerate until well chilled.

**Fill the pastry bags:** Transfer the dark pink icing to a pastry bag fitted with the #104 tip. Fit each of the remaining bags with a tip and fill each bag with a different color icing (it does not matter which color gets which tip).

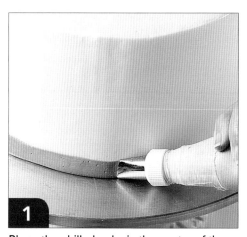

1. Place the chilled cake in the center of the turntable. ■ Using dark pink icing, pipe a ribbon border around the bottom of the cake. ■

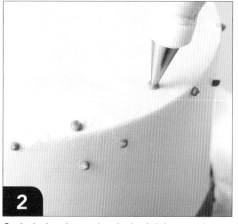

2. Switch the tip on the dark pink bag to the remaining round tip and pipe randomly placed dots in a ring around the top of the cake and spilling over the sides. ■

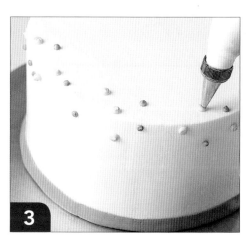

3. Using turquoise icing, pipe randomly placed dots in a ring around the top of the cake and spilling over the sides. ■

4. Using light pink icing, pipe randomly placed dots in a ring around the top of the cake and spilling over the sides. ■

## Hints and Tips

If you don't have all the round tips listed, use whichever round tips you do have. If you have fewer than eight round tips, you can switch tips between bags; just make sure to rinse and dry the tips between colors.

Using a coordinated and slightly muted color palette and restricting the dots to the top edges keeps the cake from becoming too busy (and looking like it has a severe case of the measles).

### Variation

This cake is also fun when iced in simple ivory buttercream with dots in bright primary and secondary colors.

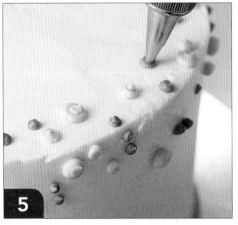

Using purple icing, pipe randomly placed dots in a ring around the top of the cake and spilling over the sides. ■

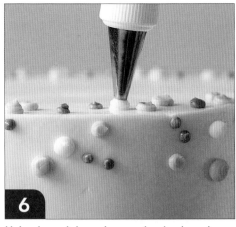

Using ivory icing, pipe randomly placed dots in a ring around the top of the cake and spilling over the sides. ■

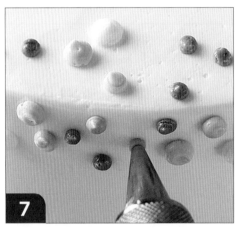

Using periwinkle icing, pipe randomly placed dots in a ring around the top of the cake and spilling over the sides. ■

Using green icing, pipe randomly placed dots in a ring around the top of the cake and spilling over the sides. ■

Using yellow icing, pipe randomly placed dots in a ring around the top of the cake and spilling over the sides. ■

# Daisies

*There's no flower more cheerful than the modest daisy. With its blue background, this cake will remind you of the endless blue skies and abundant days of summer.* **Makes one 8-inch (20 cm) layer cake.**

## Getting Started

**Ice and chill the cake:** Use light blue icing and the Smooth Icing technique to ice the cake. Transfer the cake to the presentation surface and refrigerate until well chilled.

**Fill the pastry bags:** Transfer the remaining light blue icing to a pastry bag fitted with the #6 tip, the ivory icing to a bag with the #104 tip, the yellow icing to a bag with a #10 tip, and the green icing to a bag with the #352 tip.

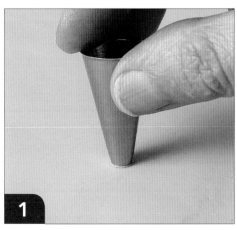

**1** Place the chilled cake in the center of the turntable. ■ Use the small end of a #10 tip to make circle impressions scattered over the top and the sides of the cake. ■ Cluster some of the circles near each other in groups of two or three. ■

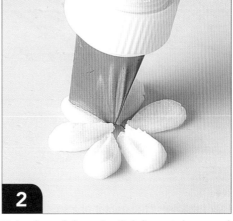

**2** Using ivory icing, pipe 6 daisy petals around an imprinted circle. ■ Continue to add petals to half of the imprinted circles. ■

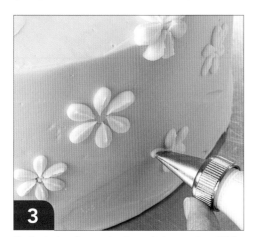

**3** Switch the tip on the ivory icing to the #102 tip and pipe petals around the remaining imprinted circles. ■

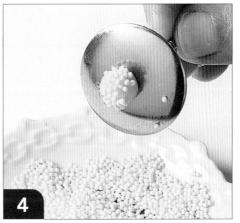

**4** Pour a mound of nonpareils into a small, shallow dish. ■ Using yellow icing and the rose nail, make a fat sprinkled rolled dot. ■

## What You Need

- 8-inch (20 cm) layer cake, sliced, filled and crumb-coated
- 4½ cups (1.125 L) light blue icing
- 1 cup (250 mL) ivory icing
- 1 cup (250 mL) yellow icing
- 1 cup (250 mL) green icing
- Turntable
- Presentation surface
- 4 pastry bags
- 4 couplers
- #6 round tip
- #104 rose tip
- 2 #10 round tips
- #352 leaf tip
- #102 rose tip
- #8 round tip
- #2 round tip
- Yellow nonpareils
- Rose nail
- Kitchen scissors

## Techniques Used

- Smooth Icing (page 82)
- Transferring an Iced Cake (page 96)
- Petal Daisy petals (page 118)
- Sprinkled Rolled Dots (page 105)
- Leaves (page 112)
- Triad Dots (variation, page 103)

## Hints and Tips

Use the index finger of your non-dominant hand to lend support when placing the sprinkle rolled dots on the side of the cake. Once they're placed, give the dots a gentle pat with your fingertip to make sure they are securely attached.

If you don't have yellow nonpareils (or other yellow sprinkles) on hand, simply use the yellow icing, fitted with the #10 tip for the large daisies and the #8 tip for the small daisies, to make center dots for the daisies directly on the cake.

## Variations

To make matching cupcakes or mini cupcakes, use light blue icing and the Smooth Cupcake Icing technique (page 85) to ice them. Make one large daisy or two to three small daisies on top and scatter leaves and triad dots around the daisies. Alternatively, simply press yellow nonpareils around the outer edge of the icing.

Pipe yellow petals and make black centers to create the cheerful and much beloved black-eyed Susan daisy.

**5** Using the scissors, place the dot in the center of a large daisy. ■ Make and place a center dot for each large daisy. ■

**6** Switch the tip on the yellow icing to the #8 tip and make a smaller sprinkled rolled dot. ■

**7** Place the dot in the center of a small daisy. ■ Make and place a center for each small daisy. ■

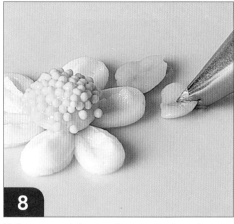

**8** Using green icing, make one to three leaves for each flower or flower cluster. ■

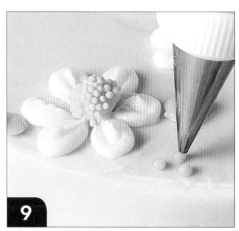

**9** Switch the tip on the yellow icing to the #2 tip and pipe one or two triad dots near each flower or flower cluster. ■

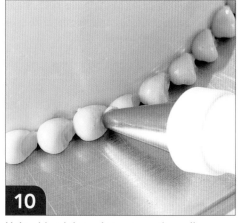

**10** Using blue icing, pipe a smooth scallop border around the bottom of the cake. ■

182

# Embroidered Tattoo

*The art of embroidery has changed little since its invention over 2300 years ago. In fact, there is nothing in technique or material that could be considered an advancement from the high standard of craftsmanship found in ancient works. Here, fine lines of buttercream icing simulate the satiny thread of embroidery — a tasty advancement your friends are sure to rave about.* **Makes one 6-inch (15 cm) layer cake.**

## Getting Started

**Ice and chill the cake:** Use beige icing and the Smooth Icing technique to ice the cake. Transfer the cake to the presentation surface and refrigerate until well chilled.

**Fill the pastry bags:** Fit a pastry bag without a coupler with the #125 tip and fill with half of the medium red icing. Transfer the black icing and half of the burgundy icing to bags fitted with #3 tips. Transfer the ivory icing to a bag with the #1 tip. Transfer the remaining medium red icing, the remaining burgundy icing and the light red, light green, medium green and dark green icings to bags fitted with #2 tips.

**1** Place the chilled cake in the center of the turntable. ■ Angle the rose template slightly off center and place it on the cake so that a small portion of the rose hangs over the edge. ■

**2** Using the toothpick, trace around the rose. ■

**3** Remove the template from the cake and, using scissors, cut off the outer ring of petals. ■ Place the center portion of the template in the center of the traced rose and trace around it. ■

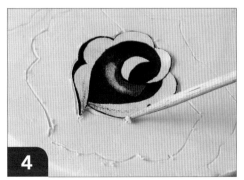

**4** Remove the template and cut out the center cluster of petals. ■ Place this portion of the template in the center of the traced rose and trace around it. ■ Remove the template. ■

## Hints and Tips

The light red and medium red shades I used are very similar, for a subtle color gradation. If you prefer, you can make them more noticeably different.

For a softer appearance, one that leans more toward embroidery and less toward tattoo, change the outline from black to one of the red colors.

If you don't have enough #2 round tips, you can switch tips between bags; just make sure to rinse and dry the tips between colors.

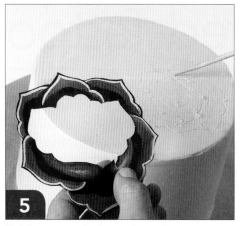

**5** Holding up each piece of template as a reference, work freehand to trace outlines within each section of the rose, defining the areas in which each color will be placed. ∎

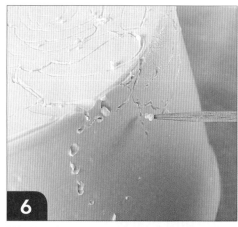

**6** Working freehand, use the toothpick to dot the outlines of scattered leaves of different sizes around the rose, then divide each leaf lengthwise into at least three parts. ∎

**7** Using black icing, pipe over all the traced and dotted lines. ∎

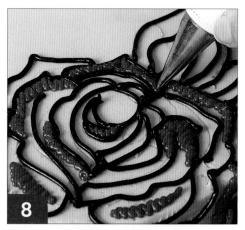

**8** Fit together the three template pieces and use the template as a reference for where to add each color. ∎ Using light red icing and the embroidery technique, fill in all the light red areas. ∎

**9** Using medium red icing from the bag with the #2 tip and the embroidery technique, fill in all the medium red areas. ∎

**10** Using burgundy icing from the bag with the #2 tip and the embroidery technique, fill in all the burgundy areas. ∎

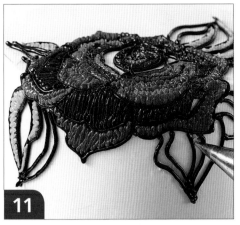

**11**

Using light green icing and the embroidery technique, fill in all the light green areas. ■

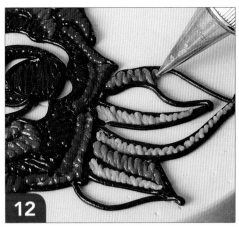

**12**

Using medium green icing and the embroidery technique, fill in all the medium green areas. ■

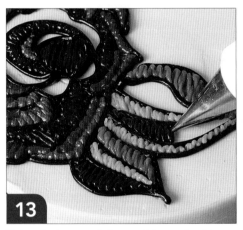

**13**

Using dark green icing and the embroidery technique, fill in all the dark green areas. ■

**14**

Using ivory icing and the embroidery technique, highlight the rose and leaves, filling in empty spaces or adding ivory on top of another color to create depth. ■

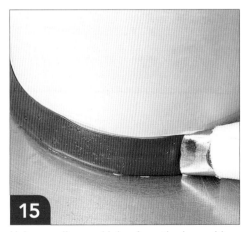

**15**

Using medium red icing from the bag with the #125 tip, pipe a ribbon border around the bottom of the cake. ■

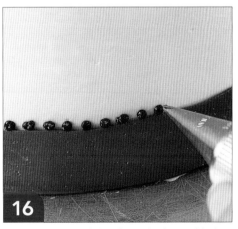

**16**

Using burgundy icing from the bag with the #3 tip, pipe evenly spaced dots immediately above the ribbon border, making a ring of dots around the cake. ■

# English Garden

English cottage gardens are highly cultivated to appear haphazard, exuberant and prolific, using different colors, textures and heights to evoke naturalism and an unstudied grace. This cake captures the spirit of these gardens, and is a wonderful way to practice making many different types of flowers. **Makes one 6-inch (15 cm) layer cake.**

## Getting Started

**Ice and chill the cake:** Use green icing and the Smooth Icing technique to ice the cake. Transfer the cake to the presentation surface and refrigerate until well chilled.

**Fill the pastry bags:** Transfer the remaining green icing to a pastry bag fitted with the #6 tip, the brown and blue icings to bags with #3 tips, the pink icing to a bag with the #16 tip, the ivory and peach icings to bags with #80 tips, the yellow icing to a bag with the #102 tip, and the purple icing to a bag with the #131 tip.

Place the chilled cake in the center of the turntable. ■ Using brown icing, pipe vines from the top edge down the side of the cake, in various lengths and proximities to each other. ■ Pipe vines all the way around the cake, making a total of 18 vines. ■

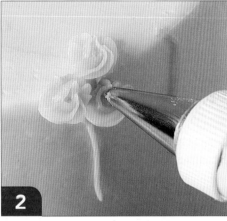

Using pink icing, pipe clusters of small rosettes cascading down a vine. ■ Add rosettes to every sixth vine. ■

## What You Need

- 6-inch (15 cm) layer cake, sliced, filled and crumb-coated
- 4 cups (1 L) pale green icing
- ¾ cup (175 mL) pale brown icing
- ¾ cup (175 mL) pale blue icing
- ¾ cup (175 mL) pale pink icing
- ¾ cup (175 mL) ivory icing
- ¾ cup (175 mL) pale peach icing
- ¾ cup (175 mL) pale yellow icing
- ¾ cup (175 mL) pale purple icing
- Turntable
- Presentation surface
- 8 pastry bags
- 8 couplers
- #6 round tip
- 2 #3 round tips
- #16 open star tip
- 2 #80 U tips
- #102 rose tip
- #131 drop flower tip

## Techniques Used

- Smooth Icing (page 82)
- Transferring an Iced Cake (page 96)
- Lines (page 106)
- Rosettes (page 120)
- Short Vertical Petals (page 114)
- Petal Daisy petals (page 118)
- Dot Daisies (page 117)
- Wisteria (variation, page 116)
- Cupped Flowers (page 119)
- Smooth Scallop Border (page 99)

## Hints and Tips

Swiss meringue buttercream icing that has not been colored is a neutral ivory color.

I have found that 18 vines gives a nice lush but not overpacked look to the cake, but feel free to create more or fewer vines, as desired.

To save time, you can skip piping the vines in step 1. Just make sure to pipe the individual flowers close enough together that each cluster has the appearance of a cascading bundle of blossoms.

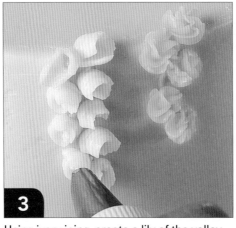

**3**

Using ivory icing, create a lily of the valley blossom by piping two short vertical petals, face to face, at the top of a vine. ■ Pipe clusters of these blossoms cascading down every sixth vine. ■

**4**

Using yellow icing, pipe daisy petals, thin side toward the vine, down both sides of every sixth vine. ■

**5**

Using blue icing, pipe clusters of dot daisies cascading down every sixth vine. ■

**6**

Using purple icing, pipe wisteria cascading down every sixth vine. ■

**7**

Using peach icing, pipe cupped flowers cascading down every sixth vine. ■

**8**

Using green icing, pipe a smooth scallop border around the bottom of the cake. ■

# Fairy Ring

*This cake is a showcase for all of the simple flower techniques. The riot of brilliant colors creates a truly magnificent display.* Makes one 6-inch (15 cm) layer cake.

## Getting Started

**Ice and chill the cake:** Use ivory icing and the Smooth Icing technique to ice the cake. Transfer the cake to the presentation surface and refrigerate until well chilled.

**Fill the pastry bags:** Transfer the remaining ivory icing to a pastry bag fitted with a #2 tip. Fit a bag without a coupler with the #125 tip and fill with half of the bright green icing. Transfer the remaining bright green icing to a bag with a #352 tip, the yellow icing to a bag with the #104 tip, the red icing to a bag with the #18 tip, the teal icing to a bag with the #131 tip, the orange and pink icings to bags with #102 tips, the purple icing to a bag with the #4 tip, the turquoise and black icings to bags with #2 tips, and the light green icing to a bag fitted with the #1 tip.

### What You Need

- 6-inch (15 cm) layer cake, sliced, filled and crumb-coated
- 3½ cups (875 mL) ivory icing
- ½ cup (125 mL) bright green icing
- ½ cup (125 mL) bright yellow icing
- ½ cup (125 mL) red icing
- ½ cup (125 mL) teal icing
- ½ cup (125 mL) orange icing
- ½ cup (125 mL) pink icing
- ½ cup (125 mL) purple icing
- ½ cup (125 mL) turquoise icing
- ½ cup (125 mL) black icing
- ½ cup (125 mL) light green icing
- Turntable
- Presentation surface
- 12 pastry bags
- 11 couplers
- 3 #2 round tips
- #125 rose tip
- 2 #352 leaf tips
- #104 rose tip
- #18 open star tip
- #131 drop flower tip
- 2 #102 rose tips
- #4 round tip
- #1 round tip
- #14 open star tip
- 2 #3 round tips

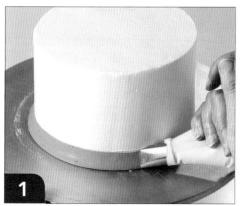

**1** Place the chilled cake in the center of the turntable. ■ Using bright green icing from the bag with the #125 tip, pipe a ribbon border around the bottom of the cake. ■

**2** Using yellow icing, pipe three pairs of petal daisies, one on the side of the cake and one on top, evenly spaced around the cake. ■ Leave the daisy centers open for now. ■

**3** Using red icing, pipe three pairs of rosettes, one on the side of the cake and one on top, evenly spaced around the cake. ■

**4** Using teal icing, pipe six clusters of wisteria cascading down the side of the cake, starting just below each of the daisies and rosettes on top of the cake. ■

195

**5** Using orange icing, pipe small petal daisies without center dots, scattering them among the other flowers on the top and sides of the cake. ■

**6** Using purple icing, pipe a cluster of dots in the shape of a bunch of grapes cascading over the edge of the cake. ■ Scatter these grape hyacinths among the other flowers on the top and sides of the cake. ■

**7** Using turquoise icing, pipe dot daisies on the top and sides of the cake, scattering them among the other flowers. ■

**8** Using pink icing, pipe rosebuds on the top and sides of the cake, scattering them among the other flowers. ■

**9** Using light green icing, pipe short curved stems from the base of each rosebud. ■

**10** Switch the tip on the red icing to the #14 tip and pipe small rosettes wherever there is a large gap in the ring of flowers. ■

**11**

Using bright green icing from the bag with the #352 tip, pipe leaves on a random selection of flowers. ∎

**12**

Switch the tip on the light green icing to a #352 tip and pipe leaves on a random selection of flowers. ∎

**13**

Using black icing, pipe multiple black dots in the center of each yellow petal daisy, stacking the dots on top of each other. ∎

**14**

Switch the tip on the yellow icing to a #3 tip and pipe a dot in the center of each turquoise dot daisy. ∎

**15**

Switch the tip on the pink icing to a #3 tip and pipe a dot in the center of each orange petal daisy. ∎

**16**

Using ivory icing, pipe simplified Swiss dots around the ribbon border. ∎

## Variations

This cake is brilliant in bright colors, but also looks beautiful in pastels or shades of ivory and beige.

To contribute to the multi-hued cheerfulness of this cake, ice it in a color other than ivory, such as a softer shade of the yellow or teal.

For added interest and complexity, use the sprinkled rolled dot technique (page 305) to make the daisy centers.

# Feathers

*When a friend showed me the team logo for the All Blacks, New Zealand's national rugby team, I knew I had found my inspiration for this whimsical cake. Two colors is all you need.* **Makes one 6-inch (15 cm) layer cake.**

## What You Need

- 6-inch (15 cm) layer cake, sliced, filled and crumb-coated
- 3½ cups (875 mL) light purple icing
- 1 cup (250 mL) ivory icing
- Turntable
- Presentation surface
- 2 pastry bags
- 2 couplers
- #6 round tip
- #104 rose tip
- Undulating leaf-shaped cookie cutter

## Techniques Used

- Smooth Icing (page 82)
- Transferring an Iced Cake (page 96)
- Petal Daisy petals (page 118)
- Smooth Scallop Border (page 99)

## Hints and Tips

Swiss meringue buttercream icing that has not been colored is a neutral ivory color.

If you don't have a cookie cutter with the right shape, use a toothpick to trace an arched line about 2 inches (5 cm) long.

## Getting Started

**Ice and chill the cake:** Use purple icing and the Smooth Icing technique to ice the cake. Transfer the cake to the presentation surface and refrigerate until well chilled.

**Fill the pastry bags:** Transfer the remaining purple icing to a pastry bag fitted with the #6 tip, and the ivory icing to a bag with the #104 tip.

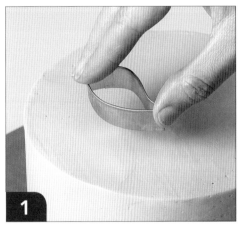

Place the chilled cake in the center of the turntable. ■ Use the long side of the cookie cutter to imprint the spine of a feather on the top of the cake. ■

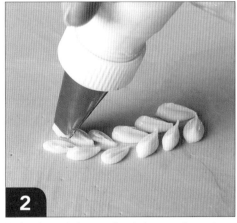

Using ivory icing, make daisy petals as the barbs of the feather, with the narrow end near the spine and the wide end angled toward the top of the feather. ■ Line both sides of the spine with barbs. ■

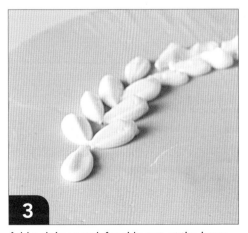

Add a daisy petal, fat side out, at the base of the feather. ■

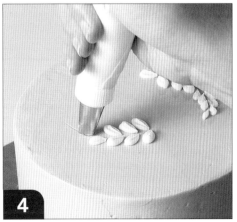

Repeat steps 1 to 3 to create another feather on the top of the cake, randomly placed in relation to the first feather. ■

## Hints and Tips

Sometimes it can be helpful to get an idea of how a design will look before continuing to decorate. Instead of making all the spine imprints at once, then all the barbs, then all the shafts, for this cake I found it was a better strategy to complete a feather before moving on to the next one.

In addition to feathers that are fully on the top of the cake or on the side of the cake, make some that drape over the edge from top to side, or climb over the edge from side to top. You can also make some partial feathers that look like they are emerging from the border at the bottom of the cake.

### Variation

For a different effect, use icing in three shades of the same color to make ombré feathers (feathers that get gradually lighter as the barbs progress from base to tip).

5

Continue to make feathers, scattering them randomly over the top and sides of the cake, until you are satisfied with the effect. ■

6

Using purple icing, pipe a smooth scallop border around the bottom of the cake. ■

# Gerbera Daisy

*Like a real gerbera daisy, the bright colors and unfussy beauty of this buttercream version just makes me happy. The cheerful flower covers the entire surface of a cupcake or small cake, and is so spectacular that I opted to ice the cake and pipe the border and Swiss dots in a single color.* **Makes one 4-inch (10 cm) layer cake.**

## Getting Started

**Ice and chill the cake:** Use brown icing and the Smooth Icing technique to ice the cake. Transfer the cake to the presentation surface and refrigerate until well chilled.

**Fill the pastry bags:** Transfer the remaining brown icing to a pastry bag fitted with a #6 tip, the dark and light green icings to bags with #352 tips, the very dark pink icing to a bag with the #80 tip, the dark pink icing to a bag with a #6 tip, and the yellow icing to a bag with the #4 tip.

## What You Need

- 4-inch (10 cm) layer cake, sliced, filled and crumb-coated
- 3½ cups (875 mL) light brown or chocolate icing
- ¾ cup (175 mL) dark green icing
- ¾ cup (175 mL) light green icing
- ¾ cup (175 mL) very dark pink icing
- ¾ cup (175 mL) dark pink icing
- ¾ cup (175 mL) yellow icing
- Turntable
- Presentation surface
- 6 pastry bags
- 6 couplers
- 2 #6 round tips
- 2 #352 leaf tips
- #80 U tip
- #4 round tip
- #3 round tip
- 2-inch (5 cm) round cookie cutter

## Techniques Used

- Smooth Icing (page 82)
- Transferring an Iced Cake (page 96)
- Leaves (page 112)
- Long Horizontal Petals (page 113)
- Short Vertical Petals (page 114)
- Dots (page 102)
- Swiss Dots (page 104)
- Smooth Scallop Border (page 99)

**1** Place the chilled cake in the center of the turntable. ■ Using dark green icing, pipe a ring of evenly spaced leaves around the top of the cake, leaving enough space between the dark green leaves to place light green leaves. ■

**2** Using light green icing, pipe leaves in the spaces between the dark green leaves, completing the ring of leaves. ■

**3** Use the cookie cutter to imprint a circle in the center of the cake. ■

**4** Using very dark pink icing, pipe a ring of long horizontal petals that start at the imprinted circle and overlap the leaves without covering them completely. ■ The petals should butt up against each other at the base, but angle away from each other as they move out. ■

205

## Hints and Tips

If you are right-handed, it is easiest to work on steps 1 and 2 with your piping hand in the East (E) position on the cake, and steps 4 and 5 with your piping hand in the Northeast (NE) position.

If you are left-handed, it is easiest to work on steps 1 and 2 with your piping hand in the West (W) position, and steps 4 and 5 with your piping hand in the Northwest (NW) position.

## Variations

Gerbera daisies come in many different bright colors. Try making them in orange, yellow or red instead of pink.

To make matching cupcakes, use brown icing and the Smooth Cupcake Icing technique (page 85) to ice them. Pipe leaves around the top of each cupcake as in steps 1 and 2. In step 3, use the back end of a large tip (#124 or #125) to imprint a circle (about the size of a quarter) in the center of the cupcake. Pipe two rings of long horizontal petals, as in steps 4 and 5, but just one ring of short vertical petals in step 6. Continue with steps 7 to 9 as directed.

**5** Pipe a second ring of petals above the first, staggered so that each petal in the second ring lies between two petals in the first ring. ■

**6** Pipe a ring of short vertical petals just inside the first two rings, with the petals at a 45-degree angle to the cake rather than vertical. ■ Pipe two more rings of petals, one inside the other, with the angle of each ring increasing toward but not all the way to 90 degrees. ■

**7** Use the back end of a standard-size tip to mark a small circle in the center of the cake. ■

**8** Using yellow icing, fill the small circle with a layer of dots, working from the outside in. ■ Make sure no cake icing shows between the dots. ■

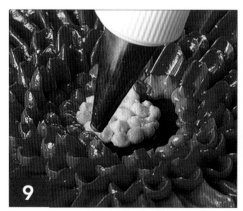

**9** Using dark pink icing, fill in the space between the yellow circle and the petals with rings of dots. ■

**10** Using brown icing, pipe a smooth scallop border around the bottom of the cake. ■ Switch the tip on the brown icing to the #3 tip and decorate the sides of the cake with Swiss dots. ■

206

# Golden Tassels

*Silk embroidery thread, macramé and the lavish decor of a sultan's palace combine to inspire this brassy cake.* **Makes one 6-inch (15 cm) layer cake.**

## Getting Started

**Ice and chill the cake:** Use red icing and the Smooth Icing technique to ice the cake. Transfer the cake to the presentation surface and refrigerate until well chilled.

**Fill the pastry bags:** Transfer the remaining red icing to a pastry bag fitted with the #6 tip, and the yellow icing to a bag with the #1 tip.

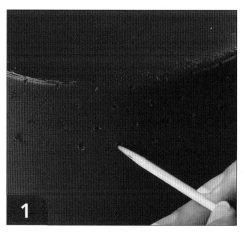

**1** Place the chilled cake in the center of the turntable. ■ Use the toothpick to make four rings of staggered dots on the side of the cake, around the top edge. ■ Place the dots about ¼ inch (5 mm) apart and space the rings about ¼ inch (5 mm) apart. ■

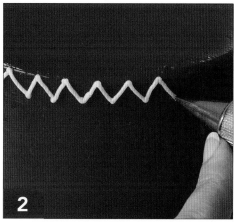

**2** Using yellow icing, pipe a zigzag line connecting the first and second rows of dots. ■

**3** Pipe a dot at the bottom of every V shape. ■

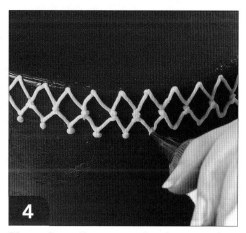

**4** Pipe a zigzag line connecting the second and third rows of dots. ■ Make a dot at the bottom of every V shape in the second row. ■

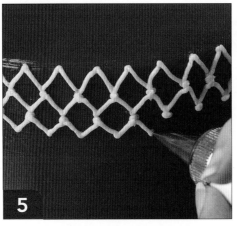

**5** Pipe a zigzag line connecting the third and fourth rows of dots. ■

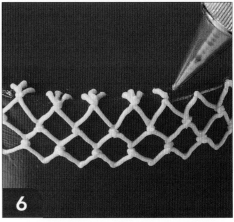

**6** At the apex of every diamond at the top of the cake, pipe a small V shape with a third line down the center. ■

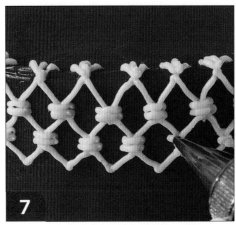

**7** Pipe two short horizontal lines over each dot at the center of each diamond. ■

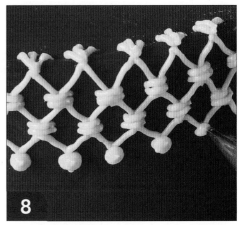

**8** Switch the tip on the yellow icing to the #3 tip and pipe a fat dot at the bottom of every V shape in the last row. ■

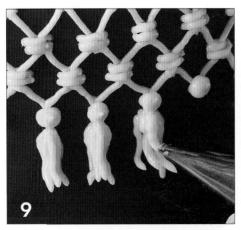

**9** Switch the tip on the yellow icing back to the #1 tip and pipe tassel strands below each fat dot. ■

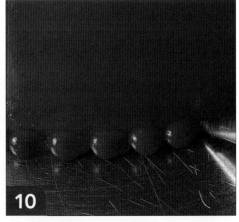

**10** Using red icing, pipe a smooth scallop border around the bottom of the cake. ■

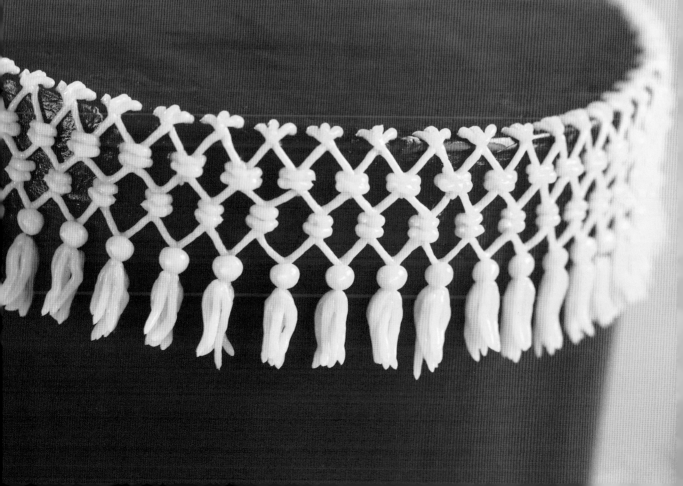

# Henna Tattoo

*Henna has been used cosmetically for millennia, and intricate henna designs still adorn the hands and feet of brides and wedding guests in a number of countries, applied to bestow luck and joy. I hope the same good fortune comes your way when you enjoy this henna-patterned cake!* **Makes one 4-inch (10 cm) layer cake.**

## Getting Started

**Ice and chill the cake:** Use orange icing and the Smooth Icing technique to ice the cake. Transfer the cake to the presentation surface and refrigerate until well chilled.

**Fill the pastry bags:** Transfer the remaining orange icing to a pastry bag fitted with the #6 tip, half the brown icing to a bag with the #2 tip, and the other half to a bag with the #1 tip.

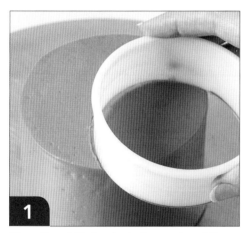

**1** Place the chilled cake in the center of the turntable. ■ Place the large cookie cutter on top of the cake so that about half of it hangs off the edge of the cake, and press gently to make an imprint in the icing. ■

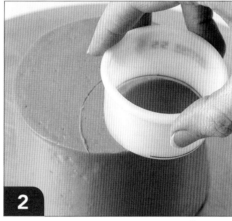

**2** Place the small cookie cutter about ½ inch (1 cm) inside the imprint from the large cookie cutter and press gently to make an imprint in the icing. ■

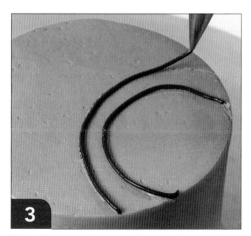

**3** Using brown icing from the bag fitted with the #2 tip, pipe over the imprints. ■

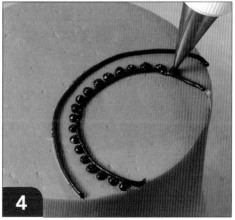

**4** Line the top of the inner arc with dots. ■

## What You Need

- 4-inch (10 cm) layer cake, sliced, filled and crumb-coated
- 3½ cups (875 mL) orange icing
- 2 cups (500 mL) dark brown icing
- Turntable
- Presentation surface
- 3 pastry bags
- 3 couplers
- #6 round tip
- #2 round tip
- #1 round tip
- 3- to 3½-inch (7.5 to 8.5 cm) round cookie cutter
- 2- to 2¼-inch (5 to 5.5 cm) round cookie cutter
- Toothpick or skewer
- Tweezers
- Large and small gold dragées

## Techniques Used

- Smooth Icing (page 82)
- Transferring an Iced Cake (page 96)
- Lines (page 106)
- Dots (page 102)
- Triad Dots (variation, page 103)
- Smooth Scallop Border (page 99)

## Hints and Tips
For this project, use three 4-inch (10 cm) baked cake layers, each sliced in half then filled and stacked.

## Hints and Tips

If you don't have cookie cutters in the right sizes, you can substitute any round objects, such as inverted drinking glasses of two different sizes, to make the imprints in steps 1 and 2.

The designs featured on these cakes are not recognizable patterns, so if yours doesn't exactly match mine, no one will know!

When it comes to making intricate lines and patterns, it helps to get as close to the cake as possible. I often place the turntable on an upside-down 10-inch (25 cm) cake pan to raise it a bit. Place a non-skid pad, cut to fit the size of the pan bottom, or a moistened paper towel under the turntable to ensure that it does not slide while you're decorating.

If you're running out of space at the top of the cake in step 9, you can make the V shapes smaller on the outer scalloped arc than on the inner arc.

When piping the dots in step 10, squeeze with added pressure for the center dots to make them larger than the others.

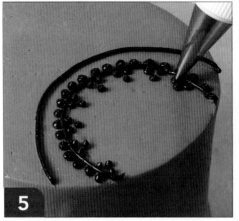

Line the bottom of the inner arc with triad dots. ■

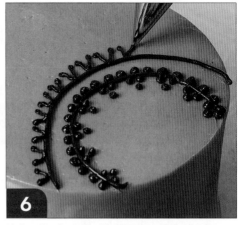

Using the bag fitted with the #1 tip, make small V shapes lining the top of the outer arc. ■

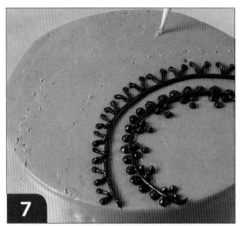

Use the toothpick to dot the outline of a scalloped arc that, at its lowest points, lies about 1/2 inch (1 cm) above the piped outer arc. ■ Dot the outline of another scalloped arc about 1/2 inch (1 cm) above the first. ■

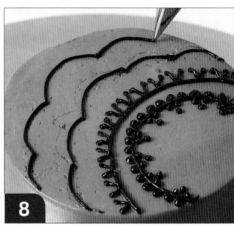

Using the bag with the #1 tip, pipe over the scalloped arcs. ■

Within the point of each scallop on both arcs, draw a V shape with a longer line in the center. ■ Add a little pressure at the end of each line to make it rounded. ■

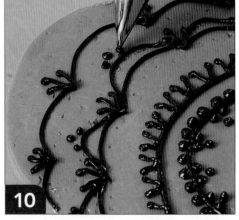

Pipe a small arc over each scallop on the inner scalloped arc and crown each arc with three dots, making the center dot a bit larger than the others (see hints and tips, at left). ■

**11** Line the bottom of the outer scalloped arc with dots. ∎

**12** Pipe a border of mini scallops above each scallop on the outer scalloped arc. ∎

**13** Using the bag with the #2 tip, pipe a loose spiral in the center of the innermost arc. ∎

**14** Using the bag with the #1 tip, make small arced lines coming off both sides of the spiral. ∎

**15** Using the tweezers, place large and small gold dragées on the cake, following the pattern in the photos above and at left. ∎

**16** Using orange icing, pipe a smooth scallop border around the bottom of the cake. ∎

## Variations

Take a cue from popular Bollywood movies and ice your cake in brilliant jewel tones, such as turquoise, hot pink or bright yellow, rather than my more muted choices.

For a more traditional, understated cake, ice it in ivory and pipe the design in an earthy red color.

Find inspiration for your own personally designed henna cake online. Search on "henna" or "henna tattoo" in Google Images, Pinterest or Instagram. You may spend more time viewing the endless images of gorgeous brides with intricate tattoos than on decorating the cake.

# Honey Bees

*These busy little bees are sure to delight as they trail from one flower to the next, up and over this charming, sunny cake. Expand the hive with cupcakes!* **Makes one 4-inch (10 cm) layer cake.**

## Getting Started

**Ice and chill the cake:** Use pale yellow icing and the Smooth Icing technique to ice the cake. Transfer the cake to the presentation surface and refrigerate until well chilled.

**Fill the pastry bags:** Transfer the remaining pale yellow icing to a pastry bag fitted with a #6 tip, the dark yellow icing to a bag with the #10 tip, the black icing to a bag with the #1 tip, the ivory and light blue icings to bags with #3 tips, and the medium blue icing to a bag with the #2 tip.

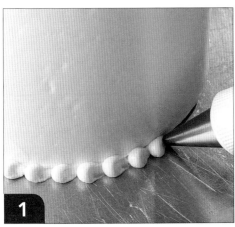

Place the chilled cake in the center of the turntable. ■ Using pale yellow icing, pipe a smooth scallop border around the bottom of the cake. ■

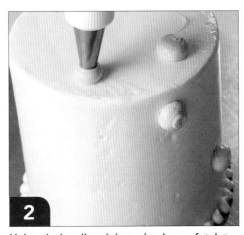

Using dark yellow icing, pipe large, fat dots that climb one side of the cake and extend along one edge of the cake top. ■ Vary the amount of space between each dot. ■

Using black icing, pipe three stripes across the back of each dot, to make the bees' bodies. ■

Pipe the stripes in a different direction for each bee (see hints and tips, page 220). ■

## What You Need

- 4-inch (10 cm) layer cake, sliced, filled and crumb-coated
- 3½ cups (875 mL) pale yellow icing
- ¾ cup (175 mL) dark yellow icing
- ½ cup (125 mL) black icing
- ½ cup (125 mL) ivory icing
- ½ cup (125 mL) light blue icing
- ½ cup (125 mL) medium blue icing
- Turntable
- Presentation surface
- 6 pastry bags
- 6 couplers
- 2 #6 round tips
- #10 round tip
- #1 round tip
- 2 #3 round tips
- #2 round tip
- Tweezers
- White sugar pearls
- Sliced almonds

## Techniques Used

- Smooth Icing (page 82)
- Transferring an Iced Cake (page 96)
- Smooth Scallop Border (page 99)
- Dots (page 102)
- Lines (page 106)
- Dot Daisies (page 117)

## Hints and Tips

Swiss meringue buttercream icing that has not been colored is a neutral ivory color.

**219**

## Hints and Tips

As you begin to pipe the stripes on the back of each bee, keep in mind that the direction of the stripes will dictate which direction the bee is facing.

If you don't like the shape of a bee or you're dissatisfied with the placement, conduct a bee-otomy. Place the cake in the refrigerator until the icing has chilled and hardened, then pop the bee off with a toothpick or the tip of a knife.

In step 5, you can either pipe the flight paths freehand or use a toothpick to dot them onto the icing, then cover the holes with icing dots.

Using tweezers makes it a great deal easier to place a pearl in the center of each dot daisy, especially those that are on the side of the cake.

### Variation

To make matching cupcakes, use pale yellow or light blue icing and the Spiral Cupcake Icing technique (page 92) to ice them, then decorate each cupcake with one or two bees and several dot daisies. Try making some of the daisies in ivory or bright yellow instead of blue.

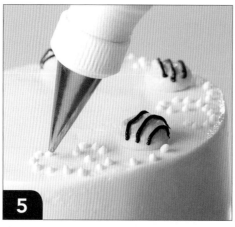

**5** Using ivory icing, pipe a dotted curlicue flight path that trails each bee (see hints and tips, at left). ■

**6** Switch the tip on the black icing to a #6 tip and pipe a head on each bee. ■

**7** Using light blue icing, pipe dot daisies that are randomly scattered but follow the general flight path of the bees. ■

**8** Using medium blue icing, pipe one or two smaller dot daisies near each pale blue daisy. ■

**9** Use tweezers to place a sugar pearl in the center of each pale blue daisy. ■

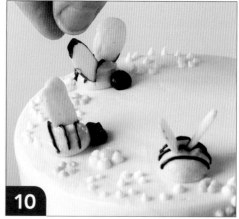

**10** Insert the narrow end of two sliced almonds into the back of each bee to represent wings, angling them so they are close together where they meet the body and wide apart at the tips. ■

# Horizontal Ruffle

*Ruffle cakes are the new darlings of the cake world, and rightfully so. They are dramatic and sweet, yet relatively fast and easy, and they allow for a merciful margin of error in the icing process.*
Makes one 8-inch (20 cm) layer cake.

## Getting Started

**Ice and chill the cake:** Use pale green icing and the Smooth Icing technique to ice the cake. Transfer the cake to the presentation surface and refrigerate until well chilled.

**Fill the pastry bags:** Transfer the remaining pale green icing and the light green icing to pastry bags fitted with just couplers, and the medium green icing to a bag with the #104 tip.

## What You Need

- 8-inch (20 cm) layer cake, sliced, filled and crumb-coated
- 5 cups (1.25 L) pale green icing
- 2½ cups (625 mL) light green icing
- 2½ cups (625 mL) medium green icing
- Turntable
- Presentation surface
- 3 pastry bags
- 3 couplers
- #104 rose tip

## Techniques Used

- Smooth Icing (page 82)
- Transferring an Iced Cake (page 96)

## Hints and Tips

This cake uses a large quantity of icing, so be sure to start with a full batch.

Make sure the cake is well chilled before beginning to add ruffles. Without the resistance of chilled icing, the tip will cut into the cake surface.

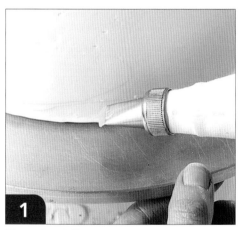

Place the chilled cake in the center of the turntable. ▪ Hold the bag of medium green icing just above the plate, almost parallel to the turntable, with the fat end of the tip touching the iced surface. ▪ The tip should be perpendicular to the cake. ▪

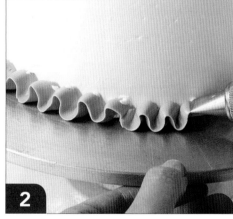

To begin the first ring of ruffles, slowly rotate the turntable with one hand and simultaneously squeeze the bag with a firm and consistent pressure, moving your hand in a rhythmic up and down motion. ▪

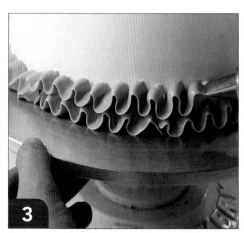

When the first ring is complete, without releasing the pressure on the bag, move your hand up to begin a second ring directly above the first. ▪

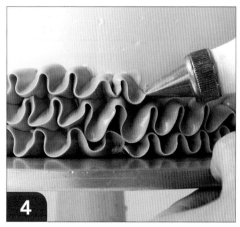

Continue until the ruffles reach a third of the way up the cake, stopping as needed to squeeze the icing down to maintain appropriate pressure. ▪

## Hints and Tips

Using the same tip for different shades of the same color ensures a gradual shift in hue. When you switch a decorating tip from one pastry bag to another, squeeze the new bag over an empty bowl to release any air bubbles before continuing to decorate.

Play with how large or small you make the up and down motions of your hand. Any change in movement will alter the appearance of the ruffle. There really is no right way to make a ruffle — make it to suit your preference.

Take as many breaks as you need. A broken ruffle is almost unnoticeable and adds to the character and handmade quality of the cake.

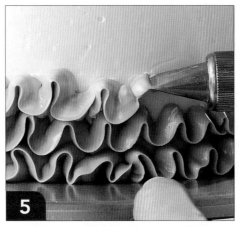

**5** Transfer the #104 tip to the bag of light green icing. ■ Placing the tip at the point where you stopped, resume making ruffles. ■

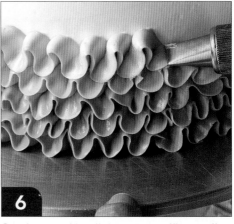

**6** Continue making light green ruffles until they reach two-thirds of the way up the cake. ■

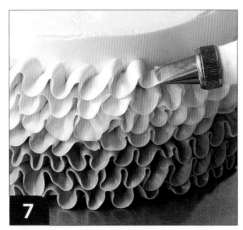

**7** Transfer the #104 tip to the bag of pale green icing. ■ Placing the tip at the point where you stopped, resume making ruffles. ■ Continue making pale green ruffles, working your way toward the top of the cake. ■

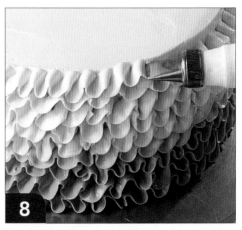

**8** For the final layer of ruffles at the top of the cake, leave just enough room so that the top arches of the ruffles meet the top edge of the cake. ■

# Hydrangea

The hydrangea's delicate beauty makes this cake an elegant choice for any special occasion. **Makes one 4-inch (10 cm) layer cake.**

## Getting Started

**Ice and chill the cake:** Use ivory icing and the Smooth Icing technique to ice the cake. Transfer the cake to the presentation surface and refrigerate until well chilled.

**Fill the pastry bags:** Transfer the remaining ivory icing to a pastry bag fitted only with a coupler. Fit a bag without a coupler with the #125 tip and fill with the light green icing. Transfer the medium and dark green icings to bags with #352 tips, and the variegated periwinkle icing to a bag with the #103 tip.

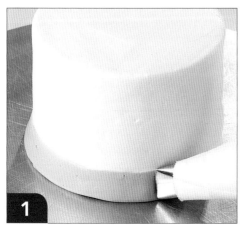

**1** Place the chilled cake in the center of the turntable. ■ Using light green icing, pipe a ribbon border around the bottom of the cake. ■

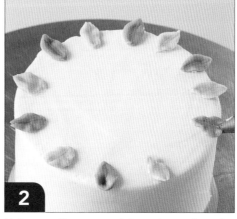

**2** Using medium green icing, pipe a ring of evenly spaced leaves around the top of the cake, leaving enough space between the medium green leaves to place the dark green leaves. ■

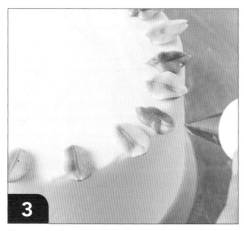

**3** Using dark green icing, pipe leaves in the spaces between the medium green leaves, completing the ring of leaves. ■

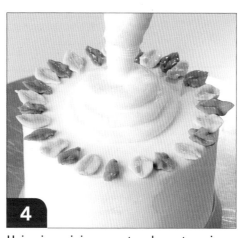

**4** Using ivory icing, create a large tapering mound in the center of the cake, leaving space between the base of the mound and the inside of the ring of leaves. ■

## What You Need

- 4-inch (10 cm) layer cake, sliced, filled and crumb-coated
- 3½ cups (875 mL) ivory icing
- 1 cup (250 mL) light green icing
- 1 cup (250 mL) medium green icing
- 1 cup (250 mL) dark green icing
- 1 cup (250 mL) periwinkle icing streaked with ivory
- Turntable
- Presentation surface
- 5 pastry bags
- 4 couplers
- #125 rose tip
- 2 #352 leaf tips
- #103 rose tip
- 2 #3 round tips

## Techniques Used

- Smooth Icing (page 82)
- Transferring an Iced Cake (page 96)
- Ribbon Border (page 98)
- Leaves (page 112)
- Mounds (page 101)
- Classic Flat Petals (page 115)
- Swiss Dots (page 104)

## Hints and Tips

For information on making variegated icing colors, see page 64.

## Hints and Tips

If you are right-handed, it is easiest to work on steps 2 and 3 with your piping hand in the East (E) position on the cake, steps 5 and 6 with your hand in the Northwest (NW) position, and steps 7, 8 and 10 with your hand in the Southeast (SE) position. If you are left-handed, use the West (W), Northeast (NE) and Southwest (SW) positions.

When piping the vines in step 10, start with the tip of the pastry bag underneath the first ring of petals. Squeeze the bag with firm pressure as you move the tip toward the edge of the cake. To make a tapered point, stop squeezing as you move your hand past the edge of the cake.

## Variations

Use just two shades of green instead of three. Use the lighter shade for the border and half of the leaves, and the darker shade for the remaining leaves.

To make matching cupcakes, use the Smooth Cupcake Icing technique (page 85) to ice them, then decorate as with a full-size cake, omitting steps 1 and 9. Use moderate pressure to make smaller petals.

**5** Using periwinkle icing, pipe a ring of classic flat petals that start at the base of the mound and overlap the leaves without covering them completely. ■ The petals can overlap each other slightly. ■

**6** Pipe a second ring of petals above the first, staggered so that each petal in the second ring lies between two petals in the first ring. ■

**7** Hold the bag horizontally, with the thin end of the tip pointing up. ■ Make a ring of vertical flat petals around the mound. ■

**8** Add a ring of four vertical flat petals to the top of the mound. ■ If necessary, add petals to the flower cluster as needed to form the mound into a pompom shape. ■

**9** Fit the ivory icing with a #3 tip and decorate the sides of the cake with Swiss dots. ■

**10** Switch the tip on the medium green icing to a #3 tip and pipe two vines between every leaf or every other leaf (see hints and tips, at left). ■

# Jungle Leaves

*This design uses the medium of buttercream in an unexpected manner. Instead of piping traditional naturalistic leaves, here they are drawn on the cake for a clean, linear and surprisingly contemporary effect.* **Makes one 6-inch (15 cm) layer cake.**

## Getting Started

**Ice and chill the cake:** Use ivory icing and the Smooth Icing technique to ice the cake. Transfer the cake to the presentation surface and refrigerate until well chilled.

**Fill the pastry bags:** Transfer the remaining ivory icing to a pastry bag fitted with the #6 tip, and the dark, medium and light green icings to bags with #3 tips.

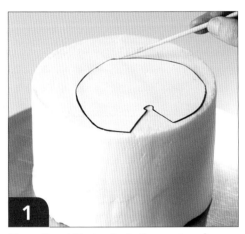

**1** Place the chilled cake in the center of the turntable. ■ Place the leaf template off-center on the top of the cake and trace around it with the toothpick. ■

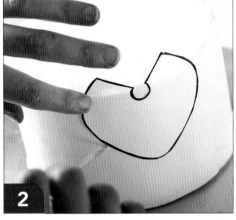

**2** Move the template so that it hangs over the edge of the cake, upside down, to the right of the first tracing. ■ Trace around it with the toothpick. ■

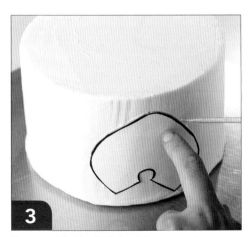

**3** Trace a third leaf, right side up, on the opposite side of the cake. ■

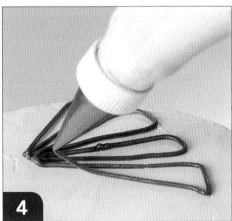

**4** Working from the bottom of the leaf on top of the cake, use dark green icing to pipe elongated triangles with the apex in the center of the leaf and the short edge aligned with the outer edge of the leaf. ■

## What You Need

- 6-inch (15 cm) layer cake, sliced, filled and crumb-coated
- 4 cups (1 L) ivory icing
- 1½ cups (375 mL) dark green icing
- 1 cup (250 mL) medium green icing
- 1 cup (250 mL) light green icing
- Turntable
- Presentation surface
- 4 pastry bags
- 4 couplers
- #6 round tip
- 3 #3 round tips
- Rounded leaf template (page 352)
- Toothpick or skewer

## Techniques Used

- Smooth Icing (page 82)
- Transferring an Iced Cake (page 96)
- Tracing and Pattern-Making (page 71)
- Lines (page 106)
- Smooth Scallop Border (page 99)

## Hints and Tips

Swiss meringue buttercream icing that has not been colored is a neutral ivory color.

## Hints and Tips

When adding vines to the cake, fill in all the large undecorated areas, but leave some empty white space so the cake doesn't look overdecorated.

Don't worry about making the leaves on the vines all look exactly the same. Just like leaves in real life, each leaf can be its own unique shape.

The leaves in step 9 also look great when piped with light green icing streaked with medium green. For information on making variegated icing colors, see page 64.

### Variation

Use the same minimalist technique to make maple, oak and beech leaves in variegated yellows, oranges, reds and browns, for a stunning autumn-themed cake.

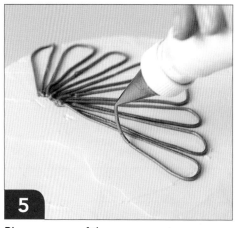

**5** Pipe as many of these segments as you need to complete one side of the leaf. ■

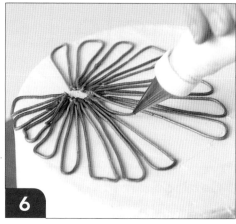

**6** Return to the bottom of the leaf and pipe triangular segments up the other side of the leaf. ■

**7** Pipe the segments on the other two leaves in the same way. ■

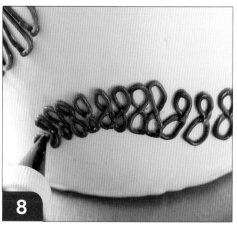

**8** Use the toothpick to dot the outlines of vines that wrap up or down and around the cake. ■ Using medium and/or dark green icing, pipe rounded leaves on half of the vines, reducing the size of the leaves as you move along the vine. ■

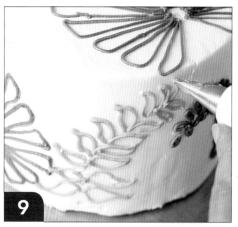

**9** Using light and/or medium green icing, pipe pointy leaves on the remaining vines, reducing the size of the leaves as you move along the vine. ■

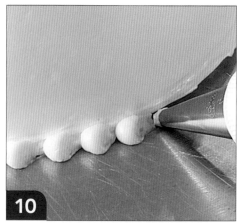

**10** Using ivory icing, pipe a smooth scallop border around the bottom of the cake. ■

232

# Ladybugs

*The vibrant colors and bold patterning, and the association with good fortune, make these ladybugs a welcome addition to any celebration.* **Makes one 6-inch (15 cm) layer cake.**

## Getting Started

**Ice and chill the cake:** Use light green icing and the Smooth Icing technique to ice the cake. Transfer the cake to the presentation surface and refrigerate until well chilled.

**Fill the pastry bags:** Transfer the medium and dark green icings to pastry bags fitted with #352 tips, the red icing to a bag with the #10 tip, and the black icing to a bag with the #1 tip.

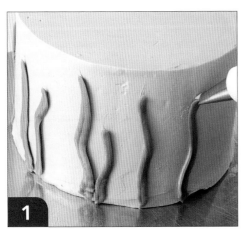

**1** Place the chilled cake in the center of the turntable. ■ Using medium green icing, pipe long, undulating leaves up the side of the cake from the base (see hints and tips, page 236), varying their heights and the distance between them. ■

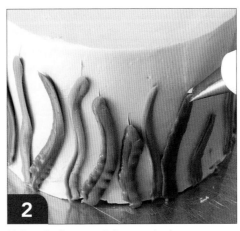

**2** Using dark green icing, make long, undulating leaves between the lighter ones. ■

**3** Switch the tip on the dark green icing to the #233 tip and pipe thick, lush grass around the base of the cake (see hints and tips, page 236). ■

**4** Pour a generous amount of sanding sugar into a shallow dish. ■ Using red icing and the rose nail, make a sprinkled rolled dot. ■ Using the scissors, place the dot on the top of the cake, near the edge. ■

## What You Need

- 6-inch (15 cm) layer cake, sliced, filled and crumb-coated
- 3½ cups (875 mL) light green icing
- 1 cup (250 mL) medium green icing
- 1½ cups (375 mL) dark green icing
- ½ cup (125 mL) red icing
- ½ cup (125 mL) black icing
- Turntable
- Presentation surface
- 4 pastry bags
- 4 couplers
- 2 #352 leaf tips
- #10 round tip
- #1 round tip
- #233 grass tip
- #12 round tip
- #6 round tip
- Red sanding sugar or sprinkles
- Rose nail
- Kitchen scissors

## Techniques Used

- Smooth Icing (page 82)
- Transferring an Iced Cake (page 96)
- Sprinkled Rolled Dots (page 105)
- Embedded Dots (variation, page 103)
- Dots (page 102)

To make the long, undulating leaves in steps 1 and 2, hold the pastry bag at a 45-degree angle to the base of the cake. Squeezing the bag with firm pressure, draw your hand up the side of the cake in an "S" or backwards "S" motion. To ensure that the leaves cling to the side of the cake and that the tips are pointy and do not flop forward, release the pressure while continuing to move your hand upward. (This motion may create an indented line in the icing above the leaf.)

To make the grass in step 3, start with the bag hovering just above the base of the cake. Squeeze the bag with firm pressure to anchor the grass to the surface before drawing your hand up and out in a quick, confident motion. Release pressure while still drawing the hand upward to create tapered, wispy grass.

### Variation
Make ladybugs in three sizes by using a #8 tip to create tiny ladybugs.

Repeat step 4 to make several ladybugs, placing them here and there around the top of the cake, near the edge, and on the leaves on the side of the cake. ■

Switch the tip on the red icing to the #12 tip and repeat step 4 to make several larger ladybugs, placing two or three around the top of the cake, near the edge, and several more on the leaves on the side of the cake. ■

Using black icing, pipe several embedded dots on the back of each ladybug, releasing pressure when the dot is level with the surface of the body. ■

Switch the tip on the black icing to the #6 tip and pipe a fat dot up against the body of each ladybug as the head, facing the ladybugs in different directions. ■

# Lily of the Valley

*The delicate bell-shaped blossoms of the lily of the valley — selected by Kate Middleton, Duchess of Cambridge, for her wedding bouquet — make for a graceful and elegant cake.* **Makes one 6-inch (15 cm) layer cake.**

## What You Need

- 6-inch (15 cm) layer cake, sliced, filled and crumb-coated
- 3¾ cups (925 mL) light green icing
- 1 cup (250 mL) ivory icing
- Turntable
- Presentation surface
- 2 pastry bags
- 2 couplers
- #6 round tip
- #2 round tip
- #80 U tip
- Toothpick or skewer
- Tweezers
- Chocolate sprinkles

## Techniques Used

- Smooth Icing (page 82)
- Transferring an Iced Cake (page 96)
- Lines (page 106)
- Short Vertical Petals (page 114)
- Smooth Scallop Border (page 99)

## Getting Started

**Ice and chill the cake:** Use green icing and the Smooth Icing technique to ice the cake. Transfer the cake to the presentation surface and refrigerate until well chilled.

**Fill the pastry bags:** Transfer the remaining green icing to a pastry bag fitted with the #6 tip, and the ivory icing to a bag with the #2 tip.

### Hints and Tips
Swiss meringue buttercream icing that has not been colored is a neutral ivory color.

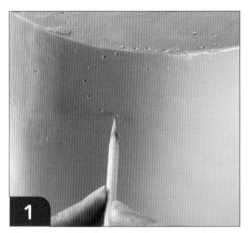

**1** Place the chilled cake in the center of the turntable. ■ Using the toothpick, dot the outlines of two small vines, crossing each other, that loop toward the center on top of the cake and curve down the side. ■

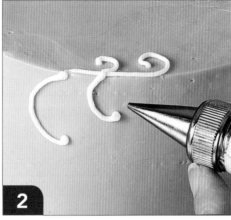

**2** Using ivory icing, pipe over the curling vines. ■

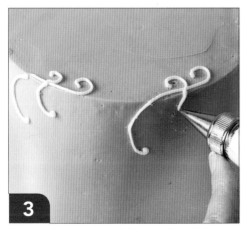

**3** Create six or seven of these pairs of vines around the top of the cake, giving each pair a slightly different shape. ■

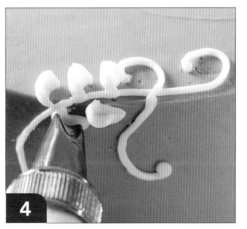

**4** Switch the tip on the ivory icing to the #80 tip and pipe rows of short vertical petals along both sides of one of the vines, starting just on top of the cake and continuing down the side. ■

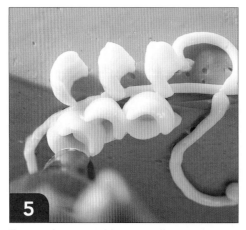

**5** To complete each blossom, pipe another short vertical petal facing the first one, so that each blossom forms a loose circle. ■

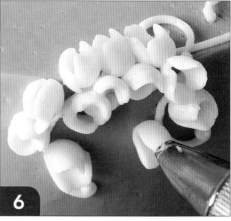

**6** Cluster the blossoms closer together at the top of the vine and taper them as you reach the end of the vine. ■

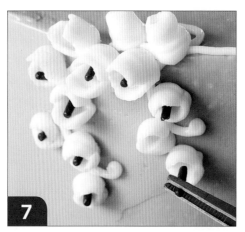

**7** Use the tweezers to place a chocolate sprinkle in the center of each blossom. ■

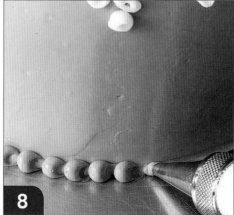

**8** Using light green icing, pipe a smooth scallop border around the bottom of the cake. ■

# Lotus Flower

*The lotus flower is a favorite of mine, not only for its exquisite beauty but for the symbolism associated with it: this graceful flower requires murky, silt-laden water to bloom and flourish.* **Makes 24 cupcakes.**

## Getting Started

**Ice the cupcakes:** Use ivory icing and the Smooth Cupcake Icing technique to ice the cupcakes.

**Fill the pastry bags:** Transfer the dark and light green icings to pastry bags fitted with #352 tips, the variegated pink and ivory icing to a bag with the #61 tip, and the yellow icing to a bag with the #2 tip.

## What You Need

- 24 cupcakes, cooled
- 4 cups (1 L) ivory icing
- ¾ cup (175 mL) dark green icing
- ¾ cup (175 mL) light green icing
- 2½ cups (625 mL) variegated pink and ivory icing
- ½ cup (125 mL) yellow icing
- Turntable
- 4 pastry bags
- 4 couplers
- 2 #352 leaf tips
- #61 petal tip
- #2 round tip

## Techniques Used

- Smooth Cupcake Icing (page 85)
- Leaves (page 112)
- Mounds (page 101)
- Long Horizontal Petals (page 113)

## Hints and Tips

For information on making variegated icing colors, see page 64.

When making a ring of leaves or petals, always rotate the turntable and keep your hand in the same position for each successive leaf or petal. This will ensure a nice round flower.

Place a cupcake in the center of the turntable. ■ Using dark green icing, pipe a ring of evenly spaced leaves around the top of the cupcake, leaving enough space between the dark green leaves to place light green leaves. ■

Using light green icing, pipe leaves in the spaces between the dark green leaves, completing the ring of leaves. ■

Using ivory icing, create a tapering mound in the center of the cupcake, leaving space between the base of the mound and the inside of the ring of leaves. ■

Using variegated pink icing, make a long horizontal petal that starts at the base of the mound and overlaps the leaves without covering them completely. ■

## Hints and Tips

If you are right-handed, it is easiest to make the leaves and petals with your piping hand in the East (E) position on the cupcake. If you are left-handed, it is easiest to work with your piping hand in the West (W) position.

To pipe each stamen in step 8, hold the bag perpendicular to the top of the cupcake and place the tip in the center of the flower (it does not need to be touching the mound). Squeeze the bag with firm pressure to create an anchor for the stamen, then rapidly draw your hand up, reducing the pressure to create a wispy, tapered end. Release the pressure when the stamen reaches the height of the inner petals.

If you plan to travel with your cupcakes, make sure the leaves do not reach past the edge of the cupcake or they could get damaged during transport.

### Variation

Replace the piped stamens with sprinkles, nonpareils or sugar pearls, or close the center by adding vertical petals.

**5** Make a ring of these petals around the cupcake. ■ The petals should butt up against each other at the base, but angle away from each other as they move out. ■

**6** Increase the angle of the pastry bag and pipe a second ring of petals above the first, angled up rather than lying flat, and staggered so that each petal in the second ring lies between two petals in the first ring. ■

**7** Pipe two or three more rings of petals, increasing the angle of the bag with each ring until it is nearly vertical for the final ring. ■ Leave the very center of the flower open. ■

**8** Using yellow icing, pipe a cluster of stamens in the center of the flower (see hints and tips, at left). ■

# Monogram

*A monogram is a great way to boldly personalize a cake. This delicate "B" combined with a daisy and vines would be especially appropriate for a girl's birthday or a bridal shower.* **Makes one 8-inch (20 cm) layer cake.**

## Getting Started

**Ice and chill the cake:** Use blue icing and the Smooth Icing technique to ice the cake. Transfer the cake to the presentation surface and refrigerate until well chilled.

**Fill the pastry bags:** Transfer the dark pink icing to a pastry bag fitted with the #3 tip, the dark green icing to a bag with the #4 tip, and the light green and ivory icings to bags with #1 tips. Transfer half of the light pink icing to a bag with the #5 tip. Fit a bag without a coupler with the #125 tip and fill with the remaining light pink icing.

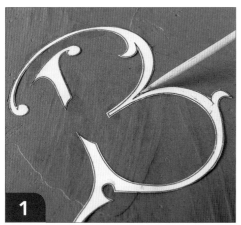

1. Place the chilled cake in the center of the turntable. ■ Place the monogram template in the center of the cake and trace around it with the toothpick. ■

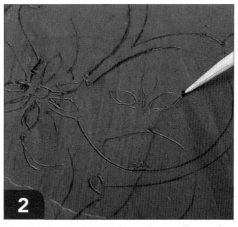

2. Use the toothpick to draw the outlines of a flower, vines and leaves winding around and through the monogram. ■

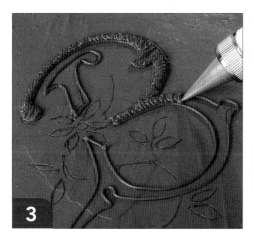

3. Using dark pink icing, pipe over the outline of the monogram. ■ Switch the tip to a #2 tip and use the embroidery technique to fill in the monogram. ■

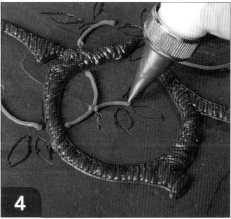

4. Using dark green icing, pipe over the outlined vines. ■

Look for monogram templates in pattern books (available at craft stores) or online (search on "free printable monogram templates"). Photocopy or print and cut out a template for the monogram you want to use. Or, if you are confident in your artistic abilities, draw the monogram freehand.

Monograms come in a vast range of font styles, ranging from looping Edwardian script to intricate Gothic typeface, each of which will create a different tone for your cake. Choose icing colors and supplementary decorations that suit the tone set by your monogram choice.

### Variations

Switch the tip on the ivory icing back to the #3 tip to decorate the sides of the cake with Swiss dots, or to pipe simplified Swiss dots on the ribbon border.

Match the colors of the cake to those chosen for the event.

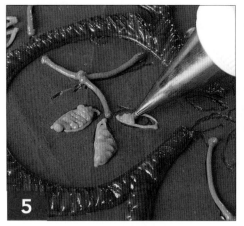

Using light green icing, pipe over the outlines of the leaves. ■ Use the embroidery technique to fill in the leaves. ■

Using ivory icing, pipe over the outlines of the flower petals. ■ Use the embroidery technique to fill in the petals. ■

Using light pink icing from the bag with the #5 tip, pipe a dot in the center of the flower. ■ Pipe single dots or clusters of dots here and there around the vines. ■

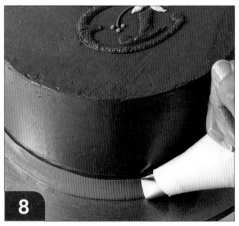

Using light pink icing from the bag with the #125 tip, pipe a ribbon border around the bottom of the cake. ■

# Nesting Birds

*These adorable cupcakes use toasted coconut to simulate the twigs of a nest. These sweet squawking chicks are so cute, you may find you have trouble eating them!* **Makes 24 cupcakes.**

## Getting Started

**Fill the pastry bags:** Transfer the beige icing to a pastry bag fitted only with a coupler, the blue icing to a bag with the #10 tip, and the yellow and brown icings to bags with #1 tips.

### What You Need

- 24 cupcakes, cooled
- 2 cups (500 mL) beige icing
- 1 cup (250 mL) pale blue icing
- 1/3 cup (75 mL) bright yellow icing
- 1/3 cup (75 mL) dark brown icing
- 4 pastry bags
- 4 couplers
- #10 round tip
- 2 #1 round tips
- #6 round tip
- Turntable
- Toasted coconut

### Techniques Used

- Dots (page 102)

**1** Place a cooled cupcake in the center of the turntable. ■ Using beige icing, pipe a thick ring around the top of the cupcake. ■

**2** Sprinkle coconut on top of the beige icing until the ring is completely coated with coconut. ■

**3** Using blue icing, fill the center of the ring halfway with buttercream, then pipe three fat dots in the center of the nest, as the birds' bodies. ■

**4** Switch the tip on the blue icing to the #6 tip and pipe a fat dot on top of each bird body, as the head. ■

### Variation

For some of the cupcakes (or if you don't have coconut on hand), fit the pastry bag of beige icing with a #233 grass tip to make the nest. Hold the bag 1/2 inch (1 cm) above the cupcake and squeeze with firm pressure. Move your hand very slowly in a ring around the top of the cupcake, allowing the icing to pile up and twist. Make a second ring on top of the first.

**251**

## Hints and Tips

To give each bird its own personality, change how close the eyes are set and how far up or down on the head they are.

### Variation

To make a single bird atop a mini cupcake, use a #12 round tip for the body, a #8 round tip for the head and a #6 round tip for the wings and tail. The wings can stretch out and forward a bit more than on the triplet birds. After piping the beak, use the yellow icing to pipe the bird's feet.

**5**

Pipe elongated dots as wings, making a wing on each side of the bird in the front and a single wing each for the birds in the back of the nest. (These two birds are butted up against each other, so a second wing would not be visible.) ■

**6**

Pipe an elongated dot as a tail on the back of each bird in the back of the nest. ■

**7**

Using yellow icing, pipe two elongated dots, one on top of the other, as the beak for each bird. ■

**8**

Using dark brown icing, pipe two dots for eyes on each bird. ■

# Ombré Rosettes

*These fat pink rosettes make for a particularly sweet cake, and the subtle shift in hue adds to its beauty.* **Makes one 8-inch (20 cm) layer cake.**

## Getting Started

**Ice and chill the cake:** Use medium pink icing and the Smooth Icing technique to ice the cake. Transfer the cake to the presentation surface and refrigerate until well chilled.

**Fill the pastry bags:** Transfer the remaining medium pink icing and the dark and light pink icings to pastry bags fitted with #32 tips.

## What You Need

- 8-inch (20 cm) layer cake, sliced, filled and crumb-coated
- 6 cups (1.5 L) medium pink icing
- 2 cups (500 mL) dark pink icing
- 2 cups (500 mL) light pink icing
- Turntable
- Presentation surface
- 3 pastry bags
- 3 couplers
- 3 #32 open star tips

## Techniques Used

- Smooth Icing (page 82)
- Transferring an Iced Cake (page 96)
- Large Rosettes (variation, page 120)

## Hints and Tips

Spin the turntable slightly after every couple of rosettes so that you are always working directly in front of you.

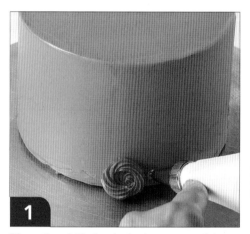

**1** Place the chilled cake in the center of the turntable. ■ Using dark pink icing, pipe a large rosette at the bottom of the cake, directly in front of you. ■

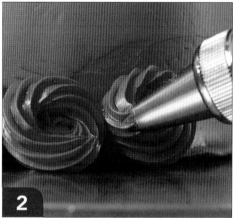

**2** Move the tip slightly to the right and make a second rosette that butts up against the first one. ■

**3** Continue to make dark pink rosettes until you have completed a ring around the bottom of the cake. ■

**4** Start to make a second ring of dark pink rosettes directly on top of the first ring, but stop halfway around the cake. ■

## Hints and Tips

If you only have one #32 tip, simply switch it between the three bags of icing. There's no need to clean the tip as you switch it.

## Variation

Use ivory icing to ice the cake and add a smooth scallop border around the bottom. Pipe 8 or 9 dark pink rosettes slanting up the side of the cake and over the top. Add a couple of medium pink rosettes near the bottom of the cake, then switch the tip to a #18 tip and intersperse medium pink rosettes among the dark pink ones. Using a #16 tip on the light pink icing, pipe small rosettes around and on top of the larger ones. Leave some random open areas to emphasize the naturalistic appearance.

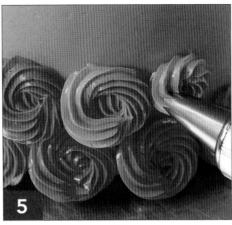

Using medium pink icing, make one and a half rings of rosettes around the cake. ■

Using light pink icing, continue making rings of rosettes, working your way toward the top of the cake. ■ For the final ring, leave just enough room so that the top edge of the rosettes meets the top edge of the cake or rises above it only slightly. ■

# Paisley

*This cake makes use of the traditional paisley motif, but the bold color and graphic pattern are anything but traditional.* **Makes one 6-inch (15 cm) layer cake.**

## Getting Started

**Ice and chill the cake:** Use ivory icing and the Smooth Icing technique to ice the cake. Transfer the cake to the presentation surface and refrigerate until well chilled.

**Fill the pastry bags:** Transfer the remaining ivory icing to a pastry bag fitted with the #6 tip, and the red icing to a bag with the #3 tip.

## What You Need

- 6-inch (15 cm) layer cake, sliced, filled and crumb-coated
- 3½ cups (875 mL) ivory icing
- ½ cup (125 mL) red icing
- Turntable
- Presentation surface
- 2 pastry bags
- 2 couplers
- #6 round tip
- #3 round tip
- #12 round tip
- #2 round tip
- Set of paisley-shaped cookie cutters in different sizes
- Small round cookie cutters

## Techniques Used

- Smooth Icing (page 82)
- Transferring an Iced Cake (page 96)
- Tracing and Pattern-Making (page 71)
- Dots (page 102)
- Lines (page 106)
- Smooth Scallop Border (page 99)

## Hints and Tips

Swiss meringue buttercream icing that has not been colored is a neutral ivory color.

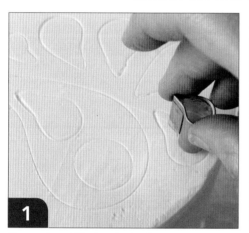

**1** Place the chilled cake in the center of the turntable. ■ Following the design in the photographs, use the paisley and round cookie cutters to make imprints on the top and one side of the cake. ■

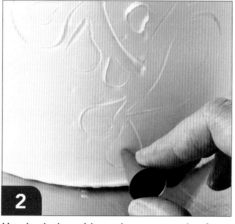

**2** Use both the wide and narrow ends of the #12 tip to add smaller imprints to the design. ■

**3** Using red icing, pipe dotted outlines over all the imprinted shapes. ■

**4** Switch the tip on the red icing to the #2 tip and pipe tiny circles and paisleys within some of the small circles and paisleys. ■

## Hints and Tips

If you don't have paisley-shaped cookie cutters, look for paisley templates in a pattern book or online, photocopy or print them, cut them out and use a toothpick to trace around them on the cake.

Feel free to come up with your own paisley design rather than following mine.

For added confidence in step 4, use the narrow end of a round tip to imprint a tiny circle, or trace a tiny paisley with a toothpick, before piping the shape.

### Variations

Try reversing the colors: ice the cake in deep red and use ivory icing to pipe the paisley design.

For a bold cake that takes its cues from the psychedelic 60s, use bright, brash colors like hot pink, sky blue, vibrant yellow and orange, and cover the entire surface of the cake with a paisley pattern.

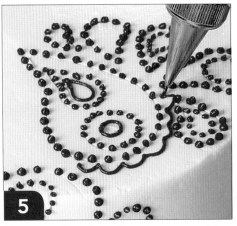

5

Pipe an outline of small scallops around the outside of three of the large paisleys. ■

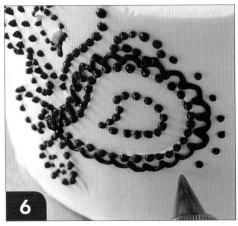

6

Pipe a dotted outline of small, widespread dots around the outside of the scalloped paisleys. ■

7

Pipe a second dotted outline around the first, staggering the dots so that each one lies halfway between two dots in the inner dotted outline. ■

8

Using ivory icing, pipe a smooth scallop border around the bottom of the cake. ■

# Pansy

*Here, the buttercream pansy flaunts its beauty as the centerpiece on a cupcake.* **Makes 24 cupcakes.**

## Getting Started

**Ice the cupcakes:** Use ivory icing and the Smooth Cupcake Icing technique to ice the cupcakes.

**Fill the pastry bags:** Transfer the purple icing to a pastry bag fitted with the #104 tip, the light yellow icing to a bag with the #103 tip, the black and dark yellow icings to bags with #1 tips, and the light and dark green icings to bags with #352 tips.

## What You Need

- 24 cupcakes, cooled
- 4 cups (1 L) ivory icing
- 2 cups (500 mL) dark purple icing
- 1 cup (250 mL) light yellow icing
- ⅓ cup (75 mL) black icing
- ⅓ cup (75 mL) dark yellow icing
- ¾ cup (175 mL) light green icing
- ¾ cup (175 mL) dark green icing
- Turntable
- 6 pastry bags
- 6 couplers
- #104 rose tip
- #103 rose tip
- 2 #1 round tips
- 2 #352 leaf tips

## Techniques Used

- Smooth Cupcake Icing (page 85)
- Classic Flat Petals (page 115)
- Lines (page 106)
- Leaves (page 112)

## Hints and Tips
Swiss meringue buttercream icing that has not been colored is a neutral ivory color.

Place an iced cupcake in the center of the turntable. ■ Using purple icing, pipe two classic flat petals side by side. ■

Using light yellow icing, pipe two classic flat petals that overlap the purple petals and touch in the center of the flower. ■

Spin the turntable so that the petals are upside down. ■ Pipe two light yellow petals side by side, directly across from and touching the first pair of yellow petals. ■

Using black icing, pipe two thin black lines down the center of each yellow petal. ■

## Variations

Yellow and purple pansies are my favorite, but pansies come in many different color combinations, all of which would make beautiful cupcakes. Try yellow and burgundy, ivory and purple, light purple and deep purple, orange and red, or any color combination that appeals to you.

To make two or three smaller flowers on each cupcake, use a #103 rose tip for the purple icing and a #102 rose tip for the light yellow icing. See the Violet cupcakes (page 329) for ideas on how to group the flowers.

**5** Using dark yellow icing, pipe a small circle in the center of the flower. ■

**6** Using light and dark green icing, pipe scattered leaves around the flower. ■

# Peachy Rosettes

*Together, the masses of rosettes on this cake become more a texture than a collection of individual flowers. This is a wonderful way to decorate a cake quickly without the need to make the icing perfectly smooth or to mix multiple colors.* **Makes one 8-inch (20 cm) layer cake.**

## Getting Started

**Ice and chill the cake:** Use peach icing and the Smooth Icing technique to roughly ice the cake. Transfer the cake to the presentation surface and refrigerate until well chilled.

**Fill the pastry bag:** Transfer the variegated pale peach and ivory icing to a pastry bag fitted with the #32 tip.

## What You Need

- 8-inch (20 cm) layer cake, sliced, filled and crumb-coated
- 4 cups (1.5 L) pale peach icing
- 6 cups (1.5 L) variegated pale peach and ivory icing
- Turntable
- Presentation surface
- Pastry bag
- Coupler
- #32 open star tip

## Techniques Used

- Smooth Icing (page 82)
- Transferring an Iced Cake (page 96)
- Rosettes (page 120)

## Hints and Tips

For information on making variegated icing colors, see page 64.

As you are making each column of rosettes, keep an eye on the top of the cake. You want to space the rosettes so that the top edge of the last rosette meets the top edge of the cake or rises above it only slightly.

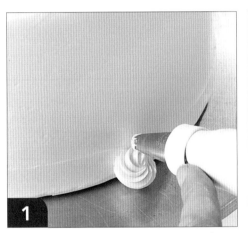

**1** Place the chilled cake in the center of the turntable. ■ Using variegated peach and ivory icing, pipe a small rosette at the base of the cake. ■

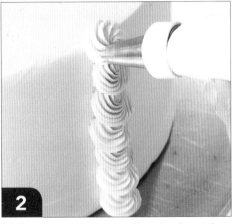

**2** Make a second rosette directly above the first. ■ Continue to stack rosettes until they reach the top of the cake. ■

**3** Make a second column of rosettes directly beside the first. ■

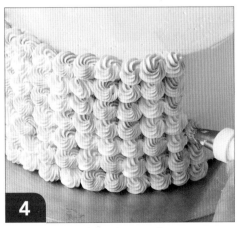

**4** Continue to make columns of rosettes until the sides of the cake are completely covered with them. ■

## Variation

To make matching cupcakes, pipe a small mound of ivory or peach icing in the center of each cupcake (see Mounds, page 101). Cover the mound with tightly packed rosettes. The #32 open star tip works well for standard-size cupcakes; for mini cupcakes, use a #18 open star tip.

**5**

Pipe a ring of rosettes on the top of the cake, around the outer edge. ■

**6**

Pipe another ring of rosettes inside the first. ■ Continue to make smaller and smaller rings until the top of the cake is completely covered with rosettes. ■

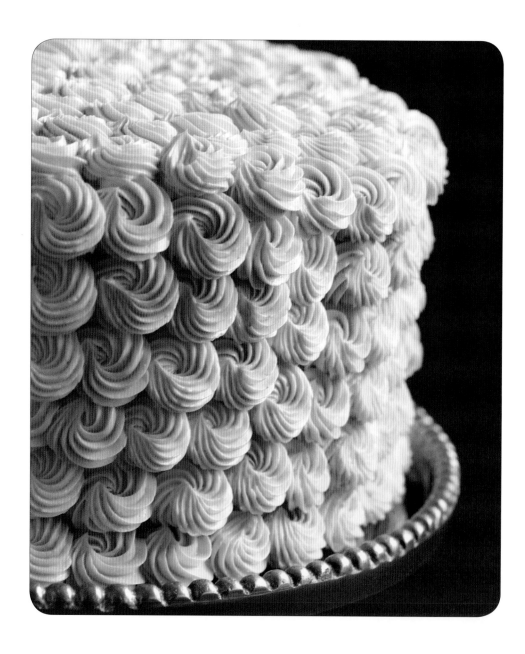

# Pearls

*It's amazing that a cake so exquisite and luxurious could be so simple to create. A handful of sugar pearls transforms a simply iced cake into an opalescent marvel.* **Makes one 6-inch (15 cm) layer cake.**

## Getting Started

**Ice and chill the cake:** Use ivory icing and the Smooth Icing technique to ice the cake. Transfer the cake to the presentation surface and refrigerate until well chilled.

**Fill the pastry bag:** Fit a pastry bag without a coupler with the #125 tip and fill with the remaining icing.

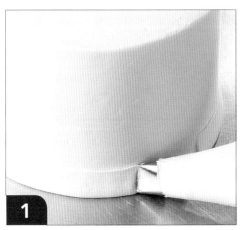

**1** Place the chilled cake in the center of the turntable. ■ Using ivory icing, pipe a ribbon border around the bottom of the cake. ■

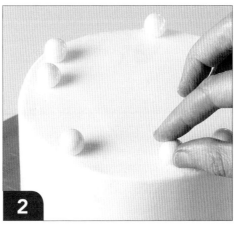

**2** Use your fingers to scatter large sugar pearls around the edge on top of the cake. ■

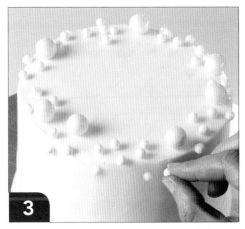

**3** Scatter medium sugar pearls around the top and spilling over the edge of the cake. ■

**4** Use the tweezers to scatter small sugar pearls around the top and spilling over the edge of the cake. ■

## What You Need

- 6-inch (15 cm) layer cake, sliced, filled and crumb-coated
- 4 cups (1 L) warm ivory icing
- Turntable
- Presentation surface
- 1 pastry bag
- #125 tip
- Large, medium and small white or ivory sugar pearls
- Tweezers

## Techniques Used

- Smooth Icing (page 82)
- Transferring an Iced Cake (page 96)
- Ribbon Border (page 98)

## Hints and Tips

Swiss meringue buttercream icing that has not been colored is naturally off-white or ivory. If you want to deepen the ivory tones, add a bit of egg yellow food coloring.

For a more vintage look, ice the cake in beige.

Brilliant pink or shocking purple icing would be fabulous for a sweet 16 or quinceañera party.

For a winter wonderland cake, use pale blue icing.

Replace the pearls with bright multicolored candies and gumballs for a fun, festive cake.

Use silver sugar pearls for a stunning anniversary cake.

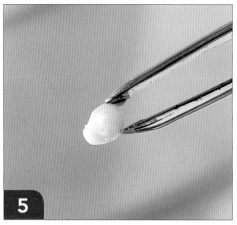

**5**

Use the tweezers to dip one side of a small pearl in icing, which will act as glue. ■

**6**

Place the pearl on top of other pearls. ■ Continue to stack, overlap and pile pearls until the cake top drips with gravity-defying pearls. ■

# Poppies

*These stylized blossoms evoke the delicate, papery petals of the brilliant red poppy. Poppies always make me think of the adventures of Dorothy and her friends, so this cake would be a great choice for a* Wizard of Oz *theme party.* **Makes one 8-inch (20 cm) layer cake.**

## Getting Started

**Ice and chill the cake:** Use purple icing and the Smooth Icing technique to ice the cake. Transfer the cake to the presentation surface and refrigerate until well chilled.

**Fill the pastry bags:** Transfer the green icing to a pastry bag fitted with the #4 tip. Fit a bag without a coupler with the #125 tip and fill with the red icing. Transfer the black icing to a bag with the #6 tip.

### What You Need

- 8-inch (20 cm) layer cake, sliced, filled and crumb-coated
- 4 cups (1 L) medium purple icing
- ½ cup (125 mL) green icing
- ¾ cup (175 mL) red icing
- ¾ cup (175 mL) black icing
- Turntable
- Presentation surface
- 3 pastry bags
- 2 couplers
- #4 round tip
- #125 rose tip
- #6 round tip

### Techniques Used

- Smooth Icing (page 82)
- Transferring an Iced Cake (page 96)
- Lines (page 106)
- Smooth Scallop Border (page 99)

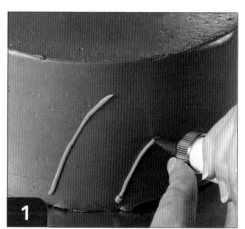

Place the chilled cake in the center of the turntable. ■ Using green icing and starting ¼ inch (5 mm) from the bottom of the cake, pipe stems of various heights leaning to the right up the side of the cake (see hints and tips, page 276). ■

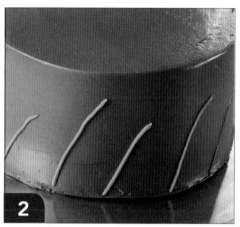

Vary the distance between the stems, but pipe them all at about the same angle. ■ Continue piping stems all the way around the sides of the cake. ■

## Hints and Tips

If you are left-handed, it is easier to make stems that lean to the left in steps 1 and 2. In step 3, start with the tip angled toward 1 or 2 o'clock, and in step 4, rotate the wide end of the tip counterclockwise.

If your poppy blossoms are coming out small because you are unable to rotate your wrist much, feel free to stop in the process of making the blossom, adjust the angle of your arm and continue. The pause will just make it look like there's another petal!

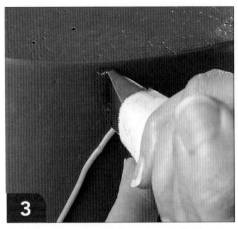

Hold the bag of red icing perpendicular to the side of the cake, with the narrow end of the tip at the top of a stem and the wide end angled toward 10 or 11 o'clock (imagining the side of the cake as the face of a clock). ■

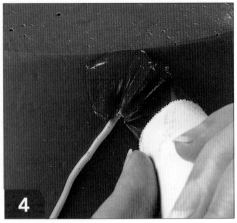

Squeeze the bag with moderate pressure, keeping the narrow end of the tip in place and rotating the wide end of the tip clockwise as far as your wrist will allow. ■

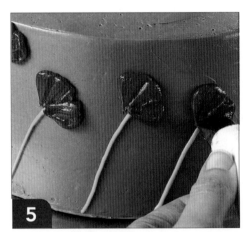

Continue to make poppies until all the stems have blossoms. ■

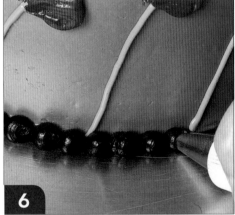

Using black icing, pipe a smooth scallop border around the bottom of the cake. ■

# Roses and Ribbons

*Sweet rosettes and matching sugar pearls are the perfect complement to simple swags, combining to create an absolutely darling cake.* **Makes one 8-inch (20 cm) layer cake.**

## What You Need

- 8-inch (20 cm) layer cake, sliced, filled and crumb-coated
- 4½ cups (1.125 L) pale pink icing
- 1 cup (250 mL) pale green icing
- Turntable
- Presentation surface
- 3 pastry bags
- 2 couplers
- 2 #3 round tips
- #125 rose tip
- #352 leaf tip
- #16 open star tip
- 1½-inch (4 cm) round or oval cookie cutter
- Tweezers
- Small pink sugar pearls

## Techniques Used

- Smooth Icing (page 82)
- Transferring an Iced Cake (page 96)
- Ribbon Border (page 98)
- Swags (page 107)
- Rosettes (page 120)
- Dots (page 102)

## Getting Started

**Ice and chill the cake:** Use pink icing and the Smooth Icing technique to ice the cake. Transfer the cake to the presentation surface and refrigerate until well chilled.

**Fill the pastry bags:** Transfer the remaining pink icing to a pastry bag fitted with a #3 tip. Fit a bag without a coupler with the #125 tip and fill with half of the green icing. Transfer the remaining green icing to a bag with the #352 tip.

**1** Place the chilled cake in the center of the turntable. ■ Using green icing from the bag with the #125 tip, pipe a ribbon border around the bottom of the cake. ■

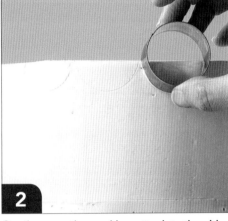

**2** Gently press the cookie cutter into the side of the cake to mark off 1½-inch (4 cm) wide and 1-inch (2.5 cm) deep swag imprints side by side around the top edge of the cake. ■

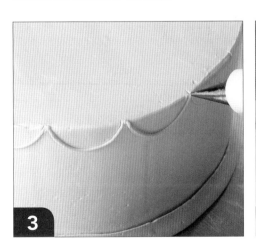

**3** Using pink icing, pipe over the swag imprints. ■

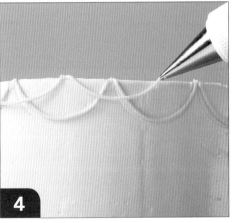

**4** Starting in the center of a swag, at the top edge of the cake, pipe a second ring of swags that are shallower than the first and that run from center to center on the first ring of swags. ■

**279**

## Hints and Tips

If you don't have a 1½-inch (4 cm) round or oval cookie cutter, you can use a toothpick to mark off the swags in step 2. Mark around the top edge of the cake at 1½-inch (4 cm) intervals, then mark the lowest point of each swag, 1 inch (2.5 cm) below the top edge. Use these points as guidelines for your piped swags.

When piping the leaves in step 6, it is easiest to pipe all the leaves that point in one direction first, then pipe all the leaves that point in the other direction.

This cake is especially appropriate for baby showers, baptisms and christenings. Change the colors to coordinate with the event. It is lovely done entirely in ivory or in soft shades of blue and yellow.

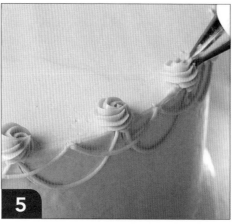

**5** Switch the tip on the pink icing to the #16 tip and pipe a rosette on top of the cake at the point of each swag from the first ring. ∎

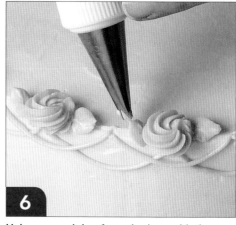

**6** Using green icing from the bag with the #352 tip, pipe a small leaf on either side of each rosette. ∎

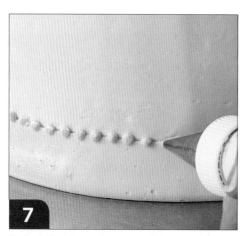

**7** Switch the tip on the green icing to a #3 tip and pipe small dots, very close together, around the top edge of the ribbon border. ∎

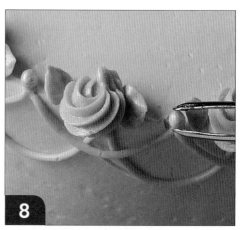

**8** Use the tweezers to place a sugar pearl on top of the cake at the point of each swag from the second ring. ∎

# Rustic Finish

*The unfussy nature of this cake — which features wear marks like a treasured antique burnished by time and use — makes it appropriate for any number of occasions, and it's an excellent backdrop for a cake topper.* **Makes one 8-inch (20 cm) layer cake.**

---

## Getting Started

**Ice and chill the cake:** Use ivory icing and the Smooth Icing technique to roughly ice the cake with a thin layer of icing. (This layer will be entirely covered.) Leave the cake on the turntable and refrigerate until well chilled.

On top of the chilled ivory icing, ice the cake with a thin layer of brown icing.
■ Leave the cake on the turntable and refrigerate until well chilled. ■

On top of the chilled brown icing, ice the cake with a thin layer of turquoise icing.
■ Leave the cake on the turntable and refrigerate until well chilled. ■

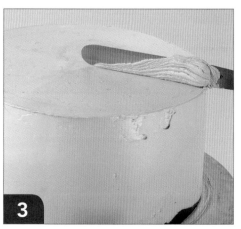

Using the edge of the straight blade spatula, scrape a thin, uneven layer of turquoise icing off the top of the cake. ■

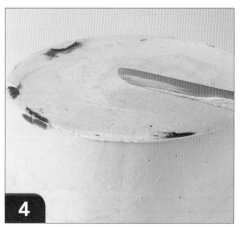

Continue scraping the top until some of the brown icing and a little of the ivory icing show through, especially around the edge. ■

## What You Need

- 8-inch (20 cm) layer cake, sliced, filled and crumb-coated
- 3⅓ cups (825 mL) ivory icing
- 3⅓ cups (825 mL) dark brown icing
- 3⅓ cups (825 mL) turquoise icing
- Turntable
- Large straight blade spatula
- Damp cloth

## Techniques Used

- Smooth Icing (page 82)

### Hints and Tips

Before icing the cake, make space in the refrigerator for the turntable with the cake on top. This cake is not transferred to the presentation surface until you are done decorating it.

Give yourself a good deal of time to create this cake. The decoration itself doesn't take long, but the cake needs to chill for 20 to 25 minutes three different times.

Don't fuss with making the icing perfectly smooth and even. It will be scraped of all ridges and flaws.

**5**

Whenever a significant amount of icing accumulates on the spatula, scrape it clean and wipe it with a damp cloth. ■

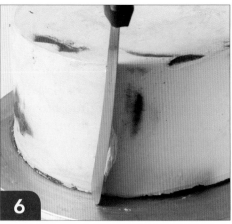

**6**

Scrape the turquoise icing off the sides of the cake until some of the brown icing and a little of the ivory icing show through, especially around the bottom edge. ■

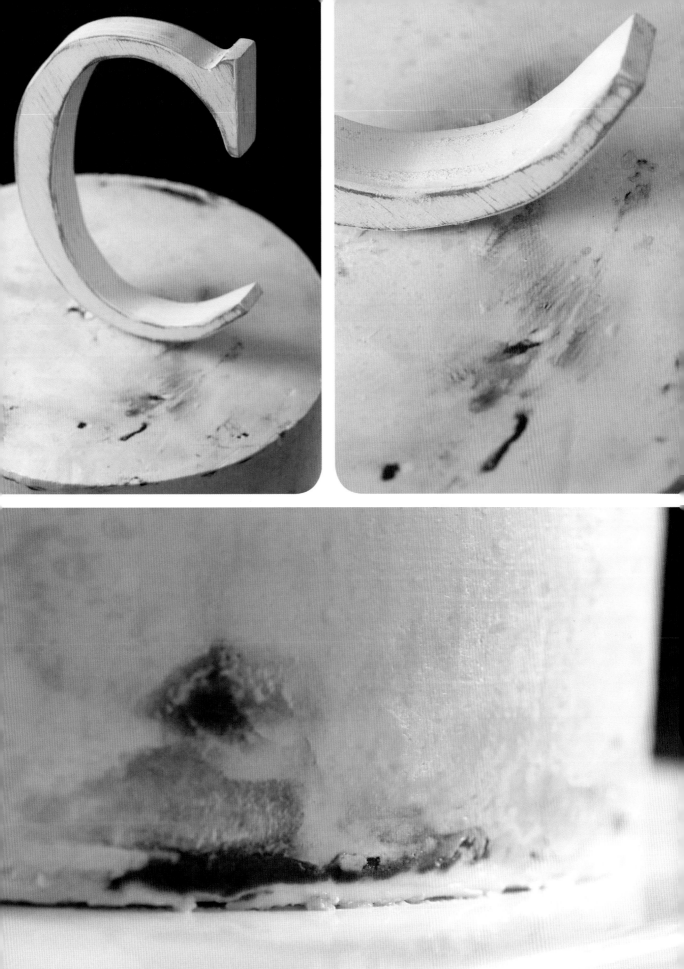

# Sheep

The fluffy white curls and expressive eyes give these sheep charm and personality even as they lounge on a grassy mound. **Makes 24 cupcakes.**

## Getting Started

**Ice the cupcakes:** Use green icing and the Spiral Cupcake Icing technique to ice the cupcakes.

**Fill the pastry bags:** Transfer the ivory and black icings to pastry bags fitted only with couplers.

**1** Place a cupcake in the center of the turntable. ■ Using ivory icing, pipe a fat and slightly elongated coupler dot in the center of the cupcake. ■

**2** Fit the ivory icing bag with the #8 tip and pipe a ring of fat dots around the bottom of the ivory coupler dot. ■

**3** Continue to add concentric rings of dots, working toward the top of the coupler dot until it is completely covered. ■

**4** Using black icing, pipe a slightly elongated coupler dot on one of the narrow sides of the sheep's body, as the head. ■ While squeezing the bag, move your hand down slightly to make a flat face. ■

## What You Need

- 24 cupcakes, cooled
- 4 cups (1 L) pale green icing
- 3 cups (750 mL) ivory icing
- 1 cup (250 mL) black icing
- Turntable
- 2 pastry bags
- 2 couplers
- #8 round tip
- #10 round tip
- #80 U tip
- #5 round tip
- #4 round tip
- #1 round tip

## Techniques Used

- Spiral Cupcake Icing (page 92)
- Mounds (page 101)
- Coupler Dots (variation, page 103)
- Dots (page 102)

## Hints and Tips

Swiss meringue buttercream icing that has not been colored is a neutral ivory color.

Using ivory icing, pipe fat dots on top of the head, as a curly pompadour. ■

Switch the tip on the ivory icing to the #10 tip and pipe an elongated dot at the back of the sheep, as the tail. ■

To make the ears, fit the black icing bag with the #80 tip. ■ Hold the bag at the side of the sheep's head and turn it so that the open part of the U faces forward. ■ Squeeze with firm pressure to anchor each ear to the head, then pull out and slightly down. ■

To make the legs, switch the tip on the black icing to the #5 tip. ■ Start at the base of the sheep's body and increase the pressure as you move the tip down, so the legs are fatter at the ends. ■

Switch the tip on the ivory icing to the #4 tip and pipe a dot for each eye. ■

Switch the tip on the black icing to the #1 tip and pipe the pupil of each eye. ■

# Sprinkles

This delightful cake is sure to get rave reviews, but don't tell anyone how easy it was to make! Because the sides are completely covered with sprinkles, you don't need to be too concerned about making them smooth. **Makes one 6-inch (15 cm) layer cake.**

## Getting Started

**Ice and chill the cake:** Use ivory icing and the Smooth Icing technique to ice the cake. Do not chill the cake before decorating.

### Hints and Tips

Swiss meringue buttercream icing that has not been colored is a neutral ivory color.

I love the contrast of the colorful sprinkled sides with the smooth top, which also allows space for an inscription, but if you're not happy with the state of your icing or you're just in the mood for more sprinkles, feel free to scatter sprinkles on the top of the cake too.

Pour a generous amount of sprinkles into the wide-mouthed bowl. ■

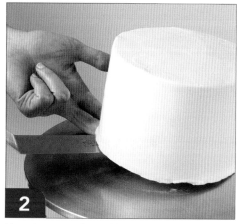

Use the spatula to lift the cake off the turntable and carefully balance the cake on the fingertips of your non-dominant hand. ■

Slide your hand all the way under the cake and balance it over the bowl of sprinkles. ■

Scoop a handful of sprinkles into your open hand and gently press the sprinkles into the side of the cake. ■

## Hints and Tips

Use any sprinkles you like. Pastel confetti sprinkles are an excellent choice, as are multicolored jimmies and heart-shaped sprinkles. Use nonpareils in the team colors for a sports-themed cake.

See Transferring an Iced Cake (page 96) for detailed instructions on the best way to pick up a cake and set it down on the presentation surface.

### Variation

Use crushed nuts or small candies in place of the sprinkles.

Cover as much of the sides of the cake as you can from this position. ■

Carefully rotate the cake in your hand to expose the side of the cake not yet covered in sprinkles. ■

Gently press sprinkles into any exposed areas. ■

Use the large offset spatula to help you transfer the cake to the presentation surface. ■

# Strands of Pearls

*Two colors and a series of dots make a decidedly elegant cake.*
Makes one 4-inch (10 cm) layer cake.

## Getting Started

**Ice and chill the cake:** Use fuchsia icing and the Smooth Icing technique to ice the cake. Transfer the cake to the presentation surface and refrigerate until well chilled.

**Fill the pastry bags:** Transfer the remaining fuchsia icing to a pastry bag fitted with the #104 tip, half the ivory icing to a bag with the #4 tip, and the other half to a bag with the #3 tip.

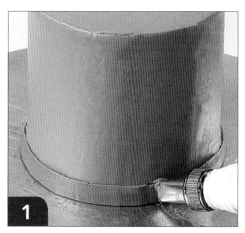

**1**

Place the chilled cake in the center of the turntable. ■ Using fuchsia icing, pipe a ribbon border around the bottom of the cake. ■

**2**

Use the toothpick to dot the outline of a strand of pearls that starts on the top of the cake, near one edge, and trails over the edge and down the side (see hints and tips, at right). ■

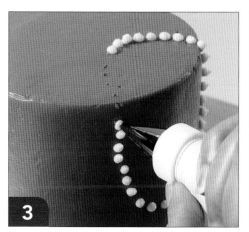

**3**

Using ivory icing from the bag with the #4 tip, pipe a dot over each dot in the outline. ■

**4**

Use the toothpick to dot the outline of another strand of pearls that overlaps the first one and extends across the top of the cake and down the other side. ■

## What You Need

- 4-inch (10 cm) layer cake, sliced, filled and crumb-coated
- 3 cups (750 mL) fuchsia icing
- ¾ cup (175 mL) ivory icing
- Turntable
- Presentation surface
- 3 pastry bags
- 3 couplers
- #104 rose tip
- #4 round tip
- #3 round tip
- Toothpick or skewer

## Techniques Used

- Smooth Icing (page 82)
- Transferring an Iced Cake (page 96)
- Ribbon Border (page 98)
- Dots (page 102)

## Hints and Tips

Swiss meringue buttercream icing that has not been colored is a neutral ivory color.

When dotting your outlines, think about how a strand of pearls draped over something might look as it dangles and sways before settling into an irregular gravity-influenced oval.

## Hints and Tips

If you have a strand of Mardi Gras beads on hand, play with draping them over other objects to get design ideas for your strands.

You can follow my design when making your strands or create your own.

## Variations

Ice the cake in classic "Tiffany Box Blue" for a chic, trendy look.

To make matching cupcakes to serve alongside the cake, use fuchsia icing and the Spiral Cupcake Icing technique (page 92) to ice the cupcakes. Using ivory icing from both the bag with the #4 tip and the bag with the #3 tip, pipe dots on top of the cupcakes, scattering them randomly.

**5**

Using ivory icing from the bag with the #3 tip, pipe a dot over each dot in the outline of the second strand. ■

**6**

Continue to outline and pipe strands of pearls on the top and sides of the cake as desired, using the bag with tip #4 for half the strands and the bag with tip #3 for the other half. ■

# Stylized Peacock

*This cake looks like it's swathed in a classic Liberty of London print one might have found in a Victorian parlor, but the audacious color palette gives it a contemporary presence.* **Makes one 6-inch (15 cm) layer cake.**

## Getting Started

**Ice and chill the cake:** Use green icing and the Smooth Icing technique to ice the cake. Transfer the cake to the presentation surface and refrigerate until well chilled.

**Fill the pastry bags:** Transfer the remaining green icing to a pastry bag fitted with the #6 tip. Transfer each of the blue, orange and yellow icings to a pastry bag fitted with a #3 tip.

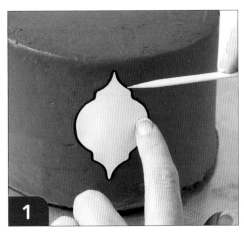

Place the chilled cake in the center of the turntable. ■ Place the stylized peacock template on the side of the cake, about ¼ inch (5 mm) above center on the vertical axis, and trace around it with the toothpick. ■

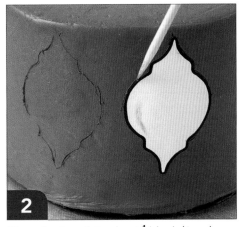

Move the template about ½ inch (1 cm) to one side of the first outline and trace another outline. ■ Continue making a ring of these outlines, about ½ inch (1 cm) apart, around the sides of the cake. ■

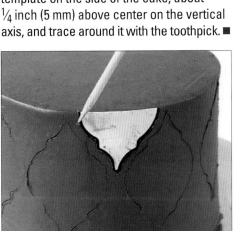

Fold the template in half, turn it so the point faces down, and place it on the top edge of the side of the cake so that the point falls halfway between two of the full outlines. ■ Trace around it with the toothpick. ■

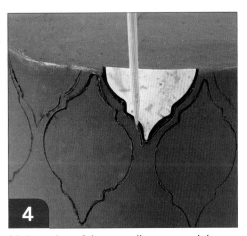

Make a ring of these outlines around the top edge of the cake. ■

## What You Need

- 6-inch (15 cm) layer cake, sliced, filled and crumb-coated
- 3¾ cups (925 mL) deep green icing
- ½ cup (125 mL) bright blue icing
- ½ cup (125 mL) orange icing
- ½ cup (125 mL) yellow icing
- Turntable
- Presentation surface
- 4 pastry bags
- 4 couplers
- #6 round tip
- 3 #3 round tips
- Stylized Peacock ornament template (page 353)
- Oval template (page 353)
- Small heart template (page 353)
- Toothpick or skewer

## Techniques Used

- Smooth Icing (page 82)
- Transferring an Iced Cake (page 96)
- Tracing and Pattern-Making (page 71)
- Lines (page 106)
- Smooth Scallop Border (page 99)

## Hints and Tips

This design works best on a cake that is 4 inches (10 cm) high.

## Hints and Tips

When tracing around a template with a toothpick or skewer, you may find it easier to make a series of small dots instead of a continuous line. This will be less disruptive to the icing surface and will still give you a clear outline to pipe the icing over.

Trace around the templates and peel them off as quickly as possible. If the cake warms up under a template, a layer of icing might peel away along with it. If that happens, carefully smooth the rough area with the tip of a small offset spatula.

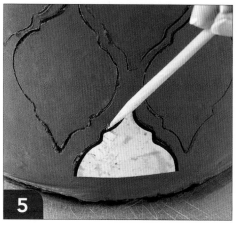

**5** Flip the template so the point faces up and place it ¼ inch (5 mm) above the bottom edge of the cake so that the point falls halfway between two of the full outlines. ■ Trace around it with the toothpick. ■

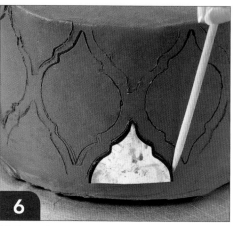

**6** Make a ring of these outlines around the bottom of the cake. ■

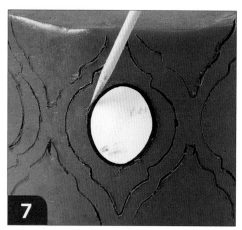

**7** Place the oval template in the center of each full stylized peacock outline and trace around it with the toothpick. ■

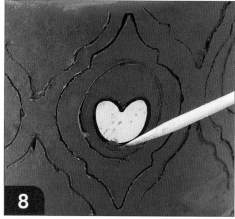

**8** Place the heart template slightly below center in each oval and trace around it with the toothpick. ■

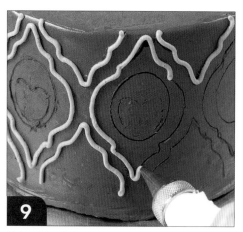

**9** Using blue icing, pipe over all the full and half stylized peacock outlines. ■

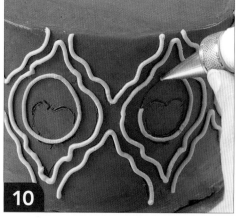

**10** Using orange icing, pipe over all the oval outlines. ■

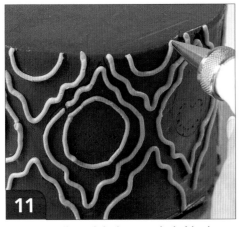

**11** Pipe a small semicircle, rounded side down, inside each of the half outlines around the top of the cake. ■

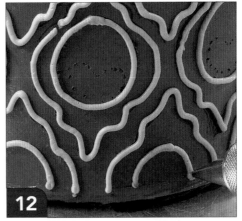

**12** Pipe a small semicircle, rounded side up, inside each of the half outlines around the bottom of the cake, making sure the ends stop 1/4 inch (5 mm) above the bottom edge. ■

**Variations**

For a more traditional peacock color palette, ice the cake in deep teal and use muted lime green, indigo blue, turquoise and medium golden brown for the lines and accents.

For a more playful look, pipe the borders in one of the accent colors.

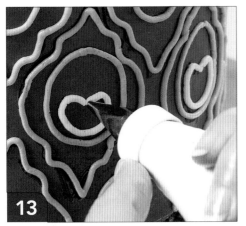

**13** Using yellow icing, pipe over all the heart outlines. ■

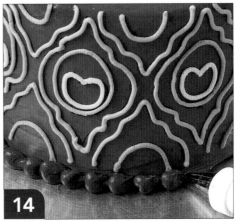

**14** Using green icing, pipe a smooth scallop border around the bottom of the cake. ■

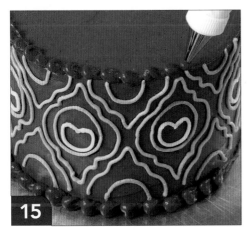

**15** Pipe a smooth scallop border around the top of the cake. ■

# Sunflower

*The sunflower, though an annual, is a perennial favorite of bakery customers. Sunflowers are also a popular option when a more masculine flower is called for. The flower is essentially just rings of simple leaves and dots.* **Makes one 6-inch (15 cm) layer cake.**

## Getting Started

**Ice and chill the cake:** Use chocolate icing and the Smooth Icing technique to ice the cake. Transfer the cake to the presentation surface and refrigerate until well chilled.

**Fill the pastry bags:** Transfer the remaining chocolate icing to a pastry bag fitted only with a coupler, the dark brown icing to a bag fitted with a #6 tip, the medium brown icing to a bag with the #3 tip, and the dark green, light green and yellow icings to bags with #352 tips.

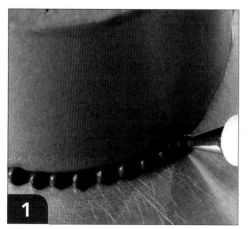

Place the chilled cake in the center of the turntable. ■ Using dark brown icing, pipe a smooth scallop border around the bottom of the cake. ■

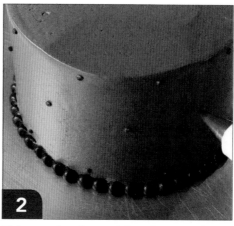

Using medium brown icing, decorate the sides of the cake with Swiss dots. ■

Turn the drinking glass upside down and use it to imprint a circle in the center of the cake. ■

Using dark green icing, pipe a ring of evenly spaced leaves around the top of the cake, with the tips of the leaves hanging just over the edge. ■ Leave enough space between the dark green leaves to place light green leaves. ■

## Hints and Tips

If you don't have a drinking glass in the right size, you can use a 3½-inch (8.5 cm) cookie cutter or any round food-safe object.

When making a ring of leaves or petals, always rotate the turntable and keep your hand in the same position for each successive leaf or petal. This will ensure a nice round flower.

If you are right-handed, it is easiest to work on steps 4 to 9 with your piping hand in the East (E) position on the cake. If you are left-handed, it is easiest to work on steps 4 to 9 with your piping hand in the West (W) position.

If your chocolate icing is too stiff to squeeze out of the bag, place the bag in a warm area to soften. Empty the bag, stir the icing, then refill the pastry bag.

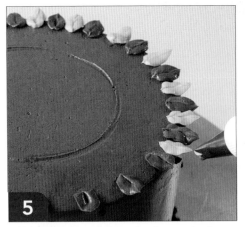

Using light green icing, pipe leaves in the spaces between the dark green leaves, completing the ring of leaves. ■

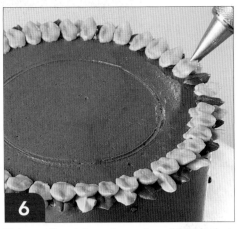

Using yellow icing, pipe a ring of petals that overlap the leaves without covering them completely. ■

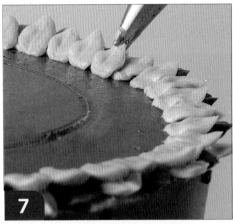

Pipe a second ring of petals above the first, staggered so that each petal in the second ring lies between two petals in the first ring. ■

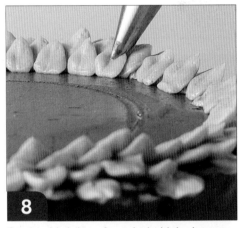

For the third ring of petals, hold the bag at a 60-degree angle to the cake and make the petals slightly shorter. ■ Stagger the petals so that each lies between two petals in the second ring. ■

Continue to make rings of shorter, more vertical petals until you reach the outline of the circle in the center of the cake. ■

Using chocolate icing, make a mound the diameter of the circle in the center of the flower. ■

**11**

Switch the tip on the medium brown icing to a #6 tip and pipe a ring of fat dots butted up against the yellow petals. ■

**12**

Pipe three more concentric rings of medium brown dots, moving up the mound. ■

**13**

Switch the tip on the dark brown icing to the #5 tip and pipe another ring of dots inside the final ring of medium brown dots. ■

**14**

Continue to make concentric rings of dark brown dots until the center of the flower is completely covered. ■

## Hints and Tips

If you're making this cake for someone special or for a special event, you may want to write an inscription. In that case, skip steps 10 to 14, leaving the center of the flower free for your message.

### Variation

This design also looks beautiful on top of ivory or vanilla icing.

# Sweet Dots

*Each time I make this cake, I am reminded that less often truly is more. It's darling as is or accentuated with a topper or fresh flowers.* **Makes one 6-inch (15 cm) layer cake.**

## Getting Started

**Ice and chill the cake:** Use blue icing and the Smooth Icing technique to ice the cake. Transfer the cake to the presentation surface and refrigerate until well chilled.

**Fill the pastry bags:** Transfer the remaining blue icing to a pastry bag fitted with the #6 tip, and the ivory icing to a bag with the #3 tip.

## What You Need

- 6-inch (15 cm) layer cake, sliced, filled and crumb-coated
- 3¾ cups (925 mL) pale blue icing
- ½ cup (125 mL) ivory icing
- Turntable
- Presentation surface
- 2 pastry bags
- 2 couplers
- #6 round tip
- #3 round tip

## Techniques Used

- Smooth Icing (page 82)
- Transferring an Iced Cake (page 96)
- Smooth Scallop Border (page 99)
- Dots (page 102)

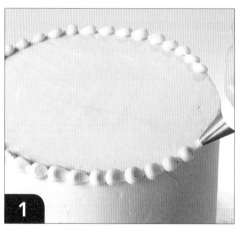

Place the chilled cake in the center of the turntable. ∎ Using blue icing, pipe a smooth scallop border around the top of the cake. ∎

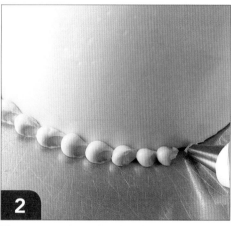

Pipe a smooth scallop border around the bottom of the cake. ∎

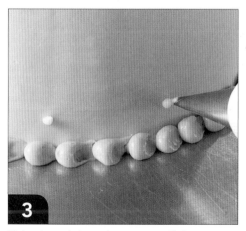

Using ivory icing, pipe two small dots an equal distance apart near the bottom edge of the cake. ∎

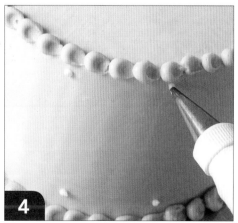

Pipe a third dot near the top edge of the cake, directly above the first dot, then a fourth dot near the top edge of the cake, directly above the second dot. ∎ You should now have a square of dots. ∎

## Variation

This cake looks beautiful in any size and color, though I particularly like it in pastels.

Use Sweet Dots cakes
as both dessert and
centerpieces at a
wedding or other large
event. Use icing that
matches the event's
color scheme and top
each cake with fresh
flowers, if desired.
Purchase coordinating
cake stands for the
guest tables and place
a cake on the stand
in the center of each
table. Write the cake
flavor in calligraphy on
a paper tent and place
the tent at the base of
each cake stand.

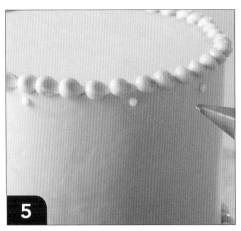

**5**

Continue piping dots around the cake, near
the top and bottom edges, until you have
two rings of dots around the sides of the
cake. ■ Make sure the dots are always an
equal distance apart. ■

**6**

Line up the cake so that a square of dots
is directly in front of you, then pipe a dot
in the exact center of the square. ■ Pipe a
ring of center dots around the cake, making
sure the dots are always an equal distance
apart. ■

# Timber

*Mimicking natural surfaces, such as wood grain, is a popular trend in cake decorating. The rustic finish of the timber cake is ideal for a western-themed party or an outdoor event. The heart on the side is the perfect space to communicate a thoughtful sentiment to someone special.* **Makes one 8-inch (20 cm) layer cake.**

## Getting Started

**Ice and chill the cake:** Use light brown icing and the Smooth Icing technique to roughly ice the cake with a thin layer of icing. Leave the cake on the turntable and refrigerate until well chilled.

**Fill the pastry bags:** Transfer the remaining light brown icing and the medium brown icing to pastry bags fitted with #6 tips.

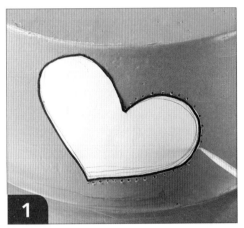

**1**

Place the heart template, tilted to one side, on the side of the cake and trace around it with the toothpick (or draw a heart freehand). ∎

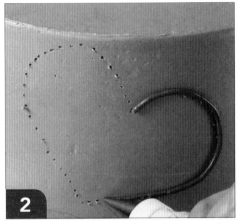

**2**

Using medium brown icing, pipe around the heart outline. ∎

**3**

Pipe lines that resemble the grain of a piece of wood around the sides and top of the cake. ∎

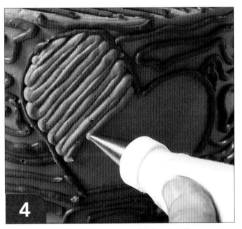

**4**

Using light brown icing, fill in the heart outline with long lines of icing. ∎

## What You Need

- 8-inch (20 cm) layer cake, sliced, filled and crumb-coated
- 4½ cups (4.125 L) light brown icing
- 2½ cups (625 mL) medium brown icing
- Turntable
- 2 pastry bags
- 2 couplers
- 2 #6 round tips
- Large heart template (page 353)
- Toothpick or skewer
- Straight blade spatula
- Damp cloth

## Techniques Used

- Smooth Icing (page 82)
- Tracing and Pattern-Making (page 71)
- Lines (page 106)

## Hints and Tips

Before icing the cake, make space in the refrigerator for the turntable with the cake on top. This cake is not transferred to the presentation surface until you are done decorating it.

## Hints and Tips

Because of the pressure exerted on the cake during the scraping process, it is important that the seal created between the cake and the turntable during the icing process not be broken, so do not remove the cake from the turntable at any time while decorating it.

In step 5, it's okay if the light brown icing pushes up against or slightly overlaps the medium brown lines. Just make sure there are no gaps remaining.

Work quickly in steps 6 to 8, so that the cake remains chilled during the entire process, and don't be shy about applying significant pressure.

Add an inscription inside the heart, using icing in a pastry bag with a #3 tip. I like medium blue against the browns of the cake, but you can use any color you like. See page 72 for guidance on creating inscriptions.

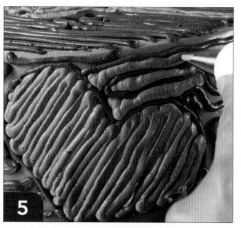

**5** Fill in all the spaces between the wood grain lines, squeezing with firm pressure to ensure that the height of the light brown icing is similar to that of the medium brown icing. ■ Place the cake, still on the turntable, in the refrigerator until well chilled. ■

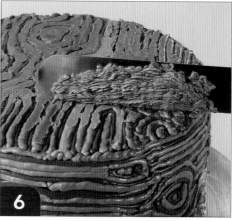

**6** Using the edge of the straight blade spatula, begin to scrape the top layer of icing off the top of the cake, either by holding the spatula steady while spinning the turntable or by scraping the spatula back and forth with the turntable still. ■

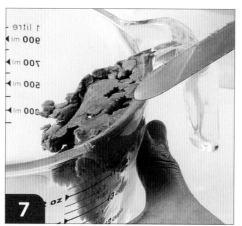

**7** Whenever a significant amount of icing accumulates on the spatula, scrape it clean and wipe it with a damp cloth. ■

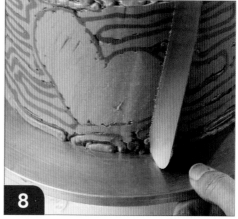

**8** Holding the edge of the spatula at an angle to the side of the cake and spinning the turntable, scrape the icing off the sides of the cake until the wood grain pattern on both the top and the sides of the cake is smooth, flat and even. ■

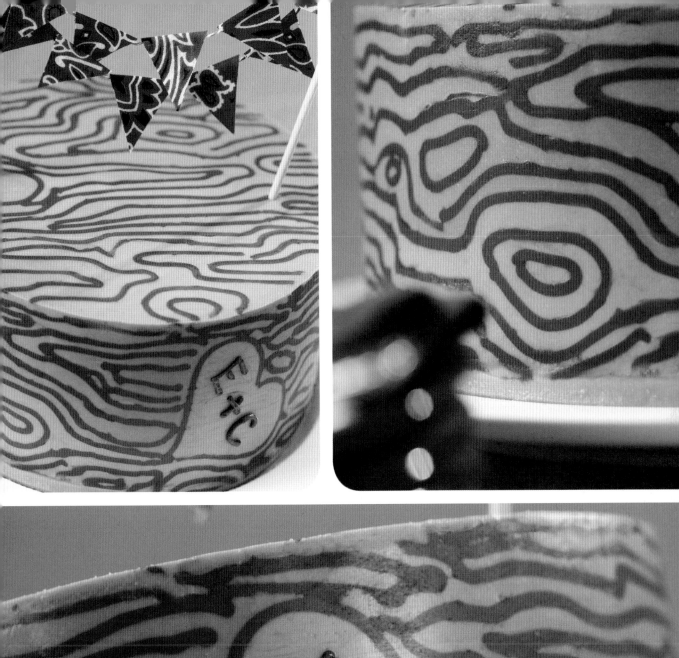

# Vertical Ribbons

*The loose vertical ribbons that adorn this cake would also be sensational in alternating blue and aqua hues or multicolored hues.* **Makes one 6-inch (15 cm) layer cake.**

## What You Need

- 6-inch (15 cm) layer cake, sliced, filled and crumb-coated
- 3½ cups (875 mL) medium yellow icing
- 3 cups (750 mL) bright yellow icing
- Turntable
- Presentation surface
- Pastry bag
- Coupler
- #104 rose tip

## Techniques Used

- Smooth Icing (page 82)
- Transferring an Iced Cake (page 96)

## Getting Started

**Ice and chill the cake:** Use medium yellow icing and the Smooth Icing technique to ice the cake. Transfer the cake to the presentation surface and refrigerate until well chilled.

**Fill the pastry bag:** Transfer the bright yellow icing to a pastry bag fitted with the #104 tip.

### Hints and Tips

It is easiest to make vertical ribbons holding the pastry bag directly in front of you, so rotate the turntable every couple of ribbons to keep your hand in the most comfortable position.

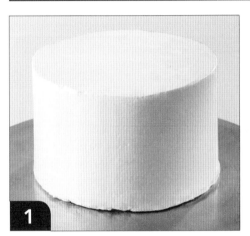

1 Place the chilled cake in the center of the turntable. ■

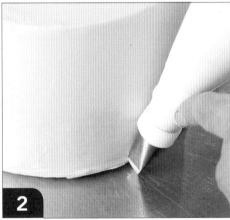

2 Hold the bag of bright yellow icing at the base of the cake, at a 60-degree angle to the turntable, with the fat end of the tip touching the side of the cake and the thin end pointing toward you. ■

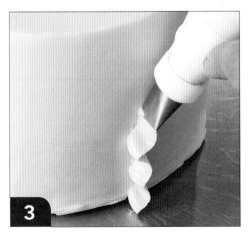

3 Squeezing the bag with moderate pressure, move your hand toward the top of the cake, keeping the fat end of the tip in contact with the cake as you move your hand in a slight back-and-forth wavy motion. ■

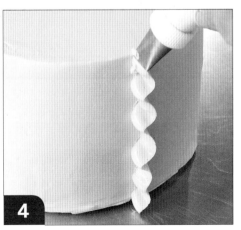

4 Release the pressure when the tip meets the top of the cake. ■

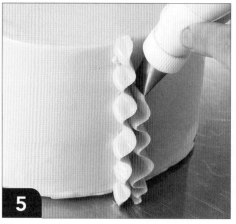

Make a second ribbon directly next to the first. ■

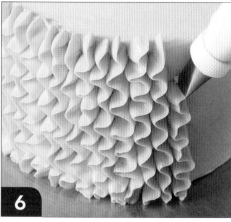

Continue to make ribbons until the sides of the cake are completely covered. ■

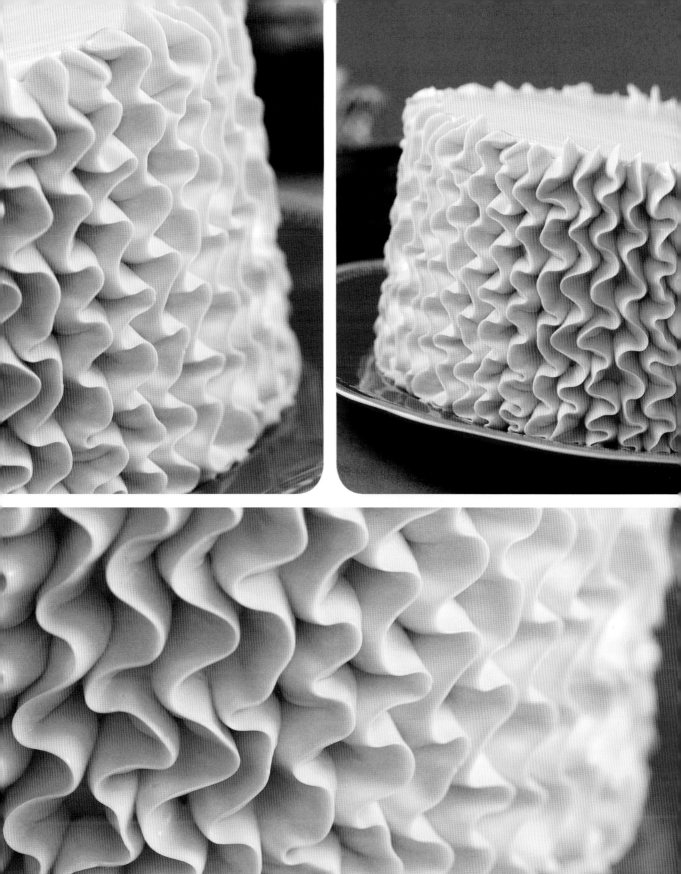

# Vintage China

This elegant cake takes inspiration from the famous blue Jasperware created by the Wedgwood company of England. Delicate ivory flowers replace the traditional neoclassical motifs found on the popular earthenware pottery. **Makes one 6-inch (15 cm) layer cake.**

## Getting Started

**Ice and chill the cake:** Use blue icing and the Smooth Icing technique to ice the cake. Transfer the cake to the presentation surface and refrigerate until well chilled.

**Fill the pastry bags:** Fit a pastry bag without a coupler with the #125 tip, and fit the remaining bags with couplers and the remaining tips. Fill all seven bags with ivory icing.

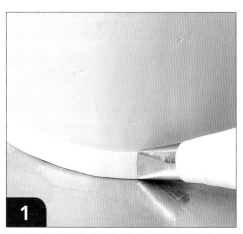

Place the chilled cake in the center of the turntable. ■ Using the pastry bag with the #125 tip, pipe a ribbon border around the bottom of the cake. ■

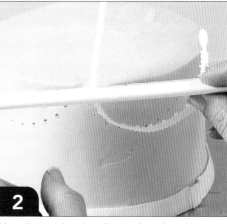

Use the garland maker to imprint six 3-inch (7.5 cm) wide and 1¼-inch (3 cm) deep garlands around the side of the cake, at the top edge, without any space between them. ■

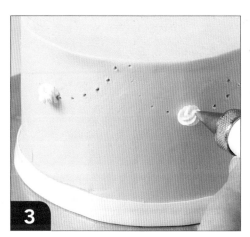

Using the bag with the #16 tip, pipe a rosette at the lowest point of each garland. ■

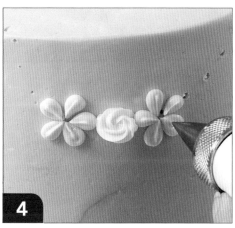

Using the bag with the #102 tip, pipe a tight petal daisy, without a center dot, on either side of each rosette, ensuring that the flowers are piped snugly up against one another. ■

## What You Need

- 6-inch (15 cm) layer cake, sliced, filled and crumb-coated
- 3½ cups (875 mL) pale blue icing
- 3½ cups (875 mL) ivory icing
- Turntable
- Presentation surface
- 7 pastry bags
- 6 couplers
- #125 rose tip
- #16 open star tip
- #102 rose tip
- #3 round tip
- #14 open star tip
- #2 round tip
- #349 leaf tip
- Garland maker (see hints and tips, page 324)
- Tweezers
- Small white sugar pearls

## Techniques Used

- Smooth Icing (page 82)
- Transferring an Iced Cake (page 96)
- Ribbon Border (page 98)
- Rosettes (page 120)
- Petal Daisies (page 118)
- Dot Daisies (page 117)
- Leaves (page 112)

## Hints and Tips

Swiss meringue buttercream icing that has not been colored is a neutral ivory color.

## Hints and Tips

If you don't have a garland maker, you can use a 3-inch (7.5 cm) round or oval cookie cutter to imprint garlands on the cake, or simply use a toothpick to draw the garlands freehand.

If you have gaps between any of your garlands, don't worry. You can fill in the gaps and stretch them out with filler flowers. No one will notice!

If empty space remains on any of the garlands after step 8, fill in the spaces with a tiny rosette or dot daisy.

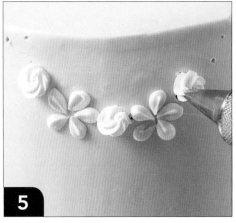

**5**

Using the bag with the #16 tip, pipe a rosette next to each daisy, following the scored arc of the garland. ■

**6**

Using the bag with the #3 tip, pipe a dot daisy next to each rosette. ■

**7**

Using the bag with the #14 tip, pipe a tiny rosette next to each dot daisy. ■

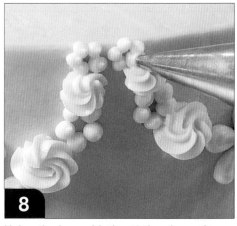

**8**

Using the bag with the #2 tip, pipe a tiny dot daisy next to each tiny rosette. ■

**9**

Using the bag with the #16 tip, pipe a rosette on the top of the cake, at the pinnacle of each garland. ■

**10**

Using the bag with the #349 tip, pipe a small leaf next to each rosette on the top of the cake. ■

**11** Use the tweezers to place a sugar pearl in the center of each petal daisy. ■

**12** Place three pearls next to each rosette on top of the cake, on the opposite side of the rosette from the leaf. ■

## Variations

Add more pearls on the side of the cake, near the center of each garland.

An ivory smooth scallop border also looks stunning on this cake.

# Violets

*Violets have a rich history of symbolism and are often associated with love, faithfulness and devotion. The Greeks even used them to make a love potion. I hope these buttercream blossoms inspire adoration in you and all who consume them.* **Makes 24 cupcakes.**

---

## Getting Started

**Ice the cupcakes:** Use the icing of your choice and the Smooth Cupcake Icing technique to ice the cupcakes.

**Fill the pastry bags:** Transfer the purple icing to a pastry bag fitted with the #102 tip, the light and dark green icings to bags with #352 tips, and the yellow icing to a bag with the #2 tip.

## What You Need

- 24 cupcakes, cooled
- 4 cups (1 L) icing of choice
- 1½ cups (375 mL) dark purple icing
- ¾ cup (175 mL) light green icing
- ¾ cup (175 mL) dark green icing
- ⅓ cup (75 mL) deep yellow icing
- Turntable
- 4 pastry bags
- 4 couplers
- #102 rose tip
- 2 #352 leaf tips
- #2 round tip

## Techniques Used

- Smooth Cupcake Icing (page 85)
- Classic Flat Petals (page 115)
- Mounds (page 101)
- Leaves (page 112)
- Dots (page 102)

**1** Place an iced cupcake in the center of the turntable. ■ Using purple icing, pipe five classic flat petals in a tight ring on one side of the cupcake, forming a violet blossom. ■

**2** Turning the cupcake so that the first flower is at the Northwest position, pipe a second flower at the Northeast position. ■

**3** In the smaller arc between the two flowers, pipe a small mound the same height as the flowers. ■

**4** On top of the mound, pipe a third flower that slightly overlaps the first two. ■

**329**

## Variations

To make an individual violet on each cupcake, first pipe a ring of alternating light and dark green leaves around the top of the cupcake. Pipe the violet in the center of the cupcake, using a #104 rose tip for the petals. (On a mini cupcake, use a #103 rose tip.)

To make two violets on each cupcake, first use a #103 rose tip to make a larger violet on one side of the cupcake. On the opposite side, pipe a small mound the same height as the violet. Use a #102 rose tip to pipe another violet on top of the mound, allowing the petals to overlap the first flower. Scatter dark and light green leaves around the flowers.

Using light and dark green icing, pipe scattered leaves around the flowers. ■

Using yellow icing, pipe three small dots in the center of each flower. ■

# Winter Birds

Many of the cakes featured in this book herald the lush colors and flowers of the warm summer months, but Winter Birds celebrates the singular enchantment of the winter season. **Makes one 6-inch (15 cm) layer cake.**

## What You Need

- 6-inch (15 cm) layer cake, sliced, filled and crumb-coated
- 4 cups (1 L) pale blue icing
- ¾ cup (175 mL) brown icing
- ½ cup (125 mL) red icing
- Turntable
- Presentation surface
- 3 pastry bags
- 3 couplers
- #6 round tip
- #4 round tip
- 2 #2 round tips
- Bird templates (page 353)
- Toothpick or skewer
- White nonpareils

## Techniques Used

- Smooth Icing (page 82)
- Transferring an Iced Cake (page 96)
- Tracing and Pattern-Making (page 71)
- Embroidery (page 109)
- Smooth Scallop Border (page 99)

## Getting Started

**Ice and chill the cake:** Use blue icing and the Smooth Icing technique to ice the cake. Transfer the cake to the presentation surface and refrigerate until well chilled.

**Fill the pastry bags:** Transfer the remaining blue icing to a pastry bag fitted with the #6 tip, the brown icing to a bag with the #4 tip, and the red icing to a bag with a #2 tip.

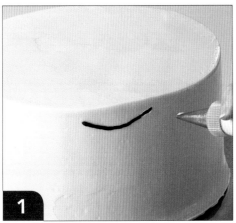

**1** Place the cake in the center of the turntable. ■ Using brown icing, pipe a shallow concave arc on the side of the cake, just below the top edge. ■

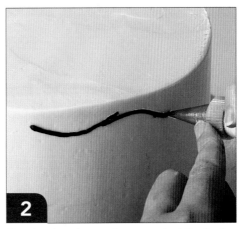

**2** Starting just beneath one end of the first arc, pipe a shallow convex arc alongside the first. ■

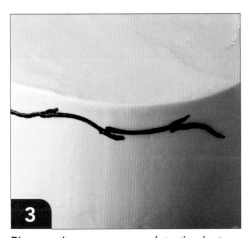

**3** Pipe another concave arc (starting just above one end of the second arc) and another convex arc to complete the branch. ■

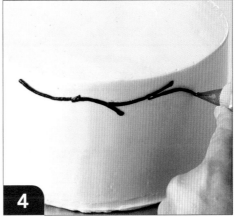

**4** Pipe these branches intermittently around the side of the cake, just below the top edge, spacing them evenly. ■

## Hints and Tips

For added confidence in making the branches, use a toothpick to draw them on the cake before beginning to pipe them.

Adding sprinkles to the branches on the side of the cake can prove challenging. You can tilt the edge of the cake up, being careful not to slide it off the turntable or presentation surface, or you can simply toss the sprinkles onto the cake.

### Variation

For a summertime version of this cake, ice it with ivory buttercream, turn the birds into yellow-breasted warblers and replace the snow with piped buttercream leaves.

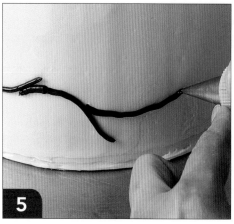

**5** Pipe an intermittent ring of branches around the side of the cake, just below center. ■

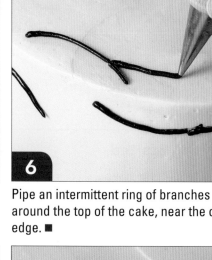

**6** Pipe an intermittent ring of branches around the top of the cake, near the outer edge. ■

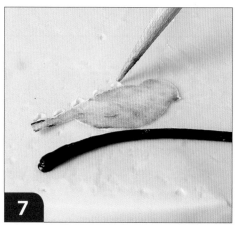

**7** Using one or both bird templates and the toothpick, trace one or two bird outlines on each branch, placing them randomly and in different directions, and making at least one pair of birds. ■

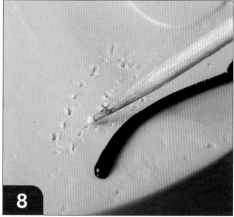

**8** Remove the template and use the toothpick to dot the outline of each bird's breast. ■

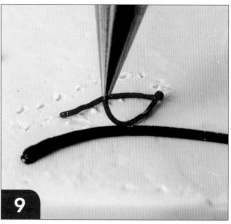

**9** Using red icing, pipe the outline of each bird's breast. ■

**10** Use the embroidery technique to fill in each bird's breast. ■

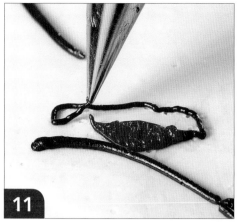

**11** Switch the tip on the brown icing to the #2 tip and pipe the outline of the top half and tail of each bird. ■

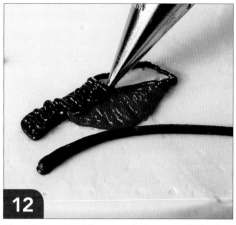

**12** Use the embroidery technique to fill in the top half and tail of each bird. ■

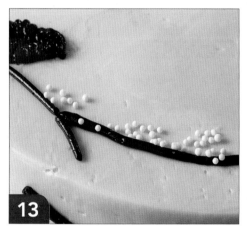

**13** Sprinkle little piles of nonpareils on the branches to represent snow. ■

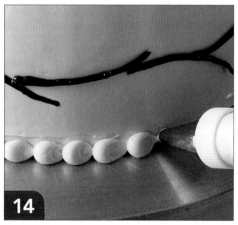

**14** Using blue icing, pipe a smooth scallop border around the bottom of the cake. ■

**Variation**

To make matching cupcakes, use pale blue icing and the Smooth Cupcake Icing technique (page 85) to ice them, then press white nonpareils around the outer edge of the icing. Decorate each cupcake with a short branch of two arcs and a bird.

# Zebra Stripes

*Just like a snowflake, no two zebras are alike: each has its own unique pattern of stripes. So there's really no wrong way to design the stripes on this cake!* **Makes one 8-inch (20 cm) layer cake.**

## Getting Started

**Ice and chill the cake:** Use pink icing and the Smooth Icing technique to ice the cake (the sides can be roughly iced with a thin layer of icing, but make sure the top has ample icing and is smooth and flat). Leave the cake on the turntable and refrigerate until well chilled.

**Fill the pastry bags:** Transfer the remaining pink icing and the black icing to pastry bags fitted with #6 tips.

## What You Need

- 8-inch (20 cm) layer cake, sliced, filled and crumb-coated
- $6\frac{1}{2}$ cups (1.625 mL) bright pink icing
- $2\frac{1}{2}$ cups (625 mL) black icing
- Turntable
- 2 pastry bags
- 2 couplers
- 2 #6 round tips
- Toothpick or skewer
- Straight blade spatula
- Damp cloth
- Presentation surface

## Techniques Used

- Smooth Icing (page 82)
- Transferring an Iced Cake (page 96)
- Smooth Scallop Border (page 99)

## Hints and Tips

Before icing the cake, make space in the refrigerator for the turntable with the cake on top. This cake is not transferred to the presentation surface until you are almost done decorating it.

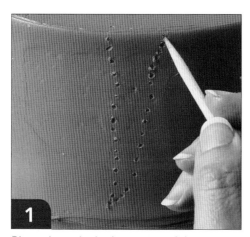

**1** Place the cake in the center of the turntable. ■ Use the toothpick to dot the outline of an irregularly shaped, thick vertical stripe on the side of the cake. ■

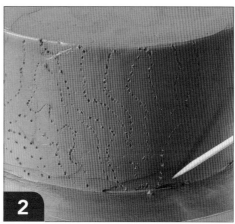

**2** Continue dotting stripe outlines around the sides of the cake, making some that start at the bottom and taper toward the top, and some that start at the top and taper toward the bottom. ■ Some stripes can interconnect; others can lean in one direction. ■

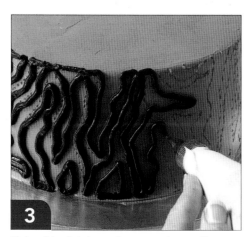

**3** Using black icing, pipe over the outlines of all the stripes. ■

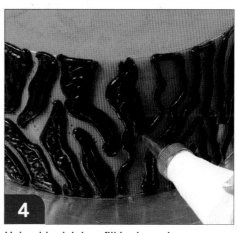

**4** Using black icing, fill in the stripes. ■

## Hints and Tips

In step 5, it's okay if the pink icing pushes up against or slightly overlaps the black icing. Just make sure there are no gaps remaining.

Because of the pressure exerted on the cake during the scraping process, it is important that the seal created between the cake and the turntable during the icing process not be broken, so do not remove the cake from the turntable at any time while decorating it.

Work quickly in steps 6 to 8, so that the cake remains chilled during the entire process, and don't be shy about applying significant pressure.

**5**

Using pink icing, fill in the empty spaces between stripes, squeezing with firm pressure to ensure that the height of the pink icing is similar to that of the black icing. ■ Place the cake, still on the turntable, in the refrigerator until well chilled. ■

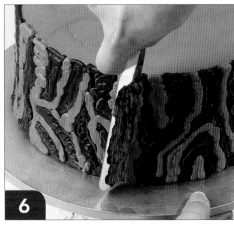

**6**

Holding the edge of the straight blade spatula at an angle to the side of the cake and spinning the turntable, scrape the top layer of icing off the side of the cake. ■

**7**

Whenever a significant amount of icing accumulates on the spatula, scrape it clean and wipe it with a damp cloth. ■

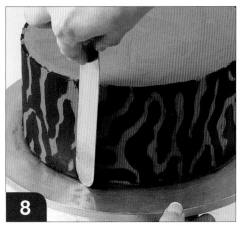

**8**

Continue scraping off icing until the zebra pattern is smooth, flat and even. ■

**9**

Transfer the cake to the presentation surface. ■ Using pink icing, pipe a smooth scallop border around the bottom of the cake. ■

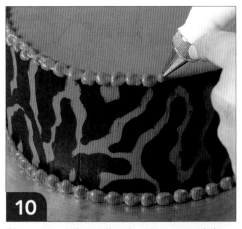

**10**

Pipe a smooth scallop border around the top of the cake. ■

**340**

# Chapter 6
# The Final Touches

# Presenting Your Cake

Creating a cake, from raw ingredients to its final decorated state, is a big accomplishment. Your cake deserves a presentation that complements the decoration and accentuates its best attributes. You've already done some of the work by selecting the presentation surface your cake now rests on, and depending on how extensive your decorations are, that alone might be enough of a presentation. But when you want to take things to the next level, there are three options to consider: toppers, fresh flowers and fresh fruit.

## Toppers

**Proportion Matters**

Be sure to select a topper that is in proportion to the size of the cake: it should accentuate the cake, not dominate it.

In my professional life as a cake decorator, I usually decorate the top of a cake rather than using a cake topper, but when I started to develop the projects for this book, I realized that some cakes can be enhanced by the use of a topper. I found the greatest selection and variety of toppers on Etsy's website (www.etsy.com), from hedgehog brides and grooms to fondant babies. Type the cake or party theme into Etsy's search bar and, more likely than not, you'll find a selection of toppers to choose from.

## Fresh Flowers

A cake simply decorated with a border and Swiss dots looks stunning adorned with fresh flowers. Flowers can be laid on top of the cake and/or around it on the presentation surface, or they can be placed in water-filled flower spikes and stuck into the cake to create an elaborate flower arrangement. The spikes secure the flowers in place, keep them fresh longer and allow them to cascade over the side.

**Glazing Fruit to Add Shine**

Combine 1/2 cup (125 mL) apricot jam and 1 tbsp (15 mL) water in a small saucepan. Heat over medium heat, stirring constantly, until the jam is liquid. Remove from heat and strain through a fine-mesh sieve to remove any fruit pieces. Let cool, then gently brush the glaze onto the fruit with a pastry brush.

## Fresh Fruit

Fruit is a wonderful way to garnish a cake — and to hint at what is secreted inside if you've used a fruit-flavored filling. Below are a few suggestions for arranging fresh fruit on a cake.

- Add a smooth or ridged scallop border around the top of the cake and place a ring of fresh berries just inside the border.
- Alternate ridged dollops and fresh berries around the perimeter of the cake.
- Cover the top of the cake with concentric rings of sliced strawberries, mangos, kiwis, raspberries, blackberries and blueberries.

- Pile berries on top of the cake for a sumptuous and carefree appearance.

- Scatter strawberries, raspberries or blackberries on top of the cake and add curling buttercream vines, leaves and white blossoms.

- Use small berries to make the bottom border of the cake.

- Slice strawberries vertically and arrange them, pointed side up, in a ring around the bottom of the cake.

When using fresh fruit as a cake topper, you'll want to take some steps to ensure that no juice leaks onto the cake. After washing them, make sure berries and other fruits are thoroughly dry before placing them on the cake. For whole strawberries, instead of cutting off the tops, grasp the leaves between your thumb and forefinger and gently twist them off. Add sliced fruit at the last minute.

# Storing Cake and Cupcakes

We all love fresh cake, but sometimes it's just not possible to make a cake and decorate it on the same day. A few handy storage tips will help ensure the preservation of your cake and an extended lifespan.

## Naked Cake

- A naked cake — one that is uncut and has yet to be frosted — can be double-wrapped snugly in plastic wrap once it is completely cool. The double wrapping keeps it from drying out or absorbing random refrigerator smells. It can be stored at room temperature for up to 3 days or in the refrigerator for up to 5 days without any significant change in moisture or texture.

- Cake freezes particularly well, but needs to be protected from freezer condensation. Again, double-wrap the cake snugly in plastic wrap before placing it in the freezer. Naked cake can remain in the freezer for up to 3 months before it begins to lose significant moisture. To thaw it, unwrap the cake, set it on a wire rack and let it come to room temperature. Do not attempt to expedite the process by warming it in the oven or microwave, as this will ruin the cake's texture.

**Sparkling Frost-Glazed Fruit and Flowers**
Using a small, soft-bristled artist's paintbrush (that has never been used with paint), gently brush the fruit and/or flower petals with egg white. (Use pasteurized liquid egg white if you have any concerns about the food safety of raw eggs.) Sprinkle with ultrafine or caster sugar. Place on a baking sheet lined with parchment paper and let dry for a couple of hours before use.

**Optimal Storage Times**
Please note that the recommended storage times are just that: recommendations. I have suggested optimal storage times for a cake that is still reliably moist and relatively similar in texture to when it was baked. The cake may be perfectly edible beyond these suggested storage times; it just may not have quite as pleasing a texture.

The less surface area exposed to air, the better. To avoid trapping excess air inside the wrapping and drying out the cake, do not wrap naked cake or sliced layers on a plate.

**Do Not Freeze**

• Cake with fresh fruit inside (jam fillings and buttercreams flavored with fruit purées are okay to freeze)

• Cake with cream cheese or whipped cream icing

• Cake filled with pastry cream or curd

• Cake with little to no fat, such as an angel food or chiffon cake

# Cake Layers

• Individual cake layers that will all be used for the same cake can be stacked together and double-wrapped snugly in plastic wrap. Layers can be stored at room temperature for up to 2 days, in the refrigerator for up to 4 days or in the freezer for up to 2 months. (Because more surface area is exposed to air, layers dry out more quickly than a naked cake.)

# Filled and Iced Cake

• A cake that has been filled and iced is essentially swathed in its own custom-fit airtight container and can remain at room temperature for up to 5 days. Store it under a cake dome or in a cake box so it doesn't attract dust, curious kids or critters.

• If you do not plan on serving the cake for several days, or if your kitchen is particularly hot or humid, refrigerate the cake to ensure that bacteria do not develop. First place it uncovered in the refrigerator to chill. When the icing has hardened, wrap the cake in plastic wrap and return it to the refrigerator, where it will keep for up to 1 week.

• A cake with cream cheese icing or any cream-based icing or filling should *always* be stored in the refrigerator and never at room temperature or in the freezer. A cake iced with cream cheese frosting can be refrigerated for up to 1 week. Cakes iced in whipped cream tend to deteriorate more rapidly and will only keep for 2 to 3 days.

• To freeze an iced cake, place it uncovered in the refrigerator to chill. When the icing has hardened, wrap the cake in plastic wrap and place it in the freezer. Iced cake can remain in the freezer for up to 2 months. To thaw it, unwrap the cake and let it thaw slowly in the refrigerator to prevent condensation from forming on the outside of the cake.

# Sliced Cake

- Once a cake has been sliced, it begins to lose moisture and goes stale more quickly. Press a piece of plastic wrap against the cut side, securing it with a couple of dabs of icing, if necessary. You can then store it at room temperature for up to 2 days or in the refrigerator for up to 4 days.

- If the sliced cake is iced in buttercream or fudge icing, it can be double-wrapped tightly in plastic wrap and frozen for up to 2 months.

# Cupcakes

- Thanks to their diminutive size, and because they are not entirely swathed in icing (and thus sealed off from the drying effects of air), cupcakes don't keep as long as iced cakes. An iced cupcake can be stored in an airtight container at room temperature for up to 3 days or in the refrigerator for up to 4 days.

- Though it's a bit of a hassle, unfrosted cupcakes keep fresh longer if individually wrapped in plastic wrap and stored snugly in an airtight container. They can be refrigerated for up to 4 days or frozen for up to 3 months.

# Returning Cake to Room Temperature

Cakes that are baked with butter and/or iced with buttercream will harden when chilled, much like a stick of butter. A butter cake served cold has the texture and mouth feel of stale cake. For a cake to be light and the icing to be glossy, it must be returned to room temperature. Here's a convenient rule of thumb: the amount of time a chilled cake needs to reach room temperature is equal to half of the cake's diameter in inches (or one-fifth of the cake's diameter in centimeters): a 4-inch (10 cm) cake will take 2 hours, a 6-inch (15 cm) cake will take 3 hours, and an 8-inch (20 cm) cake will take 4 hours.

Cakes that are oil-based, such as most carrot cakes, can be served cold or at room temperature with no difference in texture.

## Storing Buttercream Icing

Swiss buttercream icing can be stored in an airtight container at room temperature for up to 5 days, in the refrigerator for up to 1 week, or in the freezer for up to 8 weeks. Let icing thaw or warm up to room temperature, then use an electric mixer on medium speed to whip it until smooth (or, for a small amount of buttercream, mix it in a bowl with a rubber spatula).

**Call in Help as Needed**

Cakes can be surprisingly heavy, and cupcakes can add up to numerous boxes when packed up for travel. Consider whether you might need a helper when transporting your precious baked goods.

# Transporting a Cake or Cupcakes

After all the effort you put into baking and decorating a cake, you want to make sure it arrives at the event in one piece! With a few precautions and a little knowledge, you can transport your cakes (and cupcakes) worry-free.

- Ensure that the cake is securely attached to the presentation surface with glue (or with a dollop of icing that has been allowed to harden in the refrigerator).

- For added security, slide a drinking straw vertically into the center of the cake after icing and before chilling to keep the layers from sliding. Remove the straw before serving, and artfully cover the hole with fruit, flowers, toppers, a birthday candle, sprinkles or any other decoration. Alternatively, bring a small pastry bag fitted with a round tip and filled with matching icing to fill the hole on site, then smooth it with a small offset spatula.

- Carry the cake in a cake carrier or cake box. To prevent the cake from sliding around inside, the container should be as close as possible to the size of the presentation surface. If you don't have a cake supply store or craft store nearby at which to purchase a cake carrier, most bakeries will sell you a cake box for a nominal charge.

- If the presentation surface does not fit snugly in the cake container, secure it to the bottom of the container with double-sided foam mounting tape, or with masking or packing tape that has been cut and rolled sticky side out.

- If traveling in a vehicle, make sure the cake container is set on a flat surface and secured to prevent shifting.

- If the decorations on the cake are taller than the box, prop the box open and secure it with tape.

- If you must transport a decorated cake on a plate, covered with plastic wrap, prevent damage to the decorations by holding the plastic wrap above the decorations with toothpicks stuck into the cake and topped with little balls of tinfoil (resembling alien antennae).

- Cupcakes, especially mini cupcakes and decorated cupcakes, tend to be top-heavy and can threaten to topple over and roll about when transported. It is best to place them in a specially made cupcake container that has an insert with round openings to secure cupcakes in place. These containers are usually constructed from plastic, have a handle and carry 12 to 24 cupcakes.

- Alternatively, you can carry cupcakes in a bakery box. These can be purchased in bulk at cake supply stores, craft stores and online retailers, or ask your local bakery or grocery store bakery department if you can purchase one. Secure the cupcakes by lining them up in the box so that they are all touching each other and holding each other in place. If there is any remaining space in the box, use a small paper or Styrofoam cup, turned upside down, as a place saver.

- Make sure your cupcakes are well chilled before boxing them. This will help limit the damage from the inevitable finger spearing or knuckle graze as you're placing the cupcakes in the box.

**Baker's Twine**

For an especially sweet and professional look, seek out baker's twine at your local baking supply store or online. This colorfully striped string not only adds a personal touch to your boxed baked goods, but can also act as a handle. Just make sure to wrap the twine around the box multiple times, and in both directions, and tie it with a firm knot. If the cake is in the least bit heavy, support the bottom of the box with your free hand.

# Templates

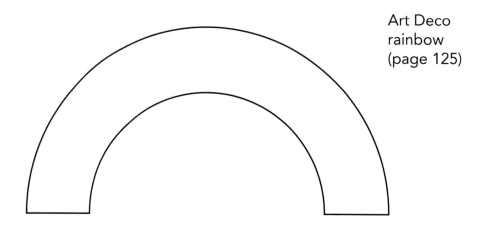

Art Deco
rainbow
(page 125)

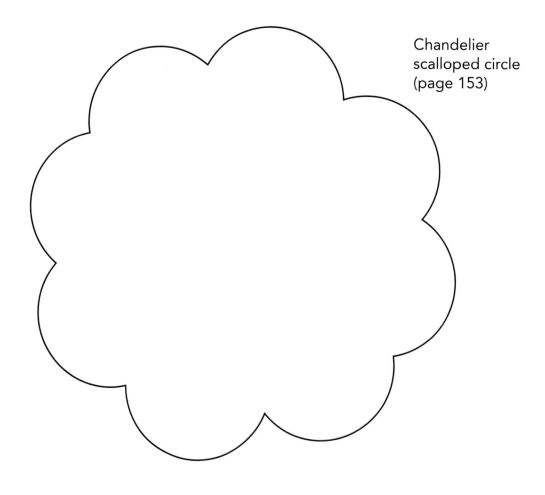

Chandelier
scalloped circle
(page 153)

Embroidered
Tattoo rose
(page 185)

Jungle Leaves
rounded leaf
(page 231)

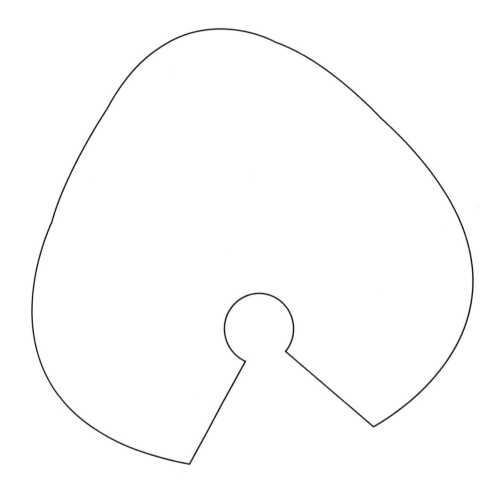

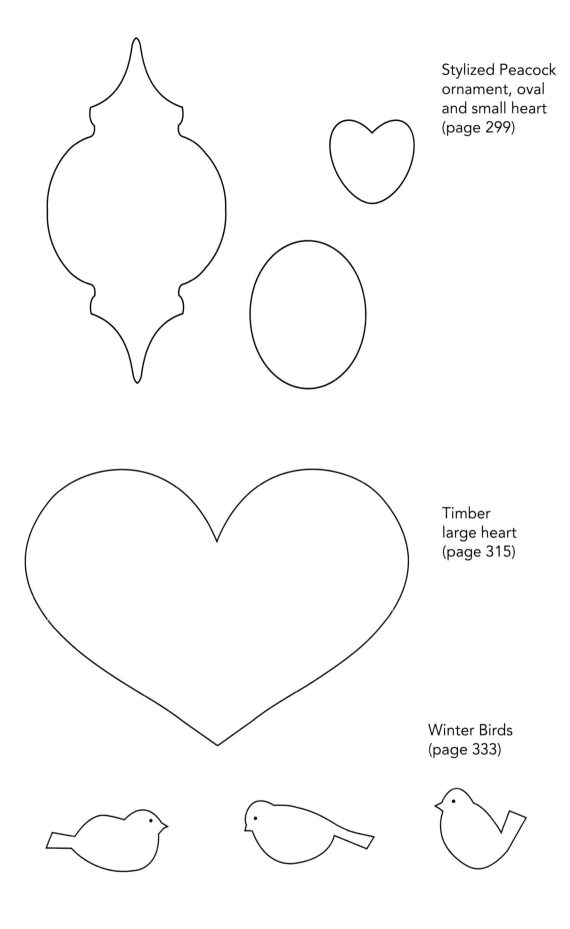

Stylized Peacock ornament, oval and small heart (page 299)

Timber large heart (page 315)

Winter Birds (page 333)

# Source Guide
## Baking Ingredients

Many baking ingredients can be purchased at your local grocery store without much consideration for brand, but for a few baking staples I have a strong preference for certain brands based on their taste, quality and/or method of production. Below you'll find information on these brands, as well as source information on some of the more unusual ingredients used in the recipes in this book.

## All-Purpose Flour

Originally founded in 1790 in Boston, Massachusetts, King Arthur is America's oldest flour company. The quality wheat used in King Arthur All-Purpose Flour is grown and milled in the United States. It's widely used by pastry chefs and bakers for consistency and performance. When I'm feeling indulgent, I purchase the organic variety offered by the company. King Arthur flour is available at many grocery stores or can be ordered directly from the company's website: www.kingarthurflour.com. If you are unable to purchase King Arthur flour, choose another high-quality name brand flour for the best results.

## Alternative Flours

I have numerous friends whose food allergies, sensitivities and preferences have led me to purchase almost every type of flour available on the market. No matter what type of flour I'm looking for, I can pretty much count on Bob's Red Mill to make it. Bob — yes, there is a Bob, and he's still alive — relies on the old-fashioned technology of stone mills and cool temperatures to grind the grain. In addition to fine flours, Bob's Red Mill carries interesting blends and mixes for easy baking. Many grocery stores carry a wide selection of Bob's Red Mill products, or you can purchase them online, directly from the manufacturer, at www.bobsredmill.com.

## Potato Starch

Potato starch is white, light, odorless and flavorless. It is made by extracting the starch from the liquid of a potato. Do not confuse it with potato flour, which is made from the entire tuber and smells and tastes like potatoes. You can often find potato starch in the baking aisle or kosher area of grocery stores. Otherwise, look for it at Asian or kosher markets.

# Dairy

When I can afford to do so, I prefer to purchase organic milk, cream, butter and cream cheese, but the recipes will work with either organic or conventional dairy products.

# Eggs

Whenever possible, I recommend purchasing eggs directly from local farmers, for the best quality and freshness. If that's not possible, grocery stores that stock eggs from small local suppliers or organic free-range eggs from larger suppliers are the next-best option. That being said, the recipes will work with any eggs that are graded as large.

# Chocolate

Scharffen Berger chocolate is an artisanal chocolate made in small batches in San Francisco, California. The flavor is complex and fruity, and the chocolate is unbelievably smooth. It can be found at upscale grocery stores or at www.scharffenberger.com. If you are unable to purchase Scharffen Berger chocolate, choose another high-quality chocolate for the best results.

I always keep a couple of varieties of chocolate on hand, with different levels of cocoa. For baking, I use 99% unsweetened baking chocolate. As for cocoa powder, I use natural unsweetened cocoa powder in my recipes.

# Freeze-Dried Strawberries

Freeze-dried strawberries, dehydrated strawberries, strawberry crunchies and strawberry crisps are different names for the same product: sliced or chopped strawberries with the moisture removed, making them feather light and perfectly crispy. Do not confuse them with dried (a.k.a. dehydrated) strawberries, which are soft, with a texture like raisins. Freeze-dried strawberries can sometimes be found at local grocery stores or health food stores, and are available at large online retailers.

# Lavender and Lavender Extract

Make sure to purchase high-quality food-grade lavender flowers that are free from pesticides and additives. Lavender flowers and lavender extract can sometimes be found at grocery stores, but you might have better luck at gourmet food stores or large online retailers.

# Decorating Supplies

Most cake decorating supplies can be found at baking supply stores, craft stores or gourmet food stores. For really specialized items and a much wider variety of options, try searching the websites of large online retailers or purchasing direct from a reputable company such as Wilton (www.wilton.com).

## Pastry Bags

Pastry bags are your primary decorating tools, and it's worth spending a little more on quality cloth bags that are easy to use, thin, durable and flexible, and will not seep oil. I like the Featherweight bags from Wilton Industries and the BakeMate bags from Bakery Crafts.

## Decorating Tips and Couplers

Although decorating tips are industry-standardized to be the same size and shape, I have noted minor differences on particular tips between brands. For example, the opening on a Wilton #1 round tip is smaller than the opening on an Atecco or Bakery Crafts #1 tip.

I highly recommend purchasing metal couplers, rather than plastic, for their durability, longevity and weight. Like a good kitchen knife that has weight and heft, a metal coupler will feel balanced and secure.

## Parchment Rounds, Cardboard Rounds, Cake Boards and Cake Boxes

Once you become accustomed to using these paper products, you'll wonder how you ever fared without them. They are all readily available at baking supply stores and craft stores, but in a pinch you can ask your local bakery to sell you singletons of these items; they will often oblige for a nominal fee.

# Food Coloring

For ease of mixing, I prefer liquid gel food coloring in a squeeze bottle. I primarily use Bakery Crafts' Bakers' Preferred Squeeze Gel, but have also heard good reviews of Americolor's Soft Gel Paste (www.americolorcorp.com). For natural food coloring, try the pretty muted colors from India Tree (www.indiatree.com). Small quantities of primary colors can usually be found at grocery stores, but for professional-grade food coloring, shop at baking supply stores, craft stores or online retailers.

# Sprinkles and Other Embellishments

Basic sprinkles can be found at most grocery stores, but craft stores, gourmet food stores and baking supply stores carry a wider selection. If you are unable to locate embellishments such as gold dragées, sugar pearls and confetti at a local retailer, you can purchase them online. Pay close attention to size when ordering online: do not order based on a photograph alone; instead, look at the actual dimensions of the sprinkle. You don't want to order what you think is a tiny, delicate pearl and end up with one the size of a gobstopper.

# Garland Maker, Cake Leveler, Cake Comb

Many people find these optional tools quite handy and innovative. To the best of my knowledge, Wilton Industries is the only manufacturer to make garland makers, and they also sell cake levelers and combs. You can purchase these items directly from www.wilton.com, or look for them at your local craft store or baking supply store.

# Cake Stands

Stands for both cakes and cupcakes can be purchased in craft stores or cake supply stores, but the selection will be limited and they tend to look mass-produced. For an amazing array of cake stands in any number of colors and materials, I recommend browsing around on Etsy's website (www.etsy.com). Or check out discount retailers such as HomeGoods, Century 21, Marshalls and T.J. Maxx.

# Cake Toppers

Etsy is also a great resource for endless cake topper options. If a particular topper featured in this book struck your fancy, you can go directly to the artist's online shop: just type the name of the shop (listed below) into the search bar on Etsy's site (www.etsy.com).

- Set of three red burlap flowers (Basket Weave, page 134): TickleberryMoon

- Green vintage lace cake bunting (Horizontal Ruffle, page 222): ApplesModernArt

- Rustic wooden "C" (Rustic Finish, page 282): TheRusticSpot

- Pale peach and blue cake bunting (Sweet Dots, page 310): ApplesModernArt

- Blue and red bandana cake bunting (Timber, page 314): GiddyGumdrops

- Rustic heart grapevine (Winter Birds, page 332): RusticDesignsByAmie

- Mommy and baby zebra (Zebra Stripes, page 338): SweetBugABoo

# Acknowledgments

I really had no idea of the enormity of the endeavor when I agreed to write this book. I feel so fortunate for the providence that landed me at Robert Rose Inc. and for the expertise those good folk offered. To a person, they were both consummate professionals and lovely people. Even with tight deadlines and unexpected mishaps, they remained steadfast in their support and belief in the project. Thank you to publisher Bob Dees for believing in me and for putting all your wisdom, experience and resources behind this project. Knowing that you were quietly operating behind the scenes and tracking the progress of the project gave me great reassurance and confidence. Thanks also to Martine Quibell, Marian Jarkovich and Nina McCreath for the effort already expended and the future assistance and expertise I know I will come to rely on.

Many thanks to Jeffrey Elliot, Robert Rose author and knife skills jedi, and his lovely wife, Jill Sloane, for recognizing my ability and seeing an opportunity, and who, out of pure good-hearted altruism, acted as patrons and advocates. (And to baby Henry, whose irresistible cuteness opened the conversation that led to all this.)

Thank you, Lou Manna, for all the beautiful photographs, artistry and hard work. I'm equally appreciative of your friendship, kind heart and generous spirit. What a trooper! Equal thanks to Lou's assistant, Joan O'Brien. Joan, I'm appreciative of your unflappable good nature and persistence, and your stellar management skills. It is people like you who keep us creative individuals from self-imploding and able to focus on producing. You are tremendously valued. I will miss the two of you.

To Daniella Zanchetta and Joseph Gisini at PageWave Graphics, thank you so much for all the dedication, time and support you gave to the project. I'm so lucky to have had on board two people who possess not only technological savvy but also creative flair and good taste. Your creative vision far surpassed anything I could have imagined for the book. Your support, kindness and availability during this process have meant a great deal to me.

Sue Sumeraj, what can I say but that we made it! I cannot express my gratitude for all you have done and all you have given to this project. I'm amazed at your editing proficiency, your ability to process and organize information, and your achievement in making my words sound reasonable, logical, clear and entertaining.

Without your unflagging dedication and encouragement, this book would not exist. I wish we lived nearer to one another so we could enjoy a much deserved glass of wine and toast to a job well done. Thank you!

Jennifer MacKenzie, you are the Florence Nightingale of cakes! I'm so appreciative of your mad baking skills and your positive attitude in the face of a desperate author and looming deadlines.

My thanks to Sheila Wawanash and Kelly Jones for your proofreading prowess, and to indexer Gillian Watts, whose very particular talent I'm in awe of.

Christina Winkler and Jamie Governale, owners of the Two Little Red Hens Bakery, saw in me a talent that didn't quite exist those many years ago. Thank you for allowing me the opportunity to develop my skills, for lending me a platform to express my creativity, for giving me a warm, comfortable and safe place to work, and for supporting me through this process and generously allowing me time away from the bakery to pursue a dream.

Marbel Martinez, my friend and co-worker, thank you for picking up the slack and covering me during these long months. Your support was vital to my finishing this project.

To the Duchess of Buttercream, Leigh Polous, you are the best assistant a girl could ever have! I'm honored to have had the opportunity to work side by side with you and to have had access to your creative brilliance. You are exceptionally talented in all your endeavors, and if I didn't love you so much, I would have to be terribly jealous of you. I'm quite certain that without your friendship, support and skill I would have suffered a breakdown long before the book was finished. You are an inspiration, and I hope this project is the first of many collaborations.

Sophie Cook, Ryan Scoble, Cara Anselmo and Megan Verenti, thank you for your assistance with this project. I feel blessed to be surrounded by so many talented people that I can claim as friends. For my other dear friends and family members, thank you for your continued encouragement, and for your patience with my self-imposed social isolation while I devoted myself to pursuing and finishing this project.

Last but not least, to Eric Slagle for his love and devotion, and for his year as "the book widower." Thank you for believing in me more than I believed in myself.

**Library and Archives Canada Cataloguing in Publication**

Madden, Carey, 1974-, author
    Sensational buttercream decorating : 50 projects for luscious cakes, mini-cakes & cupcakes /
Carey Madden.

Includes index.
ISBN 978-0-7788-0477-2 (bound)

    1. Cake decorating.  2. Icings (Confectionery).  3. Cookbooks.  I. Title.

TX771.2.M34 2014          641.86'539          C2013-908296-4

# Index

## O

Ombré Rosettes, 255
orange
    Swiss Meringue Buttercream
        Icing (variation), 46
    Vegan Coconut Decorator Icing
        (variation), 48
outlines, 71
    smoothing away, 76–77

## P

Paisley, 259
Pansy, 263
parchment paper
    for baking, 13
    for pastry bags, 18–20
pastry bags, 18–21
    air bubbles in, 68–69
    cleaning, 21
    closing, 68
    couplers for, 21, 67, 356
    cutting off tip, 67
    filling, 67–69
    holding, 21
    parchment, 18–20
    sources, 356
    tips for, 22–24, 67, 356
    using, 80–81
Peachy Rosettes, 267
peanut butter
    Swiss Meringue Buttercream
        Icing (variation), 46
    Vegan Coconut Decorator
        Icing (variation), 48
pearls (sugar), 26
    Calico, 149
    Cherry Blossoms, 161
    Chrysanthemum, 165
    Honey Bees, 219
    Pearls, 271
    Roses and Ribbons, 279
    Vintage China, 323

petals, 113–15. *See also* flowers
    flat, 115
    horizontal, 113, 118
    tips for, 23
    variegated color, 65, 66
    vertical, 114
Pink Velvet Cake, 34
plant kingdom designs. *See also*
    flower designs
    Bamboo, 131
    Birch, 141
    grass tip for, 23
    Jungle Leaves, 231, 352
    Ladybugs, 235
    Timber, 315, 353
Poppies, 275
potato starch, 30, 354
    Gluten-Free Flour Mix, 41
presentation, 28, 344–45
    supplies for, 27–28

## R

reductive technique, 66, 69
    Birch, 141
    Cheetah, 157
    Rustic Finish, 283
    Timber, 315
    Zebra Stripes, 339
ribbons. *See also* bows
    ribbon border, 98
    Roses and Ribbons, 279
    tips for, 23
    Vertical Ribbons, 319
Rich Chocolate Cake, 32
ridged dollop border, 100
rosebuds, 121
rose nails, 26
Roses and Ribbons, 279
rosettes, 120
    Ombré Rosettes, 255
    Peachy Rosettes, 267
ruffles
    Horizontal Ruffle, 223
    Vertical Ribbons, 319
Rustic Finish, 283